Michael Frayn was born in London in 1933 and began his career as a journalist on the *Guardian* and the *Observer*. His novels include *Towards the End of the Morning*, *The Trick of It* and *A Landing on the Sun*. *Headlong* (1999) was shortlisted for the Booker Prize, while his most recent novel, *Spies* (2002), won the Whitbread Novel Award. His fifteen plays range from *Noises Off* to *Copenhagen* and most recently *Afterlife*. He is married to the writer Claire Tomalin.

Further praise for *My Father's Fortune*:

'A writer who has long been one of our most engrossingly inquiring minds, Frayn has never written with more searching brilliance than in this quest for his past.' Peter Kemp, *Sunday Times*

'*My Father's Fortune* shows him at his very best. He expresses in a few words what it would take other writers several paragraphs to convey . . . And of course he is also extremely funny, possessing a quietly ironic tone that is pleasantly teasing and often self-mocking . . . In the end, Frayn has written a letter of love not just to his father, but to his mother too.' Elizabeth Day, *Observer*

'A profoundly affecting study of family myths and legends.' D.J. Taylor, *Financial Times*

'One of our best contemporary writers has now made another genre, the family memoir, his own . . . Frayn worries, as we all do, that he never managed to tell his father how much he loved him. With this marvellous book, he pays that debt in full.' Anne Chisholm, *Sunday Telegraph*

'A profound delight . . . With deft, witty touches, he resurrects the past.' Charlotte Moore, *Spectator*

'It's often very funny, always very interesting, and soaked in a wistful sort of melancholy that sometimes deepens into a compelling sadness.' Andrew Motion, *Guardian*

'A beautiful, deeply felt book . . . It's the kind of testimony that many of us wish too late our parents had left us – and, as such, admirably complete.' Benedict Nightingale, *The Times*

'A posthumous message of love that Michael had not expressed when [his father] was alive . . . a brilliant piece of writing.' Joy Lo Dico, *Independent on Sunday*

'Multi-talented Michael Frayn explored with charm and cunning his resourceful dad's wayward route from London poverty to far-from-dull suburbia.' Boyd Tonkin, *Independent* Books of the Year

'Compelling . . . this is beautiful writing.' Christopher Buckley, *New York Times*

MICHAEL FRAYN

My Father's Fortune

A Life

faber and faber

First published in 2010
by Faber and Faber Ltd
Bloomsbury House
74–77 Great Russell Street
London WC1B 3DA
This paperback edition first published in 2011

Typeset by Faber and Faber Ltd
Printed in England by CPI Bookmarque, Croydon

A CIP record for this book
is available from the British Library

ISBN 978-0-571-27059-0

2 4 6 8 10 9 7 5 3 1

Contents

Homburg

The handle of my study door softly turns. I look up from my typewriter, startled. The two older children are at school, my wife's out with the baby, the house is empty. I'm working alone on the top floor.

The door opens a few inches. Around the edge of it, with a certain deferential caution, comes a hat. A black homburg.

The year must be 1969, I realise from the internal evidence when I reconstruct the scene in my memory. No one round our way locks their front doors in 1969. But then no one still wears homburg hats. I'm looking at the last homburg in south-east London, perhaps in western Europe.

I feel a familiar touch of exasperation. Of course! Naturally! The black homburg! Just when I've got a chance to work undistracted! Why hadn't he phoned, like anyone else? Why hadn't he rung the bell, or shouted 'Anyone at home?' Why hadn't he at least taken his hat off?

The hat is followed by a pair of spectacles – a hearing aid – a trim grey moustache. And my father's familiar smile, like the sun coming up.

My exasperation evaporates in the warmth of it.

1969, yes, when I was writing my first play. It must have been. The good year, shortly before the end of his life, the year's reprieve between his first cancer and the second. He just happens to be passing, driving from somewhere in south-east London to somewhere else, on his way to put his head round the doors of building contractors and architects in Woolwich or Eltham, selling them roofing. He has always been turning up like this in my life, unannounced, on the move, a law unto himself, excused by his deafness from the usual social conventions. Not always in a black homburg – sometimes in a brown trilby. But usually in one or the other.

When he takes the hat off it reveals the last of his trim silvering hair receding above the leathery corrugations of his forehead, and brushed precisely flat. His features are as neat and well-ordered as his three-piece suit and polished toecaps. He has a touch of Fred Astaire's lightness and quickness about him.

'Not interrupting the muse, am I?' he asks, as I make him coffee. 'Not depriving the world of some great new book?'

'It's not a book this time – it's a play.'

'Are you? Where are you going?'

'A *play*. The thing I'm writing.'

'Bit crowded at this time of year, Brighton.'

He can probably hear me, actually, even if he hasn't turned his hearing aid on. It's over a quarter of a century since he first went deaf, and I've long been used both to raising my voice and to his pretending not to understand even so, for comic effect. More smiles when my wife comes in. 'Would you like some lunch?' she asks him, but after a lifetime of softly modulating her voice she finds it almost impossible to make him hear even the vowel sounds. He's rather in awe of her, though, so he doesn't like to disrupt the flow of the conversation.

'Not too bad,' he replies. 'And the children?'

'They're very well. But how about *lunch*? Something to *eat*?'

'No fear!'

'No?'

'Of course not. Up Dog Kennel Hill and across Peckham Rye.'

It's forty years since my father died. I've often thought about him since, of course. As he was when I was a child, as he was when I grew apart from him in my adolescence, as he was when we became closer again in those last years of his life. I can sometimes still feel some of his expressions on my own face and know, even without a mirror, that I'm looking like him. And yet I'm so *un*like him! Slow where he was quick, scruffy where he was dapper, head-in-the-clouds where he was feet-on-the-ground. And inside, behind our mutual expressions, in the way we think and feel, we're totally different. Aren't we? In all the years I've spent imagining myself into the heads of characters in plays and novels I've never really tried to feel what it was like to be that rather striking real character in the homburg hat. Your parents are your parents. They are what they are.

It was my children, wondering about their own origins, who first set me thinking about him in a rather different way. They wanted me to write something about my childhood – anything about the past that I could remember, before it had all vanished from my memory for ever. Rebecca, my eldest daughter, felt that she and her two sisters – all of them now older than I was when that hat came round the door – 'had risen from an unknown place'. For a long time I resisted. How could I ever contrive to lay my hands on that lost world, which had now slipped so far away even from me?

And then it occurred to me that it was my father who was one of my last links with that elusive past, and who might take us all back to it. Once again I saw his head coming round my door – the homburg, the hearing aid, the smile. Sixty-eight years of good and bad fortune were written in the corrugations of his forehead, the crinkled skin fanning back from the corners of his eyes, and the deep curving crevasses on either side of his mouth. So many things I should have asked him while he was still here to tell me. I might even have tried to talk to him about the thing he never once mentioned, the event that in one single instant broke his life in two – that broke all our lives in two – into Before and After. Did he ever wish he could have said something about it to me?

I went back to my very first conscious memory of him. I suppose I was three years old. He had appeared unexpectedly through a door, just as he did in my recollection of him at the end of his life. And – yes – wearing a homburg hat. He was coming in through the French windows of the dining room, just home from work, still carrying his files and folders. What makes this particular occasion stick in my mind is that I was crying, and that I lied to him about the reason. I'd misbehaved in some way and been scolded by my mother, but I felt so ashamed of my babyishness that I told him it was because I'd banged my head on the edge of the dining table.

Was it really the same man under that first homburg and the second, thirty-three years later? What had happened to him in between was etched not only into the skin of his face but deep into the core of the man himself. But then, if I was three when he appeared through the French windows, he must have been thirty-five. More than half a lifetime was written upon him already.

I go over that first encounter with him again, now I'm trying so hard to remember things, and what catches my attention this time is not my lying, or his sympathetic smile as he was taken in, but an odd marginal detail of the scene: the fact that he was coming in through the French windows. They were at the back of the house. If he'd just arrived home from work he'd got out of the car on the driveway by the front door. Why had he walked all the way round to the back garden before he came indoors?

Maybe he'd forgotten his keys. Or maybe he already had a penchant for appearing through doors unexpectedly. But, as I turned this tiny anomaly over in my mind, it occurred to me that there was perhaps another reason – something quite simple, that would explain a lot about him. If I was right, I should have to begin by tracing his path to the French windows that day in 1936 – all the way back, perhaps, to the unknown place from which he himself had arisen.

So back I've gone, as people often do when they get older, scrabbling among the birth and death certificates that marked my family's progress through the world. I've looked up the census returns and the electors' lists, and walked around the streets where my father grew up. I've tried to remember what little he told me, and to reconstruct the world as he saw it, with the problems he was set, and the pleasures and successes he found. I've made myself come face to face at last with that event I could never talk to him about, and its consequences for him and all of us.

The quest that I'd so reluctantly begun came to occupy my mind and heart alike. I laughed aloud to myself sometimes at the things that came back to me, and at other times could scarcely see what I was doing for tears. I also discovered many things about him – and a few about myself – that I'd never known, and that took me completely by surprise.

And now, when he puts his head round my study door again and smiles at me, as he does, I see him – and myself, and the world we shared – a little differently.

PART ONE

I

Smart Lad

I see in the *Oxford Dictionary of Surnames* that the name Frayn in all its various spellings derives from the French, *fresne*, an ash tree. We were dwellers by an ash tree, and the earliest recorded variation is a William de Fraisn in 1156, who had presumably, as some proud families like to boast, 'come over with the Conqueror'. Our branch of the family, though, arrived only four hundred years or so later, and in less exalted circumstances. We spring not from twelfth-century Norman knights but from a French pirate who was terrorising the Channel in the sixteenth century. He was captured by the English and hanged at Dover. His ship, and the cargo of gold it contained, was impounded, and both ship and gold are being held in Chancery for any Frayn who can prove his descent from the pirate.

I know this because I was told it by my mother, one rainy afternoon when I was about six. The story seized my imagination, particularly the solemnity of the phrase 'held in Chancery'. I had no clear idea of what Chancery was, but I understood that it was something to do with the law, and was dark and lofty and inaccessible. I had a picture of a gloomy panelled hall, and in it, propped on trestles, a kind of Viking longship, with the piled gold gleaming amidst the thwarts. I knew it was my task in life to reclaim it. But how would I prove that I was the legitimate heir? What tests would I be put to?

What for that matter had my father already done to secure the gold? Nothing, it turned out when I asked him some years later. The reason was simple: because he'd never heard about it. By this time my mother was no longer there to ask, but I suppose she must have made the story up to keep my sister and me entertained on a wet afternoon, just as she sometimes played the violin to us. It had never occurred to me that it didn't make any sense. Why would the pirate have had a son and heir on board with him as he raged about the Channel? Why would his ship and his illicit hoard be kept for his heirs to claim? Odd, though. The story's so circumstantial, and so out-of-nowhere. I can't recall my mother ever inventing any other piece of family history – or any other story at all.

More recently, at any rate, so I've discovered from my researches, the Frayns come from the West Country. Satisfyingly unusual as the name is in London, the nineteenth-century census returns for Devon and Cornwall are littered with Frayns, most of the men blacksmiths or locksmiths, most of the women in service. My father's father, Thomas Frayn, was born in Plymouth, the son of a general warehouseman, and rose into the world of small shop-keeping. He began his career as an assistant in a china shop, and married a greengrocer's daughter, Louisa Lavinia Allen (whose mother was illiterate – she had to make her mark when she registered Louisa's birth). Thomas progressed from working in the china shop to owning it. This turned out to be a step too high in the world, though. He apparently drank the profits, the business failed, and at some point in the last decade of the nineteenth century he brought his wife and family to London, where he found work as an assistant once more, in the china department at Whiteleys.

I can't remember now who first told me about the move from Plymouth. Not my father, who never said anything at all about his parents. I've filled out most of the details from the official records, but perhaps I got the story first from my cousin John Frayn Turner, a fellow writer. John, ten years older than me, remembered that our mutual grandmother had a rich Devon accent, and it was certainly he who first told me about our grandfather's weakness for drink. I was about sixty by then, so perhaps he felt I was old enough to be trusted with some of the family's darker secrets.

Thomas and Louisa had four children, three girls and a boy, and the six of them moved into a house in Devonshire Road, Hollo-way – chosen perhaps because the name reminded them of the old days. I recently took a walk round the district. Devonshire Road, now Axminster Road, is a turning off the Seven Sisters Road, part of the early Victorian development just to the east of the Holloway Road, and a cut above the slum streets that have long since been cleared in other parts of the borough. The terraces could pass for Georgian, with small front gardens and trees along the pavement – exactly the kind of street that in other districts developers have gentrified. It's plainly come up in the world a bit since my father's day, but the Seven Sisters Road and the Holloway Road, which flow through the history of the Frayn family like the Tigris and the Euphrates through the history of Mesopotamia, remain mostly working class, and I had the impression that gentrification was still rather hanging fire. I got talking to someone who had been brought up just round the corner from the house my grand-parents lived in. He told me that it had always been 'a rough old neighbourhood', and he catalogued a few of the more interesting local murders.

My grandparents' house had four rooms, apart from the kitchen, and according to the 1901 census there were two other couples also living there. Presumably each of these other couples occupied one of the rooms. So my grandparents and their four teenage children must have been living in the two remaining rooms. Two adults and four adolescents in two rooms – and all ten residents, presumably, sharing the kitchen. All the Frayn children were fortunately slight, wispy creatures. And they might have been packed in even tighter. In the next census, in 1911, there's a space for the total number of children born, dead as well as living, and this records two more, born alive but with no names or birth dates.

So this was my first surprise as I looked into my father's origins; quite how poor the family had been. When he at last joined the household, on 29 January 1901, he was the eleventh human being to be fitted into the four rooms, and cooked for and washed for in the communal kitchen. They named him Thomas, like his father, and Allen, after his mother's family. Thomas Allen Frayn. Tom to everyone as a boy, then Tommy to his wife's family in the years to come, and Tom still for some reason to all his colleagues and customers. Then Benjamin, with a big brother to look after him and three big sisters to fuss over him, twelve years younger than the youngest of them.

I have only one photograph of him as a baby. He's wearing a bib, and he looks as if he has just made a great discovery – the only thing that he told me about himself in these early years: if you're given bread and cheese you can eat the cheese and chuck the bread under the table. No sooner on to his first solid food than he'd discovered the first inklings of the sharpness and cheek that were going to see him through a career of salesmanship and so many of life's waiting difficulties. Parking his car in central London, for example, fifty years after this – leaving it in front of the Air Ministry and telling the attendant 'Business with the Minister', or in front of the great north door of Westminster Abbey – 'Business with the Dean'.

My second surprise, as I looked at the 1901 census, came when I understood the significance of the final column in the return. It was to be filled in, it explained at the top, if

(1) Deaf and dumb
(2) Blind
(3) Lunatic
(4) Imbecile, feeble-minded.

And it *was* filled in. Every single member of the family except for the two-month-old Thomas was tagged with a (1). The entire family were deaf and dumb.

The first thing this shows is how cautiously you have to treat even the most apparently authoritative historical records. I never knew my paternal grandfather, because he died long before I was born, and I don't remember my grandmother, because she died when I was still not two, but I'm pretty sure that they weren't dumb – and absolutely sure that my father's brother and sisters weren't, because them I did know. Deaf they certainly were, all of them – Nellie, Mabel, George, and Daisy – seriously deaf; I remember the struggle to make them hear anything I said. I was surprised, though, that they were already deaf as children. My father's deafness came on in early middle age. And his brother and sisters can't have been deaf from birth, because their speech wasn't impaired.

Or perhaps Mabel's *was* a bit, now I come to think of it. She certainly spoke in a strangely hushed way, as if she were in church. So did Daisy. Yes, and Nellie, and George.

What they were all suffering from was presumably, as I have discovered from the internet, late-onset hereditary deafness, for which apparently the gene has now been discovered, though I'm not quite sure what's happened to it in the three generations since then. A puzzle remains, though. If it's hereditary it's not surprising that one of the parents was also deaf. But *both* of them! Was this pure coincidence? Or had they been drawn to each other in the first place *because* of their deafness?

Four deaf children and two deaf parents. This is surprising enough. But one of the *other* couples sharing the house with them, a draper and his wife, are listed in the same way. The draper was from Devon, like the Frayns, so maybe he was a relative with the same heredity. But his wife, from Berkshire – *also* deaf! Maybe they, too, had picked each other because of their deafness . . . Maybe the two couples had been drawn to share a house because of the similarity of their marital arrangements . . . Or was it all just one great escalating coincidence?

Difficult to fathom this. Difficult, too, to imagine my grandfather selling china, and the other tenant drapery, to customers who couldn't make them hear what sort of china and drapery they wanted. More difficult still to imagine what life was like in the house, with two deaf parents, four deaf children, and two other deaf tenants, all either shouting or murmuring inaudibly to each other in the shared kitchen. Mabel must sometimes have made a particularly striking contribution to the proceedings. She was not only deaf but simple (although reputedly sharp at cards), and was said to be often very difficult – given to wild outbursts at certain phases of the moon, when she shouted, among other things, that she wanted a man. Every now and then she had to retire to a mental hospital.

And now here's the new baby chucking his food under the table and screaming his lungs out, with his nappies being boiled on the copper . . . In the morning everyone trying to get their breakfast, and hot water for shaving, and their clothes pressed and ready for work. All of them wanting the one lavatory, which at that time was presumably a privy in the back garden . . .

In the only photographs I have of my paternal grandparents the most noticeable things about them are his dignified but some-how weary and defeated grey walrus moustache, and her shock of resiliently springy hair. My father never mentioned their deaf-ness, any more than he said anything else about them. He never mentioned deafness at all in the various stories he told me about his childhood. Nor did he ever complain about the conditions in which he'd been brought up, or imply that in our one-family detached house in the suburbs my sister and I were being spoiled by luxury. He made life in Devonshire Road sound convivial, in a traditional working-class way. At Christmas, he said, the entire clan would gather. (How many more are there packed into these two rooms now, and queuing for the lavatory?) They would all bring their music and recitations, sleep overnight in armchairs and on the floor, and take a door off its hinges to make an extension to the dining table. Not a word about none of them being able to hear what the others were reciting or singing.

My cousin's revelation about our mutual grandfather's drinking came long after my father was dead, so it was impossible to ask him what further effect it had had on the family after the loss of the business in Plymouth. I suppose I have to imagine, in that overcrowded kitchen, not just a struggling mother, four adolescent children – one of them raving when the moon is full – four other lodgers and a squalling baby, but my grandfather coming home from the pub the worse for wear. The nearest pub, I noted on my walk around the district, was only five doors away, which may have been the amenity that recommended the house to him in the first place. When my grandmother reproached him for never worrying how they were going to manage if he spent all his wages on drink he's supposed to have asked whether it would help at all if he sat down and did worry for thirty minutes.

I look at my grandfather's picture again, and now I see him brushing the foam off that dejected moustache, and sucking the last of the beer out of it. I take another look at my grandmother Louisa, who presumably had to keep this overladen ark afloat. Unlike him, I see, she's still managing the ghost of a smile. Just.

By 1911, when the next census was taken, the house remained almost as overcrowded as before. Nellie, the eldest daughter, who worked as a needlewoman and made dresses for the wardresses in Holloway Prison (so her daughter Jean told me), had gone off to get married, to an insurance agent, but the other children were all still living at home. George was a compositor, says the census, Daisy a music-roll librarian for a pianola manufacturer, and Mabel a printer's bookfolder. The deaf draper and his deaf wife are still in residence, but the other family has been replaced by a young nephew, Courtenay, another arrival from Devon, listed as a tailor's cutter. Whether Courtenay was deaf, like the rest of the family, it's impossible to know, because in the 1911 census the disabilities column has been discreetly blanked out, but he shares some of Mabel's other problems. My father – who curiously never mentioned Courtenay's living at Devonshire Road – often talked about visiting him in a mental hospital, where he sat in silence all day watching the hands of the clock go round. According to Jean, Courtenay and Mabel were at one point sweet on each other. Whether he reacted in the same way as her to the phases of the moon I don't know, nor what life in the house must have been like if he did.

The second picture I have of my father as a child shows him at about the age of five, wearing the sailor suit in which small boys were traditionally photographed then. He looks, not wispy and self-effacing, like his siblings, but even cockier than he did as a baby. And cocky he was going to remain, for another forty years at any rate.

The only thing he told me about his education is that at the local central school he was given personal tuition in French by a master who perched on the desk in front of him and brought the register down on his head each time he made a mistake. As a teaching technique this was remarkably effective – it knocked every single word of French out of him. I never heard him essay even a humorous '*je ne sais quoi*'. He was also a boy soprano in the local church, and by the time his voice broke he had risen to become head choirboy. As an introduction to religion this served almost as well as the French lessons did to French. He retained a strong lifelong distaste for every aspect of it.

Something stuck, though, something that gave him a lot of pleasure over the years: the music. Often as we drove somewhere together he would lift up his voice, by this time tenor but still sweet and strong, and sing the soprano line from one of the old oratorios. He knew most of the great Baroque standards, but the aria that he sang over and over again was I think from Stainer's *Crucifixion*: 'Fling wide the . . . fling wide the . . . fling wide the gates, / For the Saviour awaits . . .' Whether he ever got any further than this, to a bit where the gates were at last open and the Saviour admitted, I can't now remember.

'Smart Lad Wanted.' This was the formula with which a lot of job advertisements used to begin. The smartest lad that any employer could ever wish for is now on the labour market: Tom Frayn, leaving school at the age of fourteen, and just starting out in the world to help support his family. I have a number of photographs of him taken over the next few years, and you can see – he's as smart as a whip. So handsome, so poised. Three-piece suit, hair slicked straight back, flat against his skull. In one of the pictures he has a nonchalant cigarette between his fingers. In another his adolescent face is crowned by an enormous grey homburg. Already.

His first job is as an office boy in the Hearts of Oak life assurance company in the Euston Road. Somehow each morning he emerges from the chaos of that tiny kitchen at the top of Devonshire Road with a clean collar, his suit pressed and his shoes shined, and walks down to the Seven Sisters Road to get the tram. The First World War is in its second year, and Tom Frayn is enjoying the fourth piece of good fortune in his life, though he probably doesn't appreciate it at the time. The first was the quick wits he was born with, the second was the brother and sisters who have made him such a favourite, the third was the mother who has somehow kept the family going – and the fourth is being only fourteen years old, and too young to be called up before the war ends.

At some point in the next few years he advances from office boy at the Hearts of Oak to wages clerk at McAlpines, the big building contractors. He goes to New*cast*le, as he always call it later, with a stressed short 'a', the way the people who live there do, and travels round the city every Saturday in his teenage homburg with a bag of cash, paying out the labourers who are installing sewers and culverts. He must still be in London, though, or back there again, when he has the fifth great stroke of fortune in his life. This is after the war's over, on a winter's day early in 1919, when he runs into a friend of his called Bert Crouchman. I imagine it must be a Saturday, because that evening there's a party, to which Bert is going because a girl he's seen called Vi will be there, and he's hoping to get himself introduced to her. Would my father like to come with him?

Tom is said to have only two interests in life at this point. One is dancing. He's a good dancer, deft and easy in the Fred Astaire manner. The other, no doubt exercised in tandem with the first, is girls – and I suspect, from what follows later, that he also has a certain talent in this department. I don't suppose he takes much persuading. All the same, I can't help feeling an instant of vertigo when I think about the sheer fortuitousness of this meeting with Bert Crouchman, and the arbitrariness of Tom's response. A lot is riding on this one brief moment while Tom makes up his mind. My existence, for a start, and my sister's. The lives of my three children and my sister's two. Of our eleven grandchildren . . .

He shrugs. He'll go to the party.

A close call there. Or so it seems to me now, as I write this, ninety years on, and the implications of that passing exchange finally strike me.

2

House of Straw

So there she was, the girl Bert Crouchman was after. Vi. Violet Alice Lawson. My mother.

I gaze at the old photographs of her in my album and see something of what my father saw when he walked into that party with Bert. A heart-shaped face and wide, wide eyes. Piled brown hair and plaits down to her waist. In one of the photographs she looks straight out at me as perhaps she did at him that evening. There's something touchingly wistful about her expression.

Tom looked at her, and she looked at him – and that was it. He was eighteen, and for him those few short years of girls, plural, were suddenly over. She was still only fourteen, and boys, plural, can hardly have begun. Their lives were settled for the next thirty years.

It was her younger sister, my Auntie Phyllis, who told me about how they met. In fact she wrote it down for me, seventy years later, when I asked her what she could remember of my mother. 'Tommy went straight up to Vi,' she wrote, 'and said "I'm Tom – I suppose you're Vi!" And from then on, nobody else got a look-in.' Poor Bert, said Phyllis, must have wished he'd never mentioned the party to Tom. What happened to Bert thereafter she didn't record. He had dropped away from the story like the launch stage of a space rocket.

Fourteen-year-old Vi and eighteen-year-old Tom – or Tommy, as he now became to Vi and all her side of the family. From Phyllis's account of the way he introduced himself he sounds as if he was at his most self-assured that evening, as much the cocky young man of the world as he looks in his photographs. I expect he gave her one of his irresistible smiles. Soon, I imagine, he was demonstrating his double-jointedness to her – bending his fingers backwards against the table in a sickeningly unnatural reverse curve, and pushing back the thumb on his right hand until it seemed ready to snap off. Then showing her his other special attraction, the thumb on his left hand, that couldn't be bent at all, because there was no joint in it to be even single; his brother George, the compositor, had showed him round the printing works when he was a boy, and allowed him to put his hand in a press.

I suppose she looked up at him with those wide eyes, and that hopelessly appealing plangency in her heart-shaped face. Fourteen, going on fifteen, confronting eighteen, going on twenty-five. She saw the way he was looking at her – he saw the way she was looking at him – and by the time they had finished looking the story of their lives was half-written. Together with the lives of all eighteen of their descendants so far.

They had quite a lot in common, if you went back a few years, I discovered as I worked through the records. Her father, Albert Lawson, had come from a rather similar background to Tommy's father – he was the son of a general labourer in Chatham Dockyard. Like Tommy's father he had been a shop assistant, in a draper's, and the family, like Tommy's, had been through some rocky times.

Bert had launched out from his modest beginnings with high hopes and great enterprise. He had become a travelling salesman, and left his fiancée, Eleanor Dormon, behind in England while he went out to the United States to make his fortune. He travelled all over, I think for the Irish Linen Company, and did well enough to send for Nell to come and join him. They married at City Hall in New York, in June 1903. High up in City Hall now there's a radio station that specialises in coverage of the arts, and every time I have to make the trip downtown to publicise a new book or a new play I can't help thinking of them. Bert, twenty-six, just beginning to make his fortune in this unforgiving land, and Nell, already thirty, who had overcome her lifelong fear of anything and everything to cross the Atlantic third-class or worse and join her fate to his in the summer heat of New York. Then off to Penn Station or Grand Central together, to the howling sirens and crossing-bells in the night as they chased the hard-won dollar, to Buffalo, to Cincinnati, to Saint Louis and Cleveland. That elusive dollar always just ahead of them, just out of reach. Now Nell's pregnant, and throwing up, and more nervous than ever, and still they're moving on, always moving on. Until they reach Chicago, where, on 6 August 1904, my mother is born.

I went to look at the street the first time I was in Chicago, and went again to show my daughter Susanna when she was working in the States. Anthony Avenue, way down on the South Side, a street now split in half by the elevated ramparts of the Skyway. These days the district is black, and the first time I went the friend who took me would let me out of the car only on condition that he drove alongside of me as I walked, ready for me to jump back in at the first sign of trouble. It looked peaceful enough to me. But it didn't look as if it had ever been the kind of street, even when it had had two sides to it, that suggested Bert had got very far towards making his fortune.

Within a couple of years, in 1906, with Nell pregnant again, they'd given up on the American venture, and Vi's sister Phyllis was almost born on the boat back. In the 1911 census Bert was exactly where he had started out – an assistant in a draper's shop. The house they were living in was a solid and convincing one in Dartmouth Park, half a mile west of the Holloway Road, but according to the census it belonged to Nell's father – described in her birth certificate as a house painter by trade – and they were there as his lodgers, in a single room. Spacious, of course, by the standards of my father's accommodation. In any case things began to look up. Bert got a series of well-paid jobs, said Phyllis in her note to me, as a buyer with Selfridges, John Lewis, and other West End stores. By 1912, the electoral register records, they were renting no fewer than three rooms off his father-in-law.

Then came the real turning point in Bert's fortunes, as it did for so many, one way or another – the First World War. He gave up working for other people and went into business on his own account, selling palliasses to the government. He had made it at last, not with fine linen for the comfortably-off, but with straw mattresses for the troops. He had become one of those reviled entrepreneurs who were doing well out of the war.

So well, in fact, that he was able to move his family out of the lodgings and into a detached house, which they had entirely to themselves. No father-in-law, no lodgers. He bought a car, a Ford Model T. He took Vi out of school – at fourteen, just like my father. But not, like him, to find work and help support the family. To go to the London Royal Academy of Music, to study violin and piano. She had a gift. She was to be a violinist. However similar her world and Tommy's had once been, they were now very different.

This is how things stood that Saturday evening in 1919, when Bert Crouchman and Tom Frayn came calling on Vi at her cousin's party.

After I'd looked at the setting of my father's childhood in Devonshire Road I walked, as he must have walked so many times in the next few months, to the house where my mother was now living. It's in Gatcombe Road, Tufnell Park, less than half a mile from my father's house. But it's on the other side of the Holloway Road, and sociologically it's rather more than half a mile. To the north-east of the Holloway Road are the early Victorian terraces of the 'rough old neighbourhood' that had never quite made it into middle-class respectability; to the south-west, where Bert and his family had now established themselves, is a land of late Victorian villas that seem as well cared for and genteel still as they ever were.

This is getting close to the part of Holloway where the Grossmith brothers probably located The Laurels, the home of the Pooters in *Diary of a Nobody*. The Laurels has three storeys, with a flight of steps up to a front door on the *piano nobile*. Gatcombe Road is rather different – a street not of terraces but of detached two-storey villas, their front doors not proudly elevated but waiting welcomingly at ground level. No. 1, where the Lawsons are living in 1919, has fluted columns and stained glass beyond the privet hedges. What does Tom make of this quiet and tree-lined backwater, and this comfortably desirable residence, as he calls to pay court to Vi over the coming weeks and months? What does he make of his future in-laws? I was going to get to know both of them later, unlike my paternal grandparents, and they're not much like the Pooters, in spite of their new respectability – or for that matter the usual picture of war profiteers.

Bert, for a start. Like my father he's a bit of a card. Unlike my father he's also a bit of an adventurer, who seems able to turn his hand to anything. He cycles – all over the south of England, sucking a pebble to keep his mouth moist, on a drop-handled machine which is later passed on to me, and which is built to much the same specifications as a cast-iron bedstead. He swims. While they were in Chicago, my grandmother told me, he had swum across Lake Geneva. I assumed for years that she was suffering from some fairly characteristic geographical confusion here, and that the story was another ship of gold. But when I very tentatively inquired about it the first time I was in Chicago my friends drove me there – Geneva Lake, to be precise, a noted beauty spot in Wisconsin, a mile or so across, and notoriously dangerous for swimmers. Bert had set out with a friend who gave up halfway, swum on undeterred, had a rest, and swum back. Later he took my grandmother sailing on the lake, and almost drowned them both when a sudden storm blew up.

He'd taught himself the violin. He whistles – a complex, endless flow of melody, like a songbird in summer. He's a watchmaker, and when he comes to stay with us later he gets out the old Ogdens St Bruno Flake tobacco tin in which he keeps his jeweller's tools, mostly home-made, then spreads a newspaper over the dining-room table and, whistling, whistling, repairs all the family's clocks and watches. He's a tailor, and makes suits for his two daughters. He plays chess, and plays it the way that other men drink, sometimes failing to turn up for work because he's off on a chess bender, and my grandmother has to scour the chess clubs and cafés of North London for him.

Pa, I call him, when I get to know him later, and I worship him. A lot of other people, too, are evidently charmed by him, as they are by my father, and he has a wonderful ability to find business partners and persuade them to share his enthusiasm for the opportunities he's dreamed up and the openings in the market he's identified. What he doesn't have is my father's steadiness of purpose. He's forever going off in different directions. And the associates he chooses (according to my grandmother) have a remarkable propensity to depart sooner or later with all the money. But now, at last, with the palliasses, he has broken his jinx.

His most surprising venture in life, though, and his most improbable conquest, is right there in 1 Gatcombe Road alongside him – his wife, my grandmother. Eleanor; Nell to everyone in the family; Nanny to my sister and me. I used to have a painting of her as a girl, showing her with long red-gold hair and a frail, ethereal version of my mother's appealing vulnerability. By the time I knew her the gold had turned to grey but the frailty remained, and the ethereality had become an all-consuming nervousness. She was like one of those birds which seem to spend so much time looking round for any possible danger that you can't think how they ever eat enough to stay alive. Later she lived with us for many years. I can't recall her ever going to the shops, or even to the letter box on the corner. The back garden, yes, occasionally, when she was absolutely certain that there was no chance of getting wet, or chilled, or struck by lightning. But the *front* garden? Next to the road? I don't think so.

She was fearful of gas and electricity. Also of air, fire and water, and probably of earth, too, on the rare occasions that she got within sight of any. She was nervous about the state of the world, and of any change to the arrangements of the nation or the house. She was fearful of committing some social impropriety, and would often keep a hand over her mouth as she spoke to trap any embarrassing revelations that might be emerging. She confessed to me once, with hand over mouth and many little nervous laughs, a terrible truth about her origins. She had been brought up not as an

Anglican, but as – and she made this seem such an embarrassing admission that I can scarcely bring myself to repeat it here – as a *Unitarian*.

From behind that nervously hovering hand on another occasion she confided to me an even worse family scandal. Her great-grandmother had been *Jewish*. I was too young and ignorant when she let this slip to realise quite how interesting it was. I didn't know then that Jews see Jewishness as being transmitted matrilineally, so it didn't occur to me to ask the obvious question: was she talking about her mother's mother's mother? If she was, then, in Jewish eyes, she was a Jew herself, and so am I.

I was her first grandchild, and she loved me blindly through thick and thin, in spite of my shamefully haphazard expression of the love I felt for her, and my playing cruelly, as a growing boy with trees to climb and bicycles to ride, upon her endless fears for my life and limb. As frail as a sparrow herself, in a world full of rain and draughts and electricity, she took an equally pessimistic view of her own life expectancy. 'Oh, Michael,' she would say mournfully, each time I went to visit her in later years, 'I don't think I shall see another winter through. I shan't be here this time next year.' I once reported these predictions to my father. 'She's been saying that ever since I first met her,' he replied.

So this is the life's companion that buccaneering Bert has picked out for himself. Even odder, though, is that he seems to have made the arrangement function. He has prevailed upon her to accompany him on his adventures. To embark on a ship, which might at any moment strike an iceberg or be quarantined for typhus. To enter into a foreign register office and lifelong wedlock. To trail from city to city and state to state across America. Into a sailing boat. Back from America to Tufnell Park. From Tufnell Park to Holloway. Into a villa and a motor car, strange cafés and chess clubs. He has even charmed two beautiful daughters out of her.

No wonder he's been able to talk the government into buying his palliasses.

*

Another possibility has just occurred to me – that my grandmother's nervousness was the *result* of living with Bert. That, until he had dragged her through the heat of an American summer and the cold of an American winter, almost drowned her, impoverished her, enriched her, and forced two pregnancies and two childbirths on her, she had been a flame-haired adventuress as bold as himself. It doesn't seem very likely. But then nor does the first version of the story.

I wonder what Bert and Nell make of Tom Frayn, when he comes courting their daughter. A cocky upstart from the wrong side of the Holloway Road. An office boy, or perhaps by this time a wages clerk, with no prospects in life and a poverty-stricken mother to support, from a family with an unreliable father and a hereditary disability. One look at his slicked-down hair and his sharp suit and even the most tolerant of parents would lock their daughter in her room. She's only just turning fifteen, after all – she's got her exams at the Royal Academy to think about. She's going to be a violinist. Have you ever heard of a violinist stepping out with a wages clerk? She doesn't know what she's doing – you can see she's completely besotted.

Maybe Bert recognises a few similarities between Tom and himself as a young man. Difficult to know, though, whether this would make him even more aware of the wretchedness that the lad is threatening to inflict on his daughter, or give him some hope that one day Tom, too, might find his own palliasses at the end of the rainbow.

Whatever Bert thinks, Nell must be in the most terrible twitter. She must see every possible disaster either coming or already upon them. Pregnancy . . . elopement . . . destitution . . . All that money on violin lessons wasted! All that tea and seed-cake that will have to be consumed with in-laws on the bad side of the Holloway Road! All the profits from the palliasses somehow spirited away by this cocky young chancer! Vi getting pneumonia from hovering about outside the front door to say goodnight to him! Yes, and *now* where is she? She should have been home from the Academy by six and it's nearly ten past! She's in Gretna Green! She's on a boat for South America! Oh – is that you, Vi . . .?

Do they perceive Tom as being in at all the same social class as themselves, now that they live in a detached house in Gatcombe Road? Impossible for them not to be aware of the question. It's all-pervasive, particularly in relationships that threaten to become institutionalised, even if no one mentions it. Its pervasiveness, though, is matched by its elusiveness. It seems simple enough until you try to apply it to particular families. What class *are* Tom and his parents exactly? What class are Vi and hers? Whenever I have to explain my origins I say 'lower middle'. Look at those eleven people in four rooms in Devonshire Road, though, and this seems a bit optimistic; a bit of an underestimate, on the other hand, for a palliasse merchant in a villa in Pooterland. If it's a matter of occupation then my father's sister and brother, the bookfolder and printer, surely put the family into the skilled working class – even if the office boy, the pianola-roll librarian and their shop-assistant father are struggling to lift it a few inches above.

In practice, in any case, it's surely more a matter of style and outlook than income. My father (a lifelong Labour supporter, incidentally, wherever his changing fortunes took him economic-ally) salted his speech with Cockney rhyming slang, and called his business contacts Guv'nor (though never Guv). Perhaps this was putting on a bit of a performance, though, as he did with his deafness. He didn't drop his aitches or double his negatives. For the most part he spoke more or less received English, and so did all his brothers and sisters.

And yet he had very little middle-class sense of material posses-sion, or of making provision for the future. For most of his life he drew a monthly salary, and paid it into a bank account. He never owned a house, though, probably never any of the cars he drove, or much of anything, really, except a few suits and hats, and later a hearing aid. I don't think he ever took out either insurance or assurance, and he certainly never made a will. When he died, and my sister and I concocted a tactful fiction that he had informally intended £300 of the modest balance in his account to go to his one surviving sister, I got a letter from her husband saying that it was the biggest surprise of her life to be so generously remembered – and I think the real surprise was that anyone in the family was in the business of leaving anyone anything at all.

Insofar as he thought about the future, which I'm pretty sure was not much, he assumed like Mr Micawber – and, I should think, Albert Lawson, the successful palliasse merchant – that something would turn up. But then, if you look beyond Devonshire Road and Gatcombe Road, to the further reaches of the family, the picture changes again. One of my mother's cousins was married to a stockbroker, while in my generation and my children's you find not bookfolders and shop assistants, but solicitors and academics, TV presenters and producers, not to mention three writers, all of us firmly related to the structure of society by deeds and degrees, and tethered to the future with mortages and savings.

So maybe Tom didn't seem quite so alien to Vi's family, in spite of his trans-Holloway Road origins. They must have taken to him, as everyone else did, because soon her mother was confiding to him about her tragically limited life expectancy. And in the front room behind the privet hedge at Gatcombe Road he was mutating from sharp, streetwise Tom into what he would be within the family for the rest of his life – the more domestic Tommy.

Things were finding their own level, in any case, because within six months of my father's getting a foothold in the family the Lawsons were on their way down in the world. The heyday of the house of Lawson was over. It had lasted only four years.

What had happened? 'It's a very long story,' said Phyllis in the note that she wrote me seventy years later, 'but things didn't "work out".' This was in 1919, and one of the problems must surely have been that the war was over. The civilian population was perhaps less eager to sleep on sacks of straw than the military had been. It would have been characteristic of Bert's hopeful approach to business not to have seen this coming. I imagine that there must also have been the usual problems with his associates, who had probably decamped with the last of the straw.

The anxiety of all this no doubt brought Nell even closer to her deathbed. Bert, however, seems not to have been greatly concerned. He remained, says Phyllis, the eternal optimist, and never ceased to believe that his fortunes were going to change. I imagine him continuing to whistle as he opened the final demands and distraint orders; and from now on the supply of them was going to be constant.

He sold the car. He moved the family out of Gatcombe Road into another substantial house, even closer to the Pooters' territory, but shared this time with two other families. They were back to the kind of accommodation they had left behind four years earlier.

The saddest thing about his failure was the consequences it had for the two girls. They had to become the family's breadwinners. As soon as she was fourteen Phyllis left school and trained as a shorthand typist. And at the age of sixteen, after just one year as a future violinist, Vi had to leave the Royal Academy. She had already, my father told me later, played with the Queen's Hall Light Orchestra – in what circumstances I don't know – but now, it turned out, she was not going to be a violinist after all. She was going to be a shop assistant, like her father and Tommy's father before her.

Her father's downfall, though no one realised it at the time, was not the first disaster in Vi's life – it was the second; and the effects of the first one were going to be infinitely worse. But this neither she nor anyone else would discover for another twenty-six years.

I recall my mother taking me as a treat, when I was five or six years old, to go shopping at the big stores in Kensington High Street, and I thought she told me that she had worked in at least two of them, Barkers and Pontings. Maybe this was later, though, because in Phyllis's little memoir she says that Vi started straight out at Harrods. This was certainly several steps up the ladder from the kind of places her father and future father-in-law had begun in, and I guess it must have been Bert, with his pre-war connections in the West End retail trade, who had got her the job, even if he hadn't managed to do something similar for himself.

She was in the gowns and costumes showroom, and Phyllis says she did very well there. 'They often used to take her out of her department to do special modelling for them, preferring her to their "official" models.' When, in middle age, I began to think about my origins, and about things that had long seemed more or less unthinkable, I realised that I had not one single physical memento of my mother – not so much, at that time, as a blurred snapshot. I asked Phyllis about her, and she told me where I might possibly find a picture. In the 1920s, she said, Vi had modelled Harrods gowns for their advertisements in the society papers. I went out to Colindale, to the newspaper department of what was then the British Museum Library, and searched blindly through the ancient files.

And suddenly, in an illustrated magazine called *The Bystander*, dated 18 March 1925, there she was, unidentified but unmistakable. She's sitting hand on hip, in a long silk jacket and a lace scarf. Her heart-shaped face is framed by a cloche hat, and the long plaits have been reduced to a bob. She's half-turned away from the camera, and her wide-set eyes are cast demurely down. The advertisement occupies a whole page of the magazine, and under the picture, in tasteful italics, it says:

INVITATION

Harrods Exposition of the Fashions for Spring is simply a tribute to the dress-taste and discrimination of the public Harrods serve. Visitors tell us that nowhere else is there to be found a Display so fascinating, so original, so informative. Why not accept Harrods' invitation to this enchanting spectacle?

I did, belatedly, accept it as best I could. I had the page from the *Bystander* photographed and framed, and I have only to lift my eyes an inch or two from the screen of the word processor to see it hanging on the wall. And if I look at some of the other photographs hanging around it, there she is again, in various snapshots that no one in the family had ever thought to give me copies of until I began to ask around for them.

And there's that same heart-shaped face, those same wide-set eyes, in the photographs of my daughter Rebecca. Then yet again, in the next photograph, in *her* daughter's face. Not everything is lost.

So Tommy and Vi were now socially and financially rather well-matched. Whether they had by this time already decided to get married, and if so when, I don't know. The following year, though, in 1920, any plans they had were disrupted, because Tommy's father died.

Exactly how much he had been contributing to the household in Devonshire Road in the last years of his life isn't clear. According to his death certificate he had moved on from the china shop to an ironmonger's, but he died of cancer of the stomach, which suggests that he hadn't been working for some time. He had plainly made no provision for his widow, and she was now effectively destitute. Three of the five children, Nellie, George and Daisy, had long since married and moved out, while Mabel, the simple-minded bookfolder, needed quite a lot of support herself. Daisy chipped in with the occasional ten-shilling note, says her son John, but only one of the children was really capable of doing much to help financially, and that was the baby of the family, now nineteen years old: Tommy.

Standing in for his father in this way was the first serious moral challenge of his life, and it sorts oddly with his haphazard approach to some other questions of financial responsibility that he shouldered the burden so completely. He can't have been earning much yet, and he had, says Phyllis, 'a pretty tough time'. When I think of how little was required of me at that age – and how unready I should have been to take on the task if it had been – I feel chastened. He and Vi evidently accepted that they couldn't afford to get married until his circumstances had changed. They had to wait another eleven years.

I don't know much about this decade of their lives. I have snaps of them at other people's weddings, and on the holidays they took every year, at least from 1926 onwards, with his brother George, George's wife Nelly, and George and Nelly's schoolboy son Maurice. Llandudno, Penzance, Bournemouth, Llandudno again, in George's open bull-nosed Morris Cowley, a vast haywain of a vehicle. Here they are, stuck in a ford somewhere, with the bonnet of the Morris up, and Tommy, who has presumably been trying to push the car out, leaning against the back of it, with the water halfway up his trousers. Here he is on a beach somewhere, carrying Vi across the puddles left by the receding tide. Here's Vi looking romantic on a rock, here she is smiling straight out at the camera from a crowd in front of a cockle stall, here lurking lonely and mysterious in a long dark overcoat and fur collar in front of the misty lattice of the Forth Bridge. I gaze and gaze at the soft images, unable to get enough of them.

My father's style has changed somewhat in these pictures. He's no longer the smart lad he was when he started work and met Vi. He's taken to tweed jackets and diagonal-check sweaters and a pipe, that now archaic emblem of male gravitas. He has a certain steadiness in the look on his face, even when he's smiling. In this world of holidays, though, his short-back-and-sides is always gloriously hatless, and he still seems light on his feet – Fred Astaire, just about to take the pipe out of his mouth and twinkle away with Vi across the dance floor.

And here they are together. I lift my eyes from the screen as I work and sneak another look at them, hanging on my wall beside the Harrods picture of Vi in working mode. They're on holiday somewhere, relaxed and smiling, Tommy with pipe and open-necked shirt, Vi in a modest cloche hat of her own. They look so happy.

On the twelfth of September, 1931, at Edmonton Register Office, after twelve years of waiting, Tommy and Vi finally do become man and wife. The witnesses are Vi's father and Tommy's eldest sister Nellie. Tommy is now thirty, and his Rank or Profession is given as Builders' Commercial Traveller. When he had first made this shift in his career I don't know, but he has now found the vocation to which he's going to remain faithful for the rest of his life. Vi, apparently, has no Rank or Profession. One of them evidently told the registrar that she was twenty-six, but after a little recalculation amended this to twenty-seven.

Tommy must feel he's doing quite well, because he's still not free of his family obligations, even when his mother and Mabel move out of Devonshire Road in 1933 to perhaps cheaper rooms just off the Tottenham end of the Seven Sisters Road, a couple of miles further out. Things change a bit when his mother dies in 1935, and Nellie, who lives in Stoke Newington, on the other side of the Seven Sisters Road, shoulders responsibility for Mabel and takes her in. Mabel had obviously given up her job as a bookfolder by this time because she goes back down the Seven Sisters Road each day, rain or shine, to visit her former next-door neighbour in Devonshire Road. And each day returns precisely as the clock strikes five.

Whether or not Tommy is still helping out financially, he and Vi have escaped from the Seven Sisters Road and found a flat in the north-western suburbs, over an off-licence in a new parade of shops opposite Mill Hill Station. The station, now Mill Hill Broadway, has these days been incorporated into the massive elevated bastion and ceaseless noise of the M1, as Anthony Avenue in Chicago has been into the Skyway. The shops are looking a bit run-down, and the off-licence has been replaced by a bookmaker's, but in 1931 the stylish new Tudor half-timbering, with the medieval towers above, must have seemed very up to date. Perhaps it caught their eye at once as they came out of the station looking for somewhere to live – which suggests that, even though Tommy was now a commercial traveller, he hadn't yet acquired a car. In all the time that I knew him, he to my knowledge almost literally never set foot on public transport. I'm not sure that he'd have known how to go about buying a ticket.

So here they are, married at last and with a home of their own. But by this time another set of obligations has been laid upon him:

Vi's family. The decline of the Lawsons has continued throughout the twenties. They have now lost their foothold in Pooterville completely and are reduced to a part-share in a small house out in Muswell Hill. On Tommy and Vi's wedding certificate the former palliasse magnate is now described, like his new son-in-law, as a commercial traveller. Even this, though, is probably more an aspiration than a reality. Vi and her sister, says Phyllis in her note to me, had 'managed to keep things ticking over to a certain extent, but when Vi left home to get married I couldn't do it on my own, and that was when the home definitely broke up.' Their stay in the Muswell Hill house had lasted only a couple of years; now they have lost even that. Phyllis 'went into digs,' she says, 'and my father had to "fend for himself". I know things were very rough for him.' She helped him out from her wages as a typist.

Which leaves Nell. All her nervousness has been justified, all her fears realised. She's left as destitute as Tommy's mother was. She's worse off, in fact – she hasn't even a roof over her head.

So Tommy and Vi find themselves sharing their new life together, for which they have waited so long, and their new Tudor flat at Mill Hill, with her mother. The arrangement is probably intended as a temporary stopgap. She will remain with them for the next eighteen years.

This is the second major test of my father's character. And, once again, he has risen to it, without, so far as I know, ever complaining. It's not a challenge that I should have met with any great distinction.

The flat is filling up. It must be about this time that they acquire a dog – I think, from what I remember my father saying, a wire-haired terrier. And in September 1933 the dog is joined by a baby boy (the unexpected result, according to my Auntie Elsie, of a night out together, rather than of any conscious intention, which I find rather touching, and perhaps the hidden source of my interest later in life in the random and disordered). There's rather a lot of me in the family snapshots dating from the next year or two. Or at any rate of a chunky, chubby boy with abundant blond curls, who slowly changes over the next three-quarters of a century, as I believe from my confused recollections and from a certain amount of documentary evidence, into the gaunt, balding old gent I now identify as me. The photographs show this wonderful child being held first by his mother, then by his father, then gazed at adoringly by both of them. By the age of three the boy's hair is so luxuriant and wavy that he looks like an advertisement for shampoo. It takes very little imagination on my father's part to see it flopping gracefully over his son's suntanned brow in years to come as he effortlessly sends the best that the Australian bowlers can come up with away over the Nursery End . . .

There's no sign of the dog in the photographs, nor in my conscious recollection. In a jealous fury, apparently, one day while the family's out, it attacks my cot and tears the bedding to shreds. My parents feel that they must make a choice between dog and son. They choose the son, fortunately, and the only trace of the wirehaired terrier that remains in our lives is deep in my unconscious, the cause, as I suppose, of the otherwise unexplained fear of dogs that I have suffered from ever since.

The departure of the dog must reduce the pressure on accommodation a little. And perhaps, now that the future batsman has come along, the additional presence of the batsman's grandmother doesn't seem quite so onerous. The availability of a live-in children's nurse to help change the England captain's nappies (particularly one who is as devoted to him as they are themselves, and who is too nervous ever to want to go out) is beginning to show an unforeseen return on Tommy's tolerance.

Soon, in any case, they're moving out of the flat into a house – and even further out in the suburbs. Plenty of other young families at the time are doing much the same, of course, which is why London is growing so fast in those two decades between the wars. The slightly odd thing about the move that Tommy and Vi are making, though, is that it's to the south-western suburbs, on the other side of the Thames. They have both spent their entire lives in North London, and North Londoners regard South London as a foreign country, a vague tangle of unmapped streets where only missionaries and encyclopaedia salesmen venture. Moving south of the river must feel almost as adventurous as moving to the Southern Hemisphere.

How does it come about? Well, Tommy's already working for a firm just beyond the river in Southwark, and travelling the inner boroughs round about for them. Which means that he's broken the psychological barrier of the river – and also that he must have a car. I have a hunch that they're out for a spin in it with the baby, perhaps for a day by the sea on the south coast, perhaps just to the Derby on Epsom Downs, and that they get stuck, like everybody else, in the mile-long traffic-jam that used to build up in Ewell Village on summer weekends in the twenties and thirties before the bypass was built. And that, as they sit there in the blue haze of exhaust fumes, they find themselves gazing into an estate agent's window with a sign that says the kind of thing that local estate agents' signs do at the time:

LIVE IN SURREY, FREE FROM WORRY!
Modern Homes in Old-World Ewell!
Where the fresh breezes blow straight from the Surrey Hills! Chalk upland soil! Detached residences available, erected upon approved principles, and finished to a degree of perfection!

From £975. Deposit £50. Monthly £5 18s. 9d.

However they happen upon it, one day early in 1935 they're moving in. They're not, of course, in spite of all the tempting offers in the local agents' windows, *buying* the house. They're renting, just as their parents rented before them. They have signed a lease with Stanley Charles Longhurst, a timber merchant in Epsom, at whose circular saws I later found myself labouring one summer for £3 a week (under-eighteen rate). The rent of the house is seventy-eight pounds (£78) per year; which, as anyone as quick at arithmetic as Tommy would instantly see, is approximately the same as he would be paying in instalments on a mortgage. Far though they have ventured into the wilderness of suburban South London, though, they have not gone completely native.

What more can a man want, if he has a house, a garden, a beautiful wife, and a son who will one day open for England?

A daughter, obviously, to complete the archetypal family.

On Saturday, 6 March 1937, it begins to snow. It goes on snowing hard throughout the night, as Vi goes into labour, and on the Sunday Dr Wilde, the family doctor in Epsom, has to drive through the whirling flurries and the gathering drifts to come and deliver her. The snow is still falling as the baby is born, and my father has a nightmare drive across London to fetch Florrie, the monthly nurse we're borrowing from her last clients, our rich stockbroker relations in Enfield, where for some reason she seems to have taken up permanent residence.

My parents tactfully allow me to choose my new sister's name, and even more tactfully steer me to the choice that I suppose they've already made: Gillian. Gillian Mary. Jill.

What Dr Wilde always calls her, though, for as long as he attends the family, is the Snow Baby.

3

Duckmore

So there we all finally are, in spite of the combined fecklessness of my two grandfathers, Bert Crouchman's plans, and the spring snow. Mother and father, a boy and a girl (and Nanny to fuss over them). At 3 Hillside Road, East Ewell, twelve miles out of the smoky heart of London – a detached house at last, like the palliasse magnate's villa, with no one quarrelling and banging about on the other side of the wall, no one overhead, no one underneath. In a trim green cul-de-sac where no trams clatter, and no drunks sing and vomit. Separated from even the tranquillity of the road by a front garden, with a buddleia where in summer the butterflies mass and sun themselves. With enough space on one side of the house to have a garage for the car, and on the other a shed to keep the coal in.

The house even has its own name, Duckmore, written in embossed metal letters on the green-painted gates, which are already, since the house was built eight years earlier, rotting on their hinges in the most picturesquely rural manner. Where the name came from I don't think my father ever knew or asked. Duckmore, though! As if it might be Chatsworth or Manderley.

And now, I think, I can make some sort of guess at why he was coming through the French windows round the back of the house that afternoon in 1936. Because the very first thing he wanted to do on his return from the great city was to have a look at the garden. For me Duckmore and its grounds had existed for ever, the ancestral hall of the Frayns, the only world of which I had ever been fully conscious. But for him, a year after we moved in, it was still new. And he had earned it all by his own quick wits and hard work, in the teeth of so many setbacks. It was his liberation, his great adventure in life, his triumph. In a moment he would go indoors and begin once again to enjoy the interior amenities. The dining room, the lounge. The kitchen and downstairs back bedroom, with the corridor connecting them. The separate scullery. The 'Ideal' boiler and the 'New World' gas cooker with the 'Regulo' oven. The two upstairs bedrooms, the bathroom and separate lavatory, the ample storage available in the dusty loft.

But first, the garden. That great estate, those rolling green acres, of which he is now master; lawns and glades, rose gardens and kitchen gardens, meadows and orchards. Or which one day will be. Fifty feet wide and a hundred feet long – an eighth of an acre. And over the fences, six gardens away, you can almost see the open farmland starting, with the long dip slope up to the North Downs beyond. He draws the good upland Surrey air into his lungs.

Then in through the French windows (and not even the villa in Gatcombe Road had French windows!), and there's his son and heir, already as high as the dining-room table. A chunky-looking lad, with fair hair and blue eyes. He can see him in years to come, at one of the great public schools. A cricketer, of course – a batsman. He smiles at me as I bravely make light of some childish injury, and what he sees is me strolling out to the wicket, pads gleaming, bat tucked under my arm as I pull on my gloves. And then the elegant leg glides, the effortless cover drives. The sneaked singles, the solid fours. All done with such grace, with such modesty. And now here's the ball lifting up and away for a six – over the heads of the astonished fielders, over the proud father in the applauding crowds, out into the misty blue skies over the Surrey hills . . .

How does the future cricketer himself see the world at this point? I think my first conscious memories are not of the house, or of my father as he came through the French windows that afternoon, but of myself, given objective reality and placed in the public domain by his memorialising and mythologising of me. Of my early sayings, when I was first able to speak, that he repeated over and over again, to me and no doubt to anyone else who would listen, until they passed into family lore.

'Take it round the adges' – my attempt to repeat his advice about coping with hot food. I still remind myself, faced with a bowl of scalding soup, that the adges will be the first bits to cool. And the words bring back not only him, and the small child solemnly learning how to deal with the problems of life, but – almost – an elusive deliciousness that has haunted the edges of my memory ever since, and that I think, with hindsight, must be of groats. Robinson's groats, to be precise – I remember the tin.

'I can say "steam" but I can't say "shmoke".' And now I see a locomotive labouring up the gradient from the local station. It's always the same kind of weather in my memory – a day of rolling dark clouds with a hint of rain. The line has been electrified for a decade by this time, so the locomotive must be hauling a goods train. And there watching the train, visible to me only through my reported words, is the small serious child who is being watched in turn by his equally unseen father as he exclaims upon the evanescent speakable steam hissing out of the valves and cylinders, and the unpronounceably dense shmoke piling above the funnel.

My first conscious direct memory of anything outside myself is not of Duckmore and its broad estates but of the street. I am adventuring out of our front gate and into the great world beyond. It's a summer's day – perhaps this is the very first summer after we moved in, when I'm still not yet three. I walk along the pavement, on and on into the endless distances of the street – past the gate of No. 4 – on and bravely on, until I find myself in a strange new landscape with its own exotic flora, a mass of sunlit pink blossom on a tangled rambler rose hanging over a garden fence. I have got almost as far as the garden gate of No. 5. At this point I somehow become aware of how far I am from home, and abruptly lose all my taste for exploration. I turn and and run back to No. 3.

Hillside Road, boundless as it seems to me at that age, is actually a little cul-de-sac. Seventeen detached houses of assorted design (or at any rate variations on six different themes), screened by seventeen assorted front gardens. No. 3, Duckmore, is I think a derivative from the Arts and Crafts Movement, and is trying to dissimulate its upper floor beneath a heavy wig of Dutch tiles so as to make itself look more like a cottage. The short street ends in a turning circle with a lamp post in the middle of it and loose gravel all around, a fair proportion of which is removed by myself and my friends in the years to come, embedded in our knees when we race round the circle on bicycles which skid helplessly away beneath us in the unstable surface.

Behind the luxuriant vegetation of the front gardens live mostly rather retiring neighbours, whose discreet middle-class style is in keeping with the character of the street. Between the electoral register for 1938, the last taken before the war, and the first one taken after it, in 1948, I see to my surprise that considerable churn has occurred, and that by no means all the names on either list are familiar to me. In my recollection, the neighbours have all been there since the beginning of time, and with one or two notable exceptions never change. Next door to us, behind the massed cherry and almond blossom at No. 4, are two maiden ladies, Miss Hay and Miss Fowler, who live a retired life, and who are glimpsed only through the crack of their minimally opened front door – though sometimes three or four times a day – when I ask them if I may please get our ball back. Behind the rambler rose at No. 5 are Miss Johnson, another maiden lady, and her father, then the Laverses, the Kidds, the Staineses, and round the lamp post at the top, the Milwards, the Knowleses, the Williamses and the Fieldings. Staines is in the Foreign Office, suitably enough, and Williams owns the newsagent's in Ewell Village. Shakespeare, going the other way, at No. 1 on the corner, has some connection with a firm that specialises in high-quality lithography. How Lavers, Kidd, Milward, Knowles and Fielding earn their livings I don't know. Three other families are so unobtrusive that I have completely forgotten them.

There are some anomalies in this well-ordered world. Archie Dennis-Smith and his wife, at No. 13, seem a little too grand, with their Noel Coward voices, their open Triumph Dolomite sports car, and their departure on summer weekends, he in white flannels, she in pleated white skirts, both carrying an assortment of racquets under their arms, to join the tennis parties given by Warbey, a wealthy cardboard-box manufacturer who lives in the unmade-up private avenues a quarter of a mile away. The Laverses, inconspicuous though they are, later evacuate themselves from London when war threatens and let their house to an Italian family, the Locatellis. Italians! In Hillside Road! It occurs to me now that they were probably refugees from Mussolini, but subtle distinctions of this sort are entirely beyond us, and I don't think anyone ever speaks to them. Soon, of course, they're not just aliens but enemy aliens, and I suppose this is why they and their many unspoken-to children all vanish so suddenly – into internment (taking, say the shocked neighbours, even the electric light sockets with them).

The Fieldings, almost painfully inconspicuous in themselves, become noticeable through their children. Their son John is simple-minded, and we do our best to add to his problems with our teasing. Their daughter Joan, on the other hand, later marries a fighter pilot, who will soon be one of our heroes. He looks exactly as a fighter pilot is supposed to look, with a clean-cut rugged handsomeness and determined jaw. We all worship him, just as naturally as we mock his brother-in-law.

And in the midst of them all, at No. 3, there's us. What do the Milwards and the Staineses and so on make of the Frayns? How much are they even aware of us, for a start? Jill and I are soon playing with the other children, but, until the war comes and my father has to organise everyone in the road to do fire-watching, I don't think we have much social contact with most of our neighbours. When my father comes face to face with them in the street, does he greet them with the same easy confidence with which he introduced himself to Vi fourteen years earlier? If so I don't quite share it. I suppose all children eventually become aware of their parents' embarrassing failure to be exactly like everyone else's parents, and from a very early age I'm conscious, in the unconscious way that children are conscious of things in the adult world, that we don't melt into the background quite as unobtrusively as I could wish.

Where are we going wrong? Does my father call Staines and Kidd 'Guv'nor', as he does the contractors and architects he deals with in his work? Does he ask them how the Missus is? Reveal that he votes Labour?

I don't suppose he employs exactly the same repertoire of humorous usage as he does at home; we all have different languages for different social contexts. Some of his set phrases when he's talking to anyone in the family are passing jokes that have solidified. Once, out in the car, he must have amused us by pretending to misread the warning on a road sign; now anything that threatens life and limb is danghe*rooz*. Some usages he's brought with him from Holloway or his stay in Newcastle – New*cast*le – others he's picked up from his weekend trips to the races and cricket matches. He gave old McCormick a tinkle, he tells Vi, but they'd gone all round the houses and got no forrader, because six to four on Worral in the Manchester office has been shouting the odds, so he had to go a bit canny – just hope to come up on the rails and get his nose in front. But then next day Renwick really gave McCormick what-for – hit him all round the wicket like a good 'un, which was quite a turn-up for the book.

When my father (expertly) carves the Sunday joint he quickly tosses titbits into his mouth and winks: 'Carver's perks!' One of his favourite words I've never heard on anyone else's lips: *hotchamachacha*! I imagine that this began life as a conjuror's invocation, like *abracadabra*. My father uses it, though, to create a general sense of humorous mystification ('Am I going to get a chemistry set for my birthday, Daddy?' – 'Hotchamachacha!'), or to pour scorn on what someone (usually me) is saying ('Come on – quick – seven nines!' – 'Um . . . eighty-two?' – 'Hotchamachacha!'), or to warn you urgently against doing something danghe*rooz*.

He has a brief but complex assemblage of gestures and sounds to indicate his respect for something – particularly for things with which he has no personal acquaintance. Cézanne, say, or Château Mouton Rothschild. A wink and a quick sideways twist of the head, a twitch of the mouth and a click of the tongue. Then a knowing assessment: 'Pretty good paintings, you know. Pretty good wine.'

I try to imagine Miss Hay registering her approval of something equally alien to her – a steeplechaser or a batsman, perhaps – in the same way . . . 'Mother's Ruin in the two-thirty? Put your shirt on it . . . Not half bad with a bat, you know, old Hutton.' Or Milward giving Knowles a little tinkle . . . Or Staines warning his masters against getting involved in Czechoslovakia: 'Hotcha-machacha, Foreign Secretary!'

My father's a good storyteller, and the colleagues and relatives who figure in his stories become characters like himself, slightly simplified and larger than life. Rebecca accuses me of having inherited this particular trait, even if none of his other character-istics. If there's any grain of truth in this then I suppose I should be grateful to him, as for so many other things, because I've been able to sublimate it into my professional stock-in-trade. Rebecca will raise a sceptical eyebrow at this, and produce some wildly exaggerated account of my supposed exaggeration. I listen with my jaw dropping to her tales of the things I'm supposed to have said and done. But then she, like me, now writes fiction for a liv-ing; she's inherited the same gene herself.

My father's on friendly terms with at any rate one of the respect-able neighbours, Shakespeare, at No. 1, and after the Laverses return from hiding at the end of the war they and my father are in and out of each other's houses all the time, playing bridge and making (as it seems to me) exquisitely boring non-conversation. There are two other households in the street, though, who stick out a bit, as we do, for different reasons, and these are the neigh-bours my father is closest to: the Barlows, next door at No. 2, and the Davises opposite.

The Barlows are Scots, which is a bit of an oddity in itself, and makes it difficult to assess their social standing very exactly.

She's a coloratura soprano. I have no idea where or what she sings, except at home. The characteristic sound of summer mornings, when the windows are wide, is of her practising, hours at a time, in her kitchen (or perhaps her scullery) as she clatters the dishes. He's an architect who works for Putney Council, and my father immediately recognises in him a suitable subject for his stories. Most of these turn on what my father sees as his traditional Scots carefulness with money, which forms a good complement to my father's carelessness with the literal truth.

What entertains my father most is Barlow's car. So far as I can recall, he's the only person in the street to have one, apart from my father and Archie Dennis-Smith. Barlow's old Austin, though, is distinguished from the other two by its livery of rust and filth. He's too mean (according to my father) to waste money on repairs or on leathers to wash it. He's also canny with the petrol and oil, and my father has a fund of stories about how Barlow has once again, to his surprise, had to abandon the car somewhere at the roadside between Ewell and Putney because either the tank was empty or the engine has seized up.

In the end, of course, more petrol, even more oil, has to be bought. The extravagance at which Barlow draws an absolute line (says my father) is replacing the brake linings. They wear down to the rivets, but the car goes as well as it's ever going to go without them. There's the question of stopping, of course, but there are other and less expensive ways of doing this. Slamming the car into low gear, for example. Finding a side street to turn into or an uphill slope. Running out of petrol or oil. Barlow has to go down Putney Hill each day on the way to work, and my father tells us over and over how he prevents the car from running away with him by keeping the nearside wheels rubbing against the curb, with an eventual effect on the tyres that surprises Barlow, once again, as much as it gratifies my father.

My father's other friend in the street, Davis, at No. 17 opposite us, has two distinctions. First of all, like Archie Dennis-Smith, but unlike Kidd, Milward, Staines or even Barlow, he has a first name – George. The other distinguishing characteristic of George Davis, as my father always calls him (never just George), is that he's an artist, and a famous one. He is G. H. Davis, who draws for the *Illustrated London News*, long since defunct, but at that time (or so it seems to us who are G. H. Davis's neighbours) the most important news periodical in the country.

His speciality is drawing pictures of ships and aircraft with sections of their outer skin cut away to reveal the internal workings. He does the great new ocean liners of the thirties – the *Queen Mary* and the *Queen Elizabeth*, the *France* and the *Normandie* and the *Bremen* – and you can see the teeming passengers streaming up and down the wide stairways between the decks, through suites of restaurants and saloons and ballrooms. All the gradations of the different classes are made graphic, and beneath them the mighty engines thundering away, the holds crammed with trunks and packing cases, the cold-stores hung with sides of beef and mutton and every kind of game. He does the great biplanes and flying boats of Imperial Airways, and the airships that once seemed destined to replace them. When the war breaks out he achieves even wider celebrity by taking us inside the warplanes and warships of both sides.

He's a tall, benevolent, excitable man with a tiny, benevolent, placid wife, and I'm sometimes invited into his studio at the back of the house to gaze respectfully at the artistic chaos in which he works. His painstaking constructions are imagined from sheafs of technical plans (many of which, it occurs to me now, must be highly secret). To get a realistic impression of the exteriors of the destroyers and submarines, the Hurricanes and Wellingtons, he often also uses three-dimensional models. Some of these, when he has finished with them, he impulsively donates to me. The ones I recall best now are First World War biplanes and triplanes, with meticulously detailed struts and crosswires. My favourite is a German bomber, a Gotha biplane, with a corridor, open to the night winds, leading from the cockpit to the front gunner's position in the nose, where a tiny but perfect machine gun is mounted. These models are by far the grandest toys that I will ever own, and I venerate them; but their record of survival in my muddling childish hands is considerably worse than that of their life-size counterparts in battle.

As a matter of fact Barlow is also an artist; two pale watercolours he has painted of Scottish seaside resorts hang on our dining-room wall. He and George Davis have something else in common, too – the disgraceful state of their gardens. Barlow's front garden has at any rate one feature – his rusting motor car. I don't think I'm doing George Davis an injustice when I recall that from the windows of his studio you look out through a tangle of rambler rose over a small but (to me) entrancing landscape of primeval forest and unmown savannah. Of course – he's an artist.

Was our garden also a disgrace? I'm not sure. I find it hard to know quite *what* it was. I've often told stories since of my father's ineptitude in the garden (and there are more to come). But when I think about it I realise that this isn't fair. I'm scarcely in a position to comment, in any case, since I've never even attempted to make anything grow in a garden. Whereas he planted and nurtured herbaceous borders on either side of the lawn, including banks of goldenrod that my sister and I hid behind, clumps of lupins, irises and Michaelmas daisies, and two formal beds of roses, of delphiniums and snapdragons. There were tomatoes along the sunlit south wall of the house. Beyond the rosebeds a hedge of macrocarpa concealed a kitchen garden with apple trees, blackcurrant bushes and raspberry canes, a green cathedral of runner beans, and beds that during the war kept us healthy with an endless supply of potatoes, carrots, cabbage and curly kale.

Now that I catalogue it, it begins to sound like Sissinghurst or Hidcote. All the same, there was something a bit . . . a bit funny about it all. It wasn't like most of the other gardens where I went to play. What was wrong with it? I can't put my finger on it . . . The lawn, perhaps. It was full of bumps and hollows, and plants that had some resemblance to grass but were not grass. There were odd unexplained patches of concrete and gravel. The layout of the beds was . . . unconvincing. Nothing was quite straight, or quite round, or quite lined up with anything else. The flowers looked as if they had sprung from packets of seed scattered at random, without checking the name on the packet first. There was rather a lot of elder and bindweed. Rather a lot of weeds of every sort.

It looked like . . . well, like a garden bravely planted by a man brought up in two rooms, who has never seen a garden before. I don't think anyone could ever have accused my father of keeping up with the Joneses. I'm not sure that he cared much what the Joneses were up to. Or even knew.

When I think about the unfairness of all those stories I've told people over the years past about my father as a gardener I begin to doubt the fairness of some of the other stories I'm telling here still, my father's as well as mine.

My father's stories about Barlow, for example. Had he improved them a bit in the telling? Stretched one unfortunate occasion when Barlow had run out of petrol, or the engine had seized up, into a regular pattern of comically predictable behaviour? Extended a single brief accidental graze against the kerb on Putney Hill into a daily mile-long saga? Made something light and tractable out of heavy and intractable anxieties over money?

Of course he'd improved the stories. That was his style. Have I improved them still further in retelling them, in spite of all my conscious concern for the historical truth? I can see my daughter's sardonic smile at my even asking the question.

It's everybody's style, in any case. All accounts of the past are a bit like Davis's drawings of liners and bombers. They're formalisations of what was once before us as an endlessly confusing and unformalised present. They're intended to make visible the hidden causal machinery, to show up the structure of the decks and the different classes of saloon, and to decorate it all with little models of people made small and simple enough for us to understand. The stories we tell about childhood have no more resemblance to what that childhood was like as we actually lived through it than

George Davis's neat cutaways of a Lancaster bomber had to the interior of a real Lancaster in action, stinking of aviation fuel and vomit and fear.

And when I retell my father's stories I'm moving one stage further away from the original experience, like George Davis depicting not an actual Lancaster but someone else's model of a Lancaster.

No doubt Barlow told his wife stories about my father. 'Pours petrol into that car of his. It's often standing there with half a gallon or more left in the tank, completely unused. And as for oil! He throws it about like a drunken sailor! Now he's buying new brake linings!' Perhaps George Davis does the same. 'Saw Tom Frayn mowing his front lawn again. Second time this summer. Funny fellow, Tom – killing a perfectly good crop of daisies.'

Another question occurs to me in relation to my father's stories – a strange absence among the people he told them about. Apart from Barlow and George Davis there were various colleagues and customers who were immortalised. His cousin Courtenay, watching the asylum clock. Me and my own various idiocies. His brother and sisters, occasionally.

But about his parents – never. Not a word, in all the thirty-seven years I knew him. The sons of Noah piously covered their father's nakedness. Perhaps my father was doing the same. For better or worse, that's one way in which I'm failing to follow his example.

And only now, as I write this page, does another rather fundamental question occur to me: I can remember something about my father's social relationships, but which of the neighbours were my mother's friends? Who did *she* tell stories about? Mrs Barlow? Mrs Davis? I don't think so. I can't make my mind form a picture of her talking to or about any of them. She walked to the shops, pushing my sister's pram or pushchair, and I went with her. I can remember the shops we went into. I can remember some of the weather. She must sometimes have said good day to Mrs Kidd or Mrs Knowles as we emerged from the gate, or stopped to chat with Mrs Shakespeare as we turned the corner into Queensmead Avenue . . . I can't see it, though. Her friends are her family and my father's family from North London. And of course my father himself, my sister, and me.

All four of us together, often. On a Sunday morning, perhaps, sitting outside the Tattenham Corner Hotel on Epsom Downs. My father has fetched two pints of bitter and two half-pints of ginger beer on a round nickel-plated tray. The ginger beer is in authentic pub beer glasses engraved with the measure, exact models of the glasses our parents are drinking from, and we have a packet of potato crisps with salt in a twist of blue greaseproof paper. If it's still too early in the year to sit outside we stay in the car. Our parents sit in front, chatting peacefully to each other now and then about whatever it is that parents chat to each other about. My sister and I sit behind them, on our best behaviour, not squabbling or pestering, looking out over their shoulders at the complex white rails of the empty racecourse and the soaring spring cloudscapes above the grandstand. An occasional gust of April wind rocks the car slightly. The fizz of the ginger beer in the authentic pub glasses is deliciously intoxicating.

What's our mother like? Not like anything – she's just our mother, as taken for granted and uncharacterised as the air we breathe. She's put on a bit of weight by this time, I see from the old photographs. I suppose she's shy, and feels as displaced in Hillside Road as my father does, but doesn't have his cheek to brazen it out. What the neighbours see, I should imagine, insofar as they see anything, is a placid, smiling woman who keeps herself to herself. With us, though, she can be mercurial. She sits in the dining room in the evening with my father, and my sister and I dare each other to get up and creep downstairs, further and further, before we turn and run terrified back to bed. The darer watches through the bannisters as each sortie brings the daree closer and closer to the dining-room door . . . until he or she can distinguish the voices of the BBC news announcers and comedians on the other side of it . . . is actually touching the handle . . . turning it . . . Until in the end, inevitably, the door abruptly disappears in front of our over-confident fingers and a flying mass of fury comes hurtling out, slapping wildly at whichever of us it happens to be as we run screaming back up the stairs – then slap, slap, slap – this bed, that bed – darer and daree without distinction.

But then there are the mornings when she takes us on the green 408 or 470 from the end of Queensmead Avenue to the great metropolis of Sutton, three miles away. The bus is a double-decker, with its own staircase to climb. We're going shopping in Sutton's great department store, Shinners, to buy . . . What? I never notice – only the immensely grown-up clatter of the lift gate, and the sophisticated swoosh of the little cable cars that are shot along overhead wires to carry the cash from the counter to the cashier's office and bring the change back.

Sometimes she takes us on a longer expedition still, on the 406 from Ewell Village, to Kingston and its even more palatial Bentalls, with a visit to Santa's grotto, or an ice cream amidst the dark and ancient panelling of the Tudor Lounge. Or best of all, on the electric train from Ewell East station, in the serious green livery of the Southern Railway, trailing showers of sparks. We sit in a compartment richly furnished with veneers and sepia photographs of seaside views, and luxuriously scented by dusty upholstery and the leather of the strap which you can let out to lower the window. We're going to Madame Tussauds in Marylebone Road, and our mother points out to us once again the Royal Academy of Music, almost next door, where her career as a violinist began, and was so quickly extinguished.

Then there are quiet afternoons at home, when it's too wet to go out in the garden and nothing's happening anywhere in the world; afternoons when we beg her to play the violin to us. She refuses. She has forgotten everything she ever knew, and in any case there are no strings left on the violin. Perhaps it's on one of these afternoons that she tells us about the ship of gold waiting in Chancery, to distract us from our pestering. We can't be distracted for ever, though. The gold seems a long way off; the violin's right here, in a wooden case which is kept in the impenetrable tangle of dusty junk that has accumulated in the little cupboard under the stairs. We plead, we nag, we whine. We open the cupboard and threaten to look for the violin case ourselves.

And sometimes she gives in. Probably to save us from getting killed in the hellhole under the stairs, because extracting anything from those dark seams of junk is as difficult as coal-mining – and almost as dangerous, since you have to squeeze past the fuse boxes, and most of their china covers have long since cracked and vanished. When the case is opened at last it releases a scent of the past from the dusty blue velvet lining. It's as intoxicating as the atmosphere of a Southern Railway compartment. There, exactly fitting the blue cushions, is the violin. We gaze at it with awe. Its swelling shiny woodwork is blond, the colour of pale ale. The fingerboard and the tailpiece are a mysterious ebony, the swell of the belly and the curves of the scroll imperiously idiosyncratic. It's visibly fragile, visibly precious.

Our mother's right – the strings are all snapped and curled up on themselves. She searches through little pockets in the upholstery of the case where attachments and spares are kept, and finds an E and a D, then plunges back into the junk mine under the stairs. She brings out another violin case. In it is her father's violin – dark, like a Guinness beside my mother's, an object of veneration only in so far as it can be cannibalised to keep hers going. She searches through more pockets, takes strings off the instrument itself, somehow locates a G and an A.

We watch the familiar ritual spellbound. She uncleats one of the bows from the lid of her own case and twists the little polygonal metal knob in the handle, inset with mother-of-pearl, to tighten the horsehair. She bounces the bow against her forearm to test the tension, tightens again. She takes a little circular brown cake out of one of the pockets in the case and holds it in a cloth while she draws the bow over it. 'Rosin,' she explains. She draws the bow over the G string, and briefly, magically, the instrument sings out. She sets the heel of the violin into her waist and screws the squeaking peg of the G string tighter. We flinch away, waiting for the string to break under the strain and lash all three of us. The pitch of each string in turn edges grudgingly upwards. She plays a scale or two, an arpeggio.

Then out from the inexhaustible recesses under the stairs comes a corroded nickel music stand and a mildewed leather music case. More setting up. My sister and I wait in an agony of anticipation.

Our mother takes a white-spotted, dark blue silk scarf out of the case and holds it against her collarbone as she tucks the violin between shoulder and chin, then takes her hand away from the violin to turn the pages on the music stand. The instrument remains improbably where she has put it, projecting unsupported into empty air.

And then she plays. The violin part from Rossini overtures – *William Tell*, *The Thieving Magpie*. Other light classics – *The Post Horn Gallop*, *The Blue Danube*. All things of the kind that she must have played in the Queen's Hall Light Orchestra. I recall virtuoso showpieces, too – Tartini's *Devil's Trill*, for instance. But this is scarcely possible. Not after one year at the Academy and twenty years of Harrods and housewifery. My memory is being assisted by the family talent for improvement once again.

So much about my mother I have forgotten since then. The sound of her voice. The exact words that she spoke. Even what music she played us. But not the fact that she played it. Not the excitement when she gave in to our pleading. Not the laborious restringing, the tightening of the bow, the blue silk scarf. The curve of her bent fingers on the fingerboard. The bold mellow vibrato, conjured out of nowhere but a hollow box and nothing but catgut and a swatch from a horse's tail, singing through the house.

What was *she* thinking about as she played, I wonder now. Did it take her back to the spring of 1919, when she had just met handsome Tommy and she was at the Academy, with all the time and all the music and all the happiness of the world in front of her? And what did she feel about the way things had turned out? Well, she had us, her two children. We weren't quite as big an audience as she might once have hoped for, but listening as raptly and appreciatively as any audience ever could.

And she had Tommy. It's not the kind of thing one ever wonders about as a child, but, looking back as objectively as I can, I think they loved each other. Tom Frayn and Vi Lawson. Mr and Mrs T. A. Frayn. Tommy and Vi. I remember their having one row, and how shocked by it my sister and I were, and if I can remember that one so clearly I suppose I'd also remember if there had been any others.

I've no idea which year it was, or what it was about, though I have a feeling that it was something to do with money. It's a Saturday morning, I know that, and we're having breakfast in the kitchen. Suddenly something has gone wrong with the conversation. Their voices are loud and hard, and my mother's running out of the room. My father sits on at the table in silence, too angry to look at us. My sister and I finish our breakfast without daring to speak, then creep, still chastened, upstairs to our room. And there's our mother, not in her room but in ours, sitting on my bed. She manages a smile for us. We look at her fearfully, still saying nothing. She has been crying. She sits there like a rueful child.

One row, just so as my sister and I know what a row is, in all the thirteen years I saw them together. I think that, yes, perhaps our mother *had* found something of the happiness that had seemed to be opening out in front of her that spring in 1919, in her fifteenth year.

4

Furniture and Fittings

Or is the quarrel that Saturday morning something to do with the strains of life with a mother-in-law? My grandmother must have been living with them for six or seven years by this time. Where is she when the storm breaks? I think I'd remember if she'd been with us in the kitchen. She has nervously fled, I suppose, at the first intimations of trouble. But then where is she while my mother is playing the violin to us? You might have thought she'd be proud to see her daughter resurrecting her old skills, her lost promise. The only members of the audience, so far as I can recall, though, are my sister and me. Can our mother have chosen days when Nanny's out of the house? But Nanny's *never* out of the house! The very thought of such a thing, and even I can see the bolting milk-horse that will trample her, the sudden thunderstorm that will bring her down with double pneumonia to the early grave she has so many times predicted.

So she must have chosen not to be present. Perhaps the almost human voice of the violin speaks to her too painfully of the family's lost hopes, of the way poor Bert's success in persuading her to brave the perils of the North Atlantic and the Midwest was so cruelly followed by his failure to persuade the shoppers of London to sleep on sacks of straw.

She must be in the house somewhere, and there's only one room it can be. Her own room. Her mysterious private sanctum, the downstairs back bedroom, separated from the kitchen and the rest of the house by the darkness of the windowless corridor. We get only the most occasional glimpse inside. An entire life is packed into that room – I suppose most of the contents of 1 Gatcombe Road. Étagères and chiffoniers covered in little trinkets and mementos. Faded sepia photographs of faded sepia people. The old oil painting of herself as a girl, with the converging slant of the mouth and eyes that I've inherited, and the red-gold hair that I haven't. Silver teapots, porcelain shepherdesses, religious-looking books with dark leather bindings and gilt-edged pages. Gauzy scarves and wraps and throws. Discreetly shaded lights. Everything is rose and russet, and disappears into darkness in the depths and corners of the room. Pomanders, bowls of patchouli and little bags of dried lavender make even the air delicately antique. There's a pad of the mauve paper on which Nanny writes endless letters in her sloping hand to her sister Lal. And all of it in a room twelve feet long by nine feet wide.

Do any of the other families in the street have live-in grandmothers? I can't remember any, but in the electoral register I see a number of spare female names whose owners I can't place; perhaps they're all grandmothers hidden away in dark back rooms. Having a widowed parent living in the house is after all a common enough arrangement. The oddity in this case is that Nanny *isn't* widowed. She isn't divorced – she isn't even separated in any normal sense of the word. She just happens to have a husband who can't afford to give her a home. He's 'fending for himself', as Phyllis puts it, in digs in Crouch End. And at weekends he comes to stay.

This is surely an arrangement unknown at the Kidds' or the Dennis-Smiths', even at the Davises' or the Barlows'. My poor father has got both Vi's parents on his hands. So far as I can tell, though, he gets on well with Bert. Goes off with him for a pint at the Spring Hotel in Ewell Village on a Saturday night. Takes him with us on spins in the country – us in the car, Bert following on his drop-handled iron bicycle, wearing his Harris tweed plus fours and sucking his pebble against thirst. Bert – Pa to me – sits heavily around the house in his braces whistling, often with a tangle of broken clock springs and loose brass cogwheels spread out in front of him. (How do we come to have so many defunct timepieces?) He keeps a lot of his stuff mixed up with our own chaotic arrangements. His cannibalised violin is under the stairs.

His bicycle is in the garage, making it difficult to squeeze between it and the car to get at all the junk beyond. The St Bruno Flake tin that contains his watchmaking tools lives on a shelf with the jam-jars and rusty skewers in the coal shed. His chess set is in a linen bag with our own odd loose chess pieces and defective packs of cards in the sideboard.

Where does he sleep, though? Not in Nanny's room, certainly. He's a large man; there's no room for him in there. He'd break shepherdesses and chiffoniers every time he turned round. I suppose it's on the settee. I go out into the garden on a fine, hopeful summer's morning when the air's still cool and the dew's on the grass, and there's Pa, up already, perhaps unable to sleep on that settee, since he's about the size of a settee himself. He's in his braces, with his hands in the pockets of his plus fours, contemplating the progress of the beans and the lettuces, and whistling, whistling. I stand beside him, my hands in the pockets of my shorts, also giving my father's efforts a critical once-over, also attempting to whistle. I glow in the radiance of his wonderfulness.

My father is also often playing host at the weekends to his own family as well as his wife's – all of them at once, sometimes. It's Sunday teatime, and both wings of the dining-room table have been extended. On the table are many plates of sardine sandwiches, and little jars of fish paste and meat paste, with dishes of home-made blackcurrant jam and fans of white and brown bread-and-butter to spread it on, celery and watercress, scones and teacakes, rock cakes and fairy cakes, fruit cakes and Victoria sponges.

Around the table are wedged an amazing number of people. Tommy and Vi, of course, and my baby sister. Bert, aka Pa, now with a Fair Isle sweater politely concealing his braces, taking up a good deal of what little space there is available. Nanny, or Nell of course to most of the family. A second Nell, or rather Nellie, my father's eldest sister, and her husband Frank; Uncle George and his wife, who's a third Nell, or rather Nelly with a *y*, and their son Maurice; Auntie Daisy and a second George; perhaps their sons, Philip and John; Mabel and Mrs Murkin. Mrs Murkin? Mrs Murkin is the former next-door neighbour from Devonshire Road, whom Mabel still goes back to see each day. Mabel and Mrs Murkin: the names fit together in my memory as naturally as George and Nelly.

My favourite relative among all these, apart from my grandfather, is Daisy. She's almost as deaf as Mabel, but as chirpy and restless as a baby sparrow. She has perhaps got even further away than my father has from those two rooms in Devonshire Road; the George she has married is a silent, unreadable man who began his career at sea as a naval officer, and who now has a solidly respectable job designing mines for the Admiralty. Daisy moves him and their two young sons restlessly back and forth around one address after another in the Portsmouth area. Their younger son, my writer cousin John, has been reconstructing the story for me. First there are two furnished flats in Southsea, and then two houses in Gosport, on the other side of the harbour. Here George begins an affair with a neighbour's wife, and Daisy moves the family twice more around the Gosport side to get away from her, then inland to Fareham, to get further away still. She has a breakdown. They move back to Southsea. According to my father (are we to believe this?) she tends to move without consulting George, so that he never knows from one week to the next where he's supposed to be coming home to.

Somewhere around this point he rebels. He resigns his career as a mine designer and takes off with the neighbour's wife from four or so moves back. But his liberation from the tyranny of the pantechnicon is brief. Daisy sends him a telegram, signed by their son Philip: 'Come home at once mother dying.' She then goes to the Admiralty and talks them into taking George on again. Daisy *is* in fact dying – she has leukaemia – and George grudgingly agrees to stay with her until the end comes. It's not a happy arrangement, but Daisy does her best to make a fresh start – by moving them again, all the way up the Southern main line to Guildford. So there's a painful logic to all this restlessness, though John agrees that Daisy perhaps did also like moving for its own sake. (He and his wife seem to have inherited the taste – they've moved ten times themselves.) From Guildford Daisy moves to Bramley, then on again to Liss, and she's just bought yet another house in Goring-by-Sea when death finally halts her odyssey. She's only fifty-four.

So there they all are, everyone talking at once, some of them too softly to be heard even by the ones with hearing, some of them with so little hearing that they probably don't realise that anyone else is talking. What are they all talking about? They're struggling to sort out George from George, and Nelly from Nellie and Nell. They're protesting that they're unable to eat a third or fourth rock cake, but will perhaps try a slice of that delicious-looking sponge. 'Another cup of tea, Nelly? Sorry – I don't mean Nelly – I mean *Nellie*. More tea?' – 'Four what, love?' – '*Tea*. More *tea*?' – 'Oh, I couldn't, love, but I'd love another cup of tea.' – 'And *four* lumps, is it?' – 'No, love, no more – just four.'

Apart from the eatables what they're talking about mostly is the old country – North London. Some of them are still there, around the Seven Sisters Road. Others are scattered – George's family out to Finchley, Daisy's to wherever she's got to by now in Hampshire or Surrey, Tommy and Vi to Ewell. All of them still thinking about Holloway and points north. The familiar names keep coming round. The Seven Sisters Road. Archway. Tufnell Park, Finsbury Park. Crouch End, Alexandra Palace . . .

A dozen or more people around the table, and somewhere among them there must be a chair for me. It's unoccupied, though. I'm on the floor, under the table, and refusing to come out. The trouble is not the press of people, or the din of North London place names. It's my Uncle George. Not Daisy's George – Nelly's George. Or to be precise, it's Nelly's George's eyebrows. They're enormous, and dense, and pitch black, and they beetle. They beetle most terrifyingly out from his rather small and conciliatory face, and even Richard Hannay or Bulldog Drummond would turn and run at the sight of them. Uncle George, unlike his cheeky baby brother, my father, is a shy and softly spoken man, but these qualities are completely outweighed by the horror of those terrible appendages, and I'm proposing to stay under the table until they've gone home.

My wonderful grandfather negotiates a compromise: I can sit in his lap and keep my eyes closed. I climb into that vast, warm, luxuriously upholstered human settee and eat fairy cakes by touch. After a while I feel so secure that I risk opening one eye a little and taking a peep. The great black entanglements on the other side of the table are beetling away at me just as menacingly as before. I close my eye again.

These dozen, perhaps fifteen people, are wedged around the table in a room eighteen feet long by twelve feet wide. I know the dimensions of the dining room, as I do of Nanny's room, so precisely because, many years later, I made a television film about the streets where I grew up, and I acquired the plans of the house from the local council. While I was making the film I got myself invited back by the then occupiers. Your childhood surroundings are said to look always distressingly small when you go back with an adult eye. I can't say that my old home did, though. It had been smartened up beyond recognition, but the general layout was entirely familiar – and it seemed rather spacious.

Particularly the dining room, the biggest room in the house. But then, when I went back, there weren't fourteen or fifteen people sitting in it, and a table which, with its leaves extended, must have been about nine feet long. The table wasn't the only thing occupying the available space. Against the long wall on one side of the table was a sideboard, and on Sundays, when the relatives came, a tea trolley with my grandmother hovering anxiously over it. On the other side of the table was a bureau, with a sloping lid which could be let down to make a writing surface, and which sometimes suddenly let itself down with a sharp crack under the pressure of all the junk taken off the tea table and wedged behind it.

I've been making a few rough calculations. If you add up reasonably plausible widths for the sideboard, the table and the bureau, it leaves a space of about two foot six on either side to accommodate the guests, and allow access for people bringing round the cups of tea and the slices of sponge cake. A good job, perhaps, that the Frayns are all so wispy – particularly since all fourteen or fifteen of the people at the table must be sitting along its two long sides. Why can't some of them be sitting at either end? – Because the southern end of it is hard up against the French windows, and the northern end is pressed against the back of the settee.

A settee? In the dining room? Slightly surprising, now I come to think about it after all these years. And why is it pushed up against the table? It can't be more than about three feet deep, which must leave another six feet of dining room free beyond it. Couldn't it be moved a little further away from the table?

Not really, because on the other side of the settee are two armchairs. It's not just a settee, in other words, it's a three-piece suite, and on the other side of the three-piece suite is the fireplace. There has to be a foot or two left between the fire and the knees of the people on the three-piece suite. You could safely sit with your feet in the grate in summer, it's true . . . No, you couldn't, actually, because the gap between knees and fire is also the flightpath running laterally between the darts board on the right-hand wall and the dart-launching position near the left-hand wall. Even if no burning coals were falling on your feet there would be ricocheting darts falling on your head.

Leaving aside the question of whether this is a good place to play darts, why is there a three-piece suite, upholstered in brown mock leather, studded with round-headed brass tacks, in the dining room? Because we've nowhere else to put it, obviously. But we do! We have another reception room, as an estate agent would call it, twelve feet square, called the lounge. The lounge is presumably the place where you lounge, and if you're lounging it would seem natural to have a settee and two matching armchairs to do it in. Why isn't the three-piece suite in the lounge?

Because in the lounge there's *another* three-piece suite. This one's covered not in brass-studded mock leather but in a grimy grey fabric with large green leaves sprawling across it. As prominent labels on each of the three pieces announce, it comes from Bentalls, in Kingston, where Father Christmas lives. There's something depressing about its appearance, and it's probably stuffed with material that would burn like dry tinder if you dropped a lighted cigarette on it. No one does, though, in spite of the fact that my parents and many of the relatives who come to the house work hard at smoking. They don't drop anything on it because they don't sit on it. No one sits on it. Everyone who wants to sit on a three-piece suite sits on the brown mock-leather one in the dining room. If my grandfather sleeps on a settee it certainly isn't the one in the lounge. If the dog had still been around even the dog wouldn't have slept on it.

So obviously we're keeping the lounge for best, in the time-honoured tradition of the lower classes. We're saving it for funerals, weddings and visits from the vicar.

We're not, though. There are no weddings in the house, no visits from the vicar, and only one funeral. If anyone *had* got married the wedding breakfast would have been served on the dining table. In the unlikely event that my father had admitted a minister of religion into the house, he would have been sat on the brown mock leather in the dining room like everybody else. I can't remember whether anyone ever came back to the house after the one funeral we had in the family. If they did then they would have got exactly the same treatment – dining room, brown mock leather.

So, if the lounge isn't being kept for best, why don't we sit in there ourselves? Or – another possible solution – if we like sitting on the mock brown suite, why don't we get rid of the one with the banana leaves and move the mock brown into the lounge?

Because we never do *anything* in the lounge. The front door and the staircase open directly into it, which makes it cold and draughty. The lounge is the main highway from the front door and the stairs to the rest of the house, and there are always people going back and forth through it. Even going back and forth through it is difficult, though, because the great bulk of the unused settee and the two unemployed armchairs takes up most of the space, and if you sat in them you'd have people squeezing past you and falling over your feet all the time.

We don't like the lounge. This is the long and short of it. And we do like the dining room. In the dining room we're at home.

I suppose the truth is that my father's still finding it difficult to adjust from being one of seven people living in two rooms to being one of five living in seven. He's simply not used to life in such a plethora of rooms. The jam of people on Sunday, when the family comes, is his attempt to recreate the population density of 62 Devonshire Road.

No, I'm exaggerating again, as I'm genetically programmed to. There *is* something we do in the lounge. In fact there are two things. My sister and I open our Christmas presents in it, for some mysterious reason, and it's where we telephone. We don't have a hallway, which is where the phone's traditionally kept, so we keep it in the nearest equivalent – the cold and draughty gloom of the lounge. It's the old candlestick model, and it stands on the window ledge with its nose in the air, reluctant to be spoken to by subscribers whose social origins are so dubious. You need both hands to deal with it, one to hold the heavy receiver to your ear, the other to lift the even heavier base and bring the mouthpiece into proximity with your mouth. Having a settee next to it should mean that we can at least make ourselves comfortable while we're using it, but we don't. We take telephoning too seriously for that. We perch on the arm of the sofa, keeping our backs straight. The grey fabric and green leaves on the arm are worn threadbare.

I say 'we'. The only person I can remember using the phone is my father, to talk to his customers. 'Right you are, then, guv'nor. I'll say ta-ta for now, but I'll give you another little tinkle on Friday week.' I suppose my mother must sometimes phone the local shops. I think I can recall Nanny being fetched to speak to somebody once, and getting into a terrible tangle of earpieces and mouthpieces, wires and nerves.

No, I'm still exaggerating. Or simply forgetting. There was something else that we did in the lounge – or at any rate something my mother did, all through the thirties. There must have been. She must have played the piano in here.

There's a *piano* in here? – There *was* a piano. There was a *grand* piano. I can just catch the last faint traces of it in my memory. What I remember perfectly clearly, though, is the story of what happened to it, because my father told it again and again. He got rid of the thing. He managed to choose a time when war was threatening, and apparently when war is threatening no one wants grand pianos, so he didn't get a good price for it. He didn't get a price for it at all. He had to pay someone to take it away.

Were the piano and the Bentalls three-piece suite all in here together? I don't think this is physically possible. He must have got rid of the piano to make room for the suite. The situation is this, then: they had had a piano that my mother must sometimes have played (she had been studying piano as well as violin at the Academy), on which she might have accompanied him while he sang 'Fling Wide the Gates', and on which his two children might have had piano lessons. He had got rid of it. He had paid money to get rid of it. And he had paid Bentalls more money to deliver in its place a grey three-piece suite festooned with tropical leaves on which no one was ever going to sit.

I don't suppose our neighbours realised quite how odd our arrangements were, because (with one or two exceptions much later) none of them in all the fourteen years we lived there ever set foot in the house. Is this possible? The children, certainly, but not their parents. In my imagination I try to drag each of the neighbours through the front door in turn . . . They will not come. Not even Barlow. George Davis I can get as far as the front door, but not across the threshold.

But then nor do my parents set foot in our neighbours' houses. Actually none of the adults in the street visits back and forth, only the children. I suppose, with hindsight, that every household would have had its little oddities and anomalies, if only we'd known. George Davis should have done some of his cutaway drawings for us.

Most days of the week, of course, even when my father's at home, there aren't fourteen or fifteen of us in the dining room. There are only the five of us who live there.

So what exactly are we doing? Dining, of course, except that we don't call it that (it should be the supping room), and lounging. Listening to the wireless set in the alcove on the left-hand side of the fire. On winter evenings the glowing glass valves inside it cast a warm silhouette of the fretted back panel over the wall behind it. The lighted window at the front opens on to far-off parts of the world, most of which remain as mysterious to me now as they were then: Beromünster, Athlone, Hilversum, Stuttgart, Soissons, Sundsvall, Nice-Corse. There seems to be little going on in these places except various forms of shushing and buzzing, with occasionally a human voice or a dance band struggling to make itself heard over the vast remotenesses of Europe and the perpetual tinnitus of the ether. Not that we often investigate. For the most part we listen to the BBC – to music-hall comedians, palm-court trios, light classics, adapted stage plays, the news, of course, and a magazine programme that begins with the noise of roaring buses and hooting cars, and then a mighty voice crying 'stop!' Sudden silence, followed by the important clipped public school accent of the BBC announcer: 'Once again we stop the mighty roar of London's traffic to talk to some of the interesting people who are ...' (*Pause – title:*) ' ... IN TOWN TONIGHT!'

What else? My father writes his reports. Reports on what? His sales, I assume, now I come to think about it, though I never did at the time. Reports are simply reports. They're the things my father writes. He sits at the dining-room table, or in the armchair by the wireless set, with bulging folders of loose papers in front of him. Some of the papers have printed headings with the initials of the firm, TAC, and he signs them with his own initials, TAF. He writes long columns of tiny figures with his silver

Eversharp pencil, his index finger braced against the tip in its disturbing double-jointed concave arc. He tots up the cramped sums with effortless speed, writes totals at the bottom of columns and underlines them, tots up again, marks checked totals with little ticks.

He passes on swathes of TAC's stationery to me – important blank forms headed 'Memo' and 'Expenses', sheaves of white and pink flimsy, thick foolscap volumes with interleaved tear-out report forms and blank pages, each volume with a sheet of carbon paper that can be moved from page to page. I cover the pages with inept drawings and make flicker books out of the thick volumes. Somehow, though, the movements of my laboriously repeated stick figures never have the smoothness of my favourite professional flicker book, which bears the logo of Wakefield 'Castrol' engine oil and shows George E. T. Eyston getting into his car *Thunderbolt* before his attempt on the world land-speed record in 1938, and then, if you turn the book over and flick it back the other way, *Thunderbolt* tearing across the speed-blurred Bonneville Salt Flats at 357 miles per hour. As I get older my pictures give way to words, but I never achieve anything that has the neatness, tininess, opacity and authority of the writing in my father's reports.

I suppose we also read. Read what, though? The *News Chronicle* has been read over breakfast, which we had in the kitchen. What do we read on the brown mock-leather three-piece suite in the dining room? One thing that my sister and I certainly *don't* read is comics – we aren't allowed them. We read them in other people's houses, of course, but even away from home I should never stoop to the *Beano* or the *Dandy*, which are now rated so highly by the historians of childhood. I do condescend to *Radio Fun* and *Film Fun*. The formula of the two is identical – strips featuring characters and entertainers from the respective media – but for me they're as different as suet pudding and profiteroles. The characters in *Radio Fun* are dully, almost embarrassingly, familiar from the radio shows we listen to: Old Mother Riley and her Daughter Kitty, Tommy Trinder, Arthur Askey, Flanagan and Allen. The

Furniture and Fittings

characters in *Film Fun* – Laurel and Hardy, Abbott and Costello, Joe E. Brown – have an alien and slightly threatening sophistication because they inhabit a universe almost completely closed to us. With the very occasional exception for school outings, the News Cinema on Victoria Station, and Walt Disney's more notable efforts to induce childhood trauma, we're not allowed to go to the cinema – particularly not children's Saturday morning cinema, which forms the taste of so many of my contemporaries, but which would be full of disease-ridden council-school children. Live theatre – yes. Or at any rate the panto at Christmas and music hall as a birthday treat at the Kingston or the Croydon Empire. Not to mention our own home live theatre, usually at Christmas: my efforts at conjuring, at puppets and nativity plays – and shows written by my father starring himself as a comic schoolmaster, with my sister and me as his pupils and feeds. His character is based on an original created by Will Hay, and what puzzles me now I come to think about it again is how my father managed to imitate Will Hay without ever seeing the films he was in. Is he bunking off work on his travels to pay secret visits to forbidden picture palaces in Herne Hill and Wandsworth?

Back to the three-piece suite, though, and what we read on it. Books, certainly. Though there is a certain ambivalence about them, and you have to contrive some way of reading them that doesn't involve having your *nose stuck* or *buried* in them, which is frowned upon. I think my mother looks at an occasional novel, in a detached, nose-free way, when she puts her feet up on the sofa after lunch, and Nanny certainly does, because I feel tremendously self-important when she confuses one of her books with the one that *I'm* reading, a grown-up-looking volume about the building and operation of the *Queen Mary*. I read quite a lot of books, and the danger to my nose sometimes arouses comment. I discover a small circulating library in a newsagent's in Ewell Village, and bring home endless *Just William* and Wodehouse, and novels by someone called Joan Butler about people misbehaving at country-house weekends, which I find a little too shocking for my taste. At some point I'm given a subscription to Boots Circulating Library in Epsom, and even brave the local public library, in spite of its being full of germs left on the books by the lower social orders.

What reading matter do we actually own? There are stacks of back numbers of the *Saturday Evening Post*, passed on to us each week by a neighbour, I think Shakespeare at No. 1. I'm not sure that anyone *reads* it, even me. What seizes my imagination is the America revealed in the advertisements, which is so unlike Hillside Road. Suntanned worldly men drive suntanned worldly women in enormous open Pontiacs and Studebakers to country clubs where Kriss Kraft motor boats wait dancing on sunlit blue waters. They're smoking Camels and Chesterfields with a casual distinction that seems to be impossible with English cigarettes like Players and Gold Flake. Is this how my grandfather and grand-mother lived, in the famous days in Chicago? Did they emerge into the blue American midnight from grand hotels where top-hatted doormen saluted as they held open the door of a Lincoln cabriolet with crimson upholstery and white sidewall tyres?

Books, though. Do we actually own any books? I have a few: the one about the *Queen Mary*, a children's encyclopaedia, various children's annuals passed on from Enfield and elsewhere. But as a family? Well, we have a telephone directory and *The Complete Works of William Shakespeare*; we don't read the Shakespeare. The only other books I can remember are two volumes of photographs of Switzerland. Switzerland, it appears, is a tidy kind of place. The mountains are well-organised and sharply defined, dramatic-ally lit, with clean white snow on them and well-formed banks of clouds in the background. Switzerland offers, as America does, an instructive contrast with the contents of the dining room. All the same, we have never been to Switzerland, we have no plans to go there; Switzerland is a matter of complete indifference to us. It might seem odd that no less than half of the family library is devoted to the subject.

There's a reason for this, though, just as there's a reason for the presence of a three-piece suite in the dining room. It's the same reason that another quarter of the library is a telephone directory: because all three books we were given, the telephone directory by Post Office Telephones, the volumes of Swiss photographs by Shakespeare – not of course the Shakespeare who confusingly wrote the *Complete Works* but the better-known Shakespeare who lives at No. 1 on the corner, and who's something to do with lithography. The books are presumably surplus stock, or presents intended for customers of the firm. A lot of our possessions have come to us in a somewhat similar way. Barlow's two watercolours must have been a gift from the artist, unless my father got talked into some canny Scots bargain. Much of the tangled and broken chaos in the toy cupboard upstairs began life as the carefully constructed models in George Davis's studio. My fairy cycle in the garage and my sister's pushchair are part of the overspill of largesse from our stockbroking relations in Enfield. All the stationery in the house, and all the pens, pencils, rulers and diaries, carry the logo of my father's firm.

Some people, brought up as my father was in straitened circumstances, run wild when they get a little money and spend, spend, spend. This is a pitfall that my father shows no signs of falling into. He gets razor blades off a barrow in the New Cut, at Waterloo. He gets a gross of them – only five and a tanner, a bargain – and they last for ever, because they're too blunt and nicked to shave with. We improvise out of old packaging – almost all of which, it occurs to me now, is a by-product of smoking: the large square tin of St Bruno Flake pipe tobacco in which my grandfather keeps his watchmaking tools; small round silver tins of Dobbie's Four Square, the sealing rings of which are an important source of the rubber used in the manufacture of catapults; the flat blue battery-shaped American packs of Prince Albert, particularly prized because they're so elegant, and because the lingering scent of their contents is so alluring – also because thinking of any possible practical use for them is such a challenge to the imagination; and, best of all, the even sweeter-smelling cedar-wood cigar boxes left over from Christmas, which can be used for almost anything, from the housing of home-made crystal sets to the display cases for the birds' eggs that my friends and I steal from the hedges and trees of the neighbourhood, and the butterflies that we net from the buddleia in the front garden and poison in old jam-jars with a little lighter fuel. Old jam-jars – another essential resource. The lighter fuel, of course, is yet another spin-off from the central economic activity of smoking.

All this old packaging we work with rusty tools that have turned up behind the water butt or at the back of the coal shed. Why buy a spanner to raise the saddle on the fairy cycle when you can do the job with a certain amount of barked knuckles and shouting and a pair of rusty pliers? Why use nasty shiny straight new nails from the ironmonger's when there's a jam-jar of nicely bent and well-rusted old ones on the scullery windowsill? Why spend money on a hammer to drive them into the wood recovered from the section of rotten fencing at the end of the garden when you can do it with the back of the chopper for chopping the firewood – particularly since it's too blunt for chopping firewood? Why waste space on a ladder to get into the loft, when my father can perfectly well stand on the bathroom stool, wedge his hands against the architraves above the bedroom doors on either side of the landing, flex his knees twice, then push himself up until he can get one foot on to a bedroom door handle while simultaneously lifting the lid of the trap an inch or two with his head, grab the handhold this exposes around the edge of the hatch, wedge his other foot against the architrave opposite the doorhandle, and with an almighty heave haul himself up through the hatch with the trap balanced on his head?

Even my underpants have plainly not been bought in a shop in the normal way, because they evidently once had an owner whose waist was a foot or two greater in circumference than mine, which means that they can be kept up only by folding over the spare and fixing it with a safety pin. This is what embarrasses me when Daphne Knowles, the little girl at No. 10, suggests that we retire behind some trees at the top of her garden and inspect each other's private parts. It's not my parts that I'm bashful about – it's the safety pin. I'm pretty sure that Daphne's knickers will turn out to be the right size and held up by elastic. She's that kind of girl. She has a small (extremely cold) swimming pool in her garden, in which we spend a lot of time in water wings, and she's looked after by a nanny. *Her* nanny's not her Nanny; she's a nursemaid in a starched apron. Daphne's a sensitive little girl; at the sound of Hitler's voice on the radio she has famously gone into screaming hysterics. She might go into hysterics again at the sight of the safety pin. I can't remember now what she revealed inside her snugly fitting knickers, nor how she reacted either to the safety pin or to what appeared when I finally managed to undo it. Neither the pin nor the penis, evidently, are as upsetting as Hitler, because when her nanny suddenly appears through the trees Daphne's already fully dressed and completely composed. All I can remember is that I'm still struggling unsuccessfully to get the safety pin done up again – and have to be helped (the final humiliation) by her nanny.

The fact is that my father's not greatly given to buying things. A salesman and son of a shop assistant, married to a shop assistant and daughter of a salesman; but the other central role in the commercial dialogue he shows little interest in exploring. I don't get the impression that we're poor exactly, and he isn't mean. He punctiliously lists his expenses and pays his bills. He makes the books balance. But he's just not used to possessing and spending money, or to the idea of ownership. It's not the culture he was brought up in.

The Complete Works of William Shakespeare, for instance. I don't think we were given this, but equally I can't picture the scene where my father walks into a bookshop, selects *The Complete Works of William Shakespeare* from the shelf, takes it to the counter and hands over money for it . . . The image is as outlandish as one of him breaking into the Bodleian or the British Museum to steal it. I suspect *The Complete Works* came the same way as the playing cards in the sideboard drawer – as some kind of free or cheap promotional offer from a newspaper or cigarette company.

A lot of the things in the dining room have an air that suggests the same kind of provenance. The glass biscuit barrel on the sideboard with no biscuits in, for instance. The sherry decanter with no sherry, the portless port decanter. The twisted brass candle-free candlesticks on the mantelpiece. The picture of feasting cardinals over the mantelpiece . . . Cardinals? A popular subject of domestic artwork at the time, apparently, in their full scarlet fig and various stages of over-indulgence at the dinner table. But in *our* house? Princes of the Church – of the *Roman* Church – carousing in a house where not even a C of E curate is ever invited in for a glass of sherry from the bottle in the sideboard underneath the empty decanter? They must have slipped in free, unexamined, in exchange for fifty coupons from Wills' Gold Flake packets.

Perhaps, it occurs to me now, my father didn't pay money for the Bentalls three-piece suite in the lounge. Perhaps George Davis was throwing it out. Came wheeling the settee across the road one Saturday morning. 'Tom! Any use to you?' Impossible – George Davis would never have had such a thing in his house in the first place. George Davis would never have paid money for it. No one would have. They wouldn't have taken it in for nothing. Not even the canny Barlow. Not even if someone had thrown in the two ink-and-wash pictures that were the only other objects in the lounge, one of them entitled *A Bit of Old London*, the other, of an equally ancient street, *St Gall, Switzerland*. (Switzerland again! We're obsessed with the place! Half the library and a quarter of the art collection are devoted to it!) Where did *these* come from? Not, surely, a question of money changing hands. I try to imagine my father going into the art shop . . . Or my mother, on one of our expeditions to Shinners in Sutton. 'Those two ink-and-wash townscapes in the window . . .'

I don't know the original source of the line that has been adapted to so many humorous contexts over the years: 'One day, son, this will all be yours.' It's not something my father would ever have thought of saying to me, even as a joke. The ideas of inheriting and bequeathing were as alien to him as purchasing and possessing. My father moved lightly over the earth, scarcely leaving a footprint, scarcely a shadow.

He couldn't pass the house on to his children of course, because he didn't own it. As for the contents, they'd vanished into thin air long before my father died. The brown suite, the dining table around which so many people had squeezed, the feasting cardinals, the Bentalls suite – I never saw any of it again after we finally moved out, into another house that my father didn't own. To my knowledge only two objects survived. Over sixty years later, after the death of someone who won't enter this story for another twenty years, one of the executors said to me, 'We thought you might like these.' And he handed me the two pictures, *A Bit of Old London* and *St Gall, Switzerland*, that had once hung on the lounge wall, over the Bentalls suite. I have them in my attic still, lovingly preserved inside a black rubbish bag.

5
Quick / Slow

My parents came as immigrants to Hillside Road, and immigrants they remained. My sister and I, the second generation, probably just about passed, but my father always had something about him of the cocky young man from the wrong side of the Holloway Road, while my mother (and *her* mother), in spite of their brief stay on the right side of it, had never fully recovered their social nerve after the crash in the palliasse market.

There's something else, too, that sets us apart: my father has a second home.

His second home is his car. Barlow and Archie Dennis-Smith also have cars. But theirs are not lived in the way my father's is. Barlow uses his simply to get him rustily and reluctantly to Putney and back each day. I don't think Archie Dennis-Smith's shiny Triumph Dolomite ever goes much further than the Bell in Cheam on Sunday morning. My father, though, spends half his life in his – more time, at least on weekdays, than he does with the feasting cardinals in the dining room.

It's nothing grand – an Austin saloon, I think, like Barlow's, when I'm first conscious of it, one or two models up from the perambulator-sized Austin Seven that's making motoring accessible to the mass market at the time. Later I recall a car with scalloped flutings along the bonnet, which suggests a Vauxhall, and, rather briefly, an archaic-looking Rover Twelve, which has a hand-crafted respectability that's painfully at odds with my grandfather's bicycle and the rest of the stuff it shares the garage with. My father doesn't actually *own* any of these daytime accommodations, any more than he owns the house he sleeps in at night. They aren't even rented, as the house is – they're provided free to the reps by TAC.

Quick/Slow

It's already evening when he gets home from his day in the grimy commercial back streets of his South London territory, but in summer the front garden is still alive with butterflies – tortoiseshells, peacocks and red admirals – gorging on the heavy sweetness of the buddleia. Suddenly there he is in his hot three-piece suit, unlatching the double green gates at the end of the driveway. I must have been watching for him, because already I'm out there, like the pilot meeting an incoming liner, and jumping into the waiting car to help him steer it into the driveway. If this is the Austin still it's as importantly dark blue as his suit, and inside it the scent of the baking leather upholstery and the sombre veneers of the dashboard and window trims are even more intoxicating than the fumes of the buddleia. From the back seat comes a different kind of smell, a dusty grey sourness from the samples of roofing materials and rainwater goods he's carrying. The smell is serious, like everything on the back seat. There are serious dark albums with spring clips and the TAC logo, full of serious grey photographs of TAC products installed in serious grey factories and warehouses. There are the piles of buff folders full of my father's reports. There is his black homburg hat, removed for once as a concession to the low headroom and greenhouse heat. The contents of the car have a kind of natural authority, an order and purposiveness, that the contents of the house never quite achieve.

I sit in my father's lap and press the deliciously shallow disc in the middle of the steering wheel. 'Ge-*gurgle*!' cries the car, with a suddenness that always makes me jump. I twist the elegantly geometrical lever above the disc, first left then right, and the trafficators spring out of the coachwork, left and right in their turn, shining yellow. I seize hold of the wheel, and the car glides forward. It swings wide towards George Davis's driveway, then spins my hands clockwise as it makes its precisely judged right-hand turn into ours. There are only inches to spare between the car and the gateposts, but not once do I scrape them, or fail to stop the car before it hits the garage doors.

Then next morning the exciting blue smell of exhaust from a newly started engine drowns the scent of the buddleia, and back up the driveway goes the car again, taking my father to his other life in the inner boroughs of South London – a world where he knows every inch of the greasy setts and treacherous tramlines on the main roads, every possible hold-up from policemen on point duty or the horse-drawn drays of railway companies and breweries – and every possible permutation of ways through the back streets to avoid them, even in the yellow fogs that so often in winter reduce the rest of the traffic to walking pace. At the centre of this web are the dour London offices of TAC in the Borough, where the Southwark Street tramlines cross the Southwark Bridge Road ones, and the trams lurch round at a sudden breakneck right angle from one line to another over the complexity of points, steel screaming on steel. Uncle George, with the eyebrows, who began as a printer, now like his brother works for TAC, I think in some kind of financial depart-ment, though whether it was George who got Tom into the firm or Tom George I don't know. The most familiar character in the office from my father's stories, though, is Kerry, who is I suppose his clos-est friend, a whimsical Irishman, as tall as Nelson's Column, with a thoughtful pipe in his mouth and a not entirely serious porkpie hat on his head, like Jacques Tati. He has a difficult home life, and he writes verse and stories, which he pays to have published. He takes a kindly, amused interest in me when I start to write as well, and occasionally sends me humorous birthday messages, often in verse.

My father likes being in the car. Even after he has spent the working week nipping through the side streets of Bermondsey and Battersea he's always happy to get it out again at the weekend and take us all for a drive to the noted beauty spots of Surrey and Sussex, or on our summer holidays to the West Country. Over the years the car becomes a bond between him and myself. It's something he can give me – something he's alway happy to give me: a lift. I think it's in the car, when I'm seven or eight years old, that he makes the offhand suggestion after reading one of my school essays, 'The House I Should Like to Live in When I Am Grown Up', that I should become a journalist. On his way up to Southwark in the morning he drops me at various different bus stops where I can get various different buses to school. Later he takes me all the way with him, so that I can spend the day in London. For years this is my experience of the city – first a bewilderingly complicated zigzag, always different, through the grimy districts of Tooting, Balham, Mitcham, Streatham, Herne Hill and Tulse Hill, that have no known function except to be complexly threaded through by my father, and then a walk through the Borough, its thick commercial air laden with the sour smell of warehoused Kentish hops, and across a Thames still full of barges loading and unloading along the busy quays, and tugs lowering their funnels at every bridge.

My father doesn't just like being in the car – he likes driving. He's the Smart Lad on wheels. It gives him great satisfaction to be the first away from the lights, and to dismiss scornfully as a *weekend motorist* anyone who delays him by a millisecond or two. He enjoys nipping past a motor coach on a narrow winding road, in the interval that may or may not exist before another motor coach comes over the brow of the hill in the opposite direction, and squeezing into the gap that may or may not have been left by a weekend motorist too half-witted or too timid to keep his front bumper touching the rear bumper of the car in front. He smiles into the mirror at the sudden expressions of surprise and alarm on their bumpkin faces. He's doing his bit for society by keeping his fellow motorists alert.

And he's perfectly relaxed about it all. He sings at the wheel. 'Fling Wide the Gates', of course, but also old favourites that we can all join in. 'Ten Green Bottles', 'Down at the Old Bull and Bush', 'There is a Tavern in the Town', 'Daisy Daisy', 'The Man Who Broke the Bank at Monte Carlo' – all the songs that families sing together in cars to replace the bonding effect of family prayers. Years later the car provides another link between him and me when he teaches me to drive. It's often an intense experience. We have another dog by then, a black spaniel, and driving lessons are sometimes combined with taking it for a walk. We drive up to Epsom Downs, with the dog standing on the back seat, its forepaws resting on our shoulders, blocking the rear-view mirror and barking with uncontrollable excitement six inches from my left ear. My father turns to crane around the dog to see what's happening behind us. 'Some fool trying to overtake!' he shouts over the barking. 'Keep up, keep up! Don't let him in!'

I love the lessons, though, and I somehow absorb his pleasure in driving. It becomes one of his many gifts to me. In the first few years after I have passed the test I even aspire to his smartness and competitiveness, and am lucky not to kill myself or anyone else before this part of the inheritance wears off. Not that my father's approach to driving ever causes *him* any trouble. In all the thirty-five or so years that he drove he only ever had one accident.

It had occurred probably before I was born, but he told me the story of it many times, because he found it so amusing. He had been driven into at a crossroads in the middle of the country by a very expensive sports car. It had sprung out of a side road at forty or fifty miles per hour, he said, hit him, turned over several times, and thrown the driver over a hedge. My father was unhurt, and his car scarcely dented. The sports car, however, was a write-off. No doubt its speed and the number of times it had turned over increased a little over the years, and I can't help suspecting that the hedge over which the other driver had been thrown was planted only later. What amused my father so much was that the man was a car salesman, who was delivering the expensive sports car to a customer. 'Brand new!' he complained wretchedly to my father, when he finally limped into view, ashen-faced and shaking, from a gateway in the neighbouring field. 'Just out of the showroom! What's he going to say?'

I also came to share his enjoyment in learning the geography of London. Another source of stories for him, though, was my slowness at this, as at so many other things. One night he lent me the car to visit relatives in Hampstead. Next morning, to amuse him, I told him that on the way home I'd found myself driving through the Elephant and Castle five times. 'Five' probably meant 'three', but it wasn't the number of times that caught his attention – it was the fact that I had gone through the Elephant and Castle, in south-east

London, on a journey between north-west London and the south-western suburbs, even once. I never heard the end of that. Any sub-sequent car journey that I mentioned to him, even if it was through the Highlands or the Alps, was likely to remind him of it. 'We went over the St Gotthard,' I would boast to him, 'then back over Great St Bernard.' 'Much traffic at the Elephant?' he would inquire.

My slowness is causing problems long before then. By the time I'm four or five it's already clear that the son-and-heir project is not going as well as Tommy might have hoped. Little Michael's a bit of a disappointment. Tommy coaches the lad patiently with a tennis ball in the back garden, but I think he's already scaling back his ambitions for him as a batsman. Any hopes of the boy one day playing for England, or even Surrey (the club he himself supports), must have been abandoned by this time.

There's a problem getting the bat to connect with the ball. My father runs up to the imaginary crease, about fifteen feet from where I'm standing at the imaginary wicket, and bowls no more than moderately fast, to which I respond with a perfectly well-executed off-drive – but somehow the ball's not where the bat is. It has already gone past me; it hasn't got to me yet. I can't find any snaps of myself at the crease (which may suggest that my father was waiting for me to develop my style a little before he put anything on record), so I can't see exactly what's going wrong. There are a couple of pictures of me around the age of two, not with a bat, but with a large coloured ball at my feet, and I'm not trying to hit it, or even to kick it. I don't seem to be intending violence towards it of any sort – I'm just gazing dubiously at it, as if considering the geometry of a sphere. There is, however, a picture not of me but of my father taking guard in front of the imaginary wicket which may offer a clue to the difficulties I'm having.

The problem is the bat. The picture's dated summer 1939, when I'm five. By this age other boys have been given rather solid pieces of oiled willow with sprung handles and rubber grips, serious sporting instruments that reach all the way down to the ground and a long way out to leg and off. The bat my father's holding is a toy bat. It's the only bat we possess, and it reaches about halfway down my father's shins. This is the trouble. It's too short to reach the ball.

I remember that bat. It has none of the springing in the handle that enables a real bat to leap out at an approaching ball before it has gone past, none of the oiliness that makes it bide its time until the ball has got to it. Even if this feeble mockery of a bat were somehow to connect with the ball, it doesn't have the authentic bulge at the back that gives a real one the heft to drive the ball to the boundary. Instead of a rubber grip the handle has a piece of string wound round it. The string's coming undone, and hanging down distractingly. Attempting to hit a ball with this bat is like adjusting the saddle of the fairy cycle with the rusty pliers, or hammering nails in with the back of the blunt chopper. I'm the victim once again of my father's failure to learn the usual skills of acquisition and possession.

Well, even if I can't be a batsman I can perhaps be a bowler. The inadequacies of the bat, though, affect bowling practice as well. However my father springs about, the shortness of that pathetic little paddle makes it difficult for him to reach my cunningly placed wides to leg and off, my unexpected overhead volleys. Even a good fielder's worth having, of course – and you don't need a bat for fielding practice. But you do need a ball that doesn't move about so *suddenly*, in the way that the mangy tennis ball we have acquired from our rich relations in Enfield seems to, so that it's shot past your left ear before you know what's happened, or bounced painfully off the end of your extended thumb and gone over the fence once again into Miss Hay's garden.

My father becomes a little impatient. Not with the bat or the ball, but with me. He must sometimes feel that he would have had more success in training up a cricketer if he'd got rid of me and kept the wire-haired terrier.

Family snaps weren't taken indoors in those days, and none of the photographs I have of the back garden features all the multiplicity of my father's family who would sometimes be packed into the dining room on Sundays. Perhaps they were wedged so tight that it was impossible to get the French windows open. The back garden, at any rate in the photographic record, is reserved for my parents, my sister, and me – and for my mother's side of the family. Nanny makes an occasional appearance, braving the uncertainties of the weather, nervously perching me or my sister on her knee, visibly anxious that we're at any moment about to fall off and concuss ourselves. My grandfather's sometimes there, massively overspilling a deckchair, with one of us safely clamped between his all-embracing plus fours. And in a lot of the pictures there appears another member of my mother's family, also a weekend visitor – Auntie Phyllis, my mother's younger sister.

She seems to me a dream of glamour and sophistication, as slim and ethereal as her father is large and solid. Her blonde hair is permed. She trails chiffon scarves and delicate perfumes. While she's in the garden, being photographed laughing at my father's jokes, I creep into the bathroom and intoxicate myself with the sight of all the various suavely sculpted jars and tins that she has brought for the weekend. Cold cream . . . vanishing cream . . . face powder . . . talcum powder . . . foundation . . . mascara . . . Some of the slimmest and suavest containers have the elegant cursive inscription 'Evening in Paris', and show the Eiffel Tower and other well-known landmarks silver against a velvet-blue Paris night set with a new moon as slim as my aunt, and a discreet handful of stars . . . I can almost see my aunt herself in the picture, gliding laughingly among the spires and domes, around the moon, among the stars, trailing perfume, chiffon, a hint of talcum powder . . .

Auntie Phyllis has a glamorous professional life. She's a typist, and those slim well-manicured fingers fly every working day over the keys of a gleaming black Remington or Underwood. She works not just for any old company, but for Carreras. Carreras! One of the most famous names in the world! The sound alone is as romantic as the skyline on the talcum powder. Carreras, as everyone knows, is the company that makes Craven A, the slim white cigarettes with the yellow cork tips which are manufactured, as the packet explains, 'specially to prevent sore throats'. They're packaged in brilliant scarlet, and they bear the logo of a black cat. My aunt brings packets of Craven A for my parents when she comes at the weekend, and tiny black cat charms for me and my sister.

She sometimes also brings Uncle Jack. Who Uncle Jack is no one ever explains, but he seems to be a major in a Welsh regiment, and to ride a motor bike. He's also, I think, pursuing my aunt, but with a tongue-tied bashfulness that advances his suit extremely slowly, until it comes to a halt altogether and he's replaced by Uncle Sid.

The letter from Phyllis announcing Uncle Sid's entry into my aunt's life arrives one day when my mother, my grandmother and I are eating tinned sardines for lunch. Nanny reads it and begins to laugh nervously behind her hand. 'Sidney Bubbers!' she says to my mother. 'Wouldn't it be funny if it was two *g*'s in the middle instead of two *b*'s!'

Perhaps the letter came later, the formal announcement of their subsequent engagement, because I'm evidently already fully literate. 'Buggers?' I say, as quick with words as I'm slow with bats and balls. 'Why would it be funny if he was called Buggers?'

Nanny utters a little appalled cry from behind her concealing hand, and my mother turns on me with as much fury as if she had seen the dining-room door handle move in the middle of the nine o'clock news. 'I never want to hear you utter that word again!' she shouts. 'But I only said what Nanny said . . .' I begin, stunned by the incomprehensible injustice of her anger. '*Never*, do you hear?' cries my mother.

In spite of this unfortunate beginning, Uncle Sid turns out to be the most wonderful addition to the family. He's a man of great solidity, already balding in a responsible kind of way. He has fair, reasonable opinions about everything, public and private, and he's a good deal more reliable than the Bank of England – exactly what Phyllis needs in her life after her feckless father and the dilatory Uncle Jack. Like her he works for Carreras. Perhaps he's already on his way to becoming what he was when he went back to the firm after his war service, and what he was surely born to be: a personnel officer. If you had to sum him up in one word it would be 'avuncular'. This is fortunate for the personnel of Carreras, who could scarcely have a more reassuring figure to pour out their ambitions, grievances and sorrows to – and even more fortunate for me, the nephew on whom his avuncularity can be most literally exercised.

He's a keen cyclist (like his future father-in-law, it occurs to me now that I begin to notice all these hidden connections – though what he rides is not a rusty old iron mangle like Bert's but a gleaming blue-and-chrome lightweight sports machine), and soon he's got my glamorous aunt cycling, too. They ride all the way over from North London at the weekend to stay with us. My father and the new boyfriend get on well together, rather improbably, since their temperaments are so unlike. Sid has a good loud voice, which helps, because my father's hearing is beginning to go the same way as that of all his siblings. And they're both adept at the bantering manner which is the common social currency of the English lower-middle classes. Tommy, even smarter and quicker and more Tommy-like with the slow-spoken Sid than he is with the rest of the family, joshes his future brother-in-law about the likelihood of his getting the wheels of his bicycle fatally caught in tramlines. Sid joshes Tommy slowly and loudly back. 'You want to try a bike some time, Tommy. Strap the samples on the handlebars. Get round to twice as many customers as the other reps.' 'Hotchamachacha,' says Tommy.

Some of the snaps show Phyllis and Sid in the back garden with Bert as well as Nell. So on these weekends my father has four members of his wife's family boarded on him. Where do they all sleep? One of them, I suppose, probably good-natured, uncomplaining Sid, must be lodged on the Bentalls settee in the lounge . . .

They bring presents for everyone. For me, the sets of Carreras cigarette cards that the general public can get their hands on only by patiently smoking their way through packet after packet of health-giving Craven A. What I'm even more enchanted by, though, are the little scenes from around the world that the firm produces to be stuck in the empty packets. Inside the back of the packet you paste a backcloth of the Pyramids, say. On the front of the packet you stick a foreground – the Sphinx and a caravan of camels – then cut around their outline to make a miniature theatre with two receding planes of scenery. I'm not much better at assembling them than I am at making flicker books out of my father's commercial stationery. Uncle Sid helps me, with endless avuncular patience.

Does he ever have a presentiment, I wonder, as the little stages accumulate on the sideboard – the gondolas of Venice, the skyscrapers of New York, even the sights of Paris that I know so well from the tins of talcum powder – how the work's going to escalate over the years? Does he even begin to see the long corridors of Christmas and summer weekends stretching ahead of him, or guess how many old razor blades he's going to wear blunt as he cuts and scores the printed cardboard, how many tubes of stinking fish-glue he's going to squeeze dry, how ever more complex the models he's assembling will become – locomotives with cardboard wheels glued on to matchstick axles, a cardboard Tower Bridge with working cardboard machinery, an electric motor clipped improbably to an insufficiently rigid cardboard base? His daughter Jean says he always wanted to be an engineer, so perhaps he actually enjoys the work. I hope he does.

For my parents Phyllis and Sid bring the packets that will be used to make the little theatres. First, of course, they have to be emptied of their contents, and Uncle Sid helps with this as well. Phyllis won't share in the work, so the others have to make up. Hundreds, thousands, of cigarettes they smoke their way through. Even my father, who normally smokes a pipe, and my grandmother, coughing nervously. Most of all Sid himself, even while he's at the same time helping me with the cutting and gluing. The house fills up with scenes of the world's better-known tourist destinations, and blue smoke, and ashtrays heaped with corked-tip cigarette ends. Each weekend must be as good for everyone's throats as a month in a sanatorium.

The state of my own throat probably still leaves something to be desired, and so does that of my sister and our friends. Although the cigarette ends that we collect from the overflowing ashtrays, and recycle with the help of a rolling machine and packets of Rizla cigarette papers stolen from one of my grandfather's old tobacco tins, are mostly health-giving Craven A, we can find no practical way of incorporating the cork tips. Even so they're probably better for our throats than the straws that we have smoked hitherto. They're less dry – in fact distinctly soggy. They certainly taste more authentic; probably even more authentic than the original cigarettes did, since the goodness must be so much more concentrated.

And we're so much more concentrated ourselves. We smoke not casually in the garden or in a well-lit dining room, like the adults, but in the darkness, in one of the long bedroom cupboards under the eaves, reclining on the heaps of junk stored there. The only light comes from a paraffin lamp we've found in the coal shed, and its pinprick reflections in our pupils. It's like the scene in a Chinese opium den, as shown in the engraved illustrations of Sherlock Holmes stories. The lack of cork tips is made up for by the disinfectant powers of the oily black paraffin fumes from the lamp and the acrid little firework displays of the matches as we struggle to keep the wet tobacco alight.

Any time my Uncle Sid can spare from smoking he devotes to sport. Carreras have a club for their staff out at Edgware, and Uncle Sid seizes all the opportunities it offers, particularly for tennis and riding. He also enjoys cricket, though, and he takes up the challenge, from where my father left off, of making a cricketer out of me. His patience is inexhaustible, unlike my father's, and he's perfectly prepared to go back to first principles. No run up to the crease, no overarm, no fast bumpers or leg breaks. A tennis racquet instead of a bat. Not even a tennis racquet. Just me standing with both hands outstretched and ready, while he places himself three feet in front of me, in a good light, and lobs the ball very slowly and precisely into them . . . Out it bounces again. 'You have to close your hands, you see, Michael, as soon as you've got the ball in them.' We retrieve the ball from the flower bed and he lobs it to me even more slowly. I smartly close my hands. The ball bounces off them and hits me on the nose. 'Yes, but the thing is, Michael, you need to wait until the ball's got there. Let's try again . . .'

The work continues on fine summer weekends for the next three years. I can trace it in the snapshots, from when Uncle Sid first appears, in 1939, until a solution to the problem suddenly emerges in 1942. Spectacles. My mother has taken me to S. J. Best, Chemist and Optician, in his low-ceilinged cottage shop in Ewell Village. Mr Best has gone through his entire tray of lenses and his entire stock of test cards with me, reached the end of his resources, and sent me on to Mr Cameron, Consultant Ophthalmologist and Ophthalmic Surgeon, in a large Victorian mansion in Sutton. Mr Cameron has at last discovered what the trouble is. I have an acute astigmatism. No wonder I was gazing so thoughtfully at that coloured ball when I was two – I was trying to make out whether it was a ball or a pot of geraniums. No wonder I can't hit anything, or kick anything, or catch anything. I'm engulfed in a wave of belated sympathy. Even my father's understanding.

By this time the Second World War has broken out. Uncle Sid has been called up; my father's the local Fire Captain. Whenever Sid can get a weekend's leave, though, or my father can manage a break from his duties, cricket practice resumes. Only now with our new wartime fighting spirit, and my new spectacles.

So where's the bat in this new order of things? Where it always was: somewhere the ball is not. Where's the ball, then? The ball, too, is where it always was: in the goldenrod, over the fence, bouncing off some part of me it had not expected to come in contact with, hurtling straight at where my powerful new spectacles would have been if I hadn't smartly closed my eyes and ducked. The only thing that has changed is my appearance. I no longer even look like a future cricketer. I look like a weedy small boy in specs. I have started school, and to the ferocious little Amazon there who runs the gang of which I find myself a member the glasses evidently make me appear to be some kind of intellectual, so she appoints me Gang Scientist. My job is to produce explosive. I do my best with the only materials I can find, ground-up chalk from the Downland soil and crushed elderberries from the elders by the coal shed, but even in my spectacles I can make bangs no more than runs.

By this time, in any case, my father realises that the problem with little Michael goes deeper than an astigmatism or poor coordination. Not only is the boy never going to make any runs on the cricket field – he's never going to be able to earn a living. He's the antithesis of the Smart Lad that Tommy himself already was at his son's age, and has ever since remained. He's slow-witted.

My sister also has an astigmatism, and is not all that much better at games than I am. But she's quick, like our father, and over the years she gets as impatient with my slowness as my father always was. She has no academic ability – she fails the only two GCSEs (O-Levels, as they were called at the time she took them) that her school puts her in for, whereas I could paper the walls with certificates. When in later life I try to explain all this to people they believe that I'm displaying some kind of pathological or humorously disingenuous self-deprecation. Not at all. If you'd asked my father to sum me up in one word I can tell you confidently what it would have been: 'dozy'. I'm as dozy as a weekend motorist. My father takes to calling me not Michael but Willy, after a character in a strip cartoon that features two idle tramps, Weary Willy and Tired Tim.

He's wearing specs himself by this time, and looking rather more like an academic than a sales rep, but it doesn't make him any more sympathetic to my doziness. 'Come on, Willy,' he says, sounding increasingly weary himself, while he waits for me to remember what I'm supposed to be doing, and where and when and how I'm supposed to be doing it. He tries to help me with my maths homework. The pressure of his braced concave index finger against the end of his silver pencil projects a spray of tiny figures on to the paper, and I gaze at them just as dumbly through my glasses as I did without them. The pencil suddenly pauses and hovers. I can feel his eye on me. I'm supposed to be telling him what the pencil is to write next. Nothing comes into my slow head. 'Roughly,' he says. 'You should always make a rough estimate in any case to check your answer against.' I go on gazing at the figures. 'Well,' he says, 'is it going to be something like a hundred, say? Or something more like a thousand?' I peer at the space for the answer more closely. It doesn't look to me as if it's going to be more or less like anything. The pencil twitches. 'Or ten thousand? Or a million? Come on, Willy, buck your ideas up.'

But my ideas stay unbucked. At lunchtime one Saturday I go out to the scullery to pour myself a glass of water. 'Thank you,' I say politely to the tap as I turn it off, and when I return to the table feel obliged to report this amusing misunderstanding to the rest of the family. My father's not amused, and I decide to keep to myself a later moment of absent-mindedness when I come home to change for cricket, and instead of white flannels find that I have somehow put on my pyjamas and gone to bed.

What's he going to do with me? He can see me ending up unemployable, like other members of the two families he's had to support – another Mabel. Soon I'm at a school where they play cricket with a ball which is not only invisible but hard, and my new spectacles are even less help than before because I have to take them off in case this horrible projectile breaks them. At least the moments where I cringe in front of the wicket with only a bat and pads to protect myself tend to be brought to a swift conclusion. Worse, really, are the long hours of dazed boredom standing at some arbitrarily allotted point in the middle of the landscape, with the perpetual fear at the back of my mind that voices are going to start shouting my name. Somewhere up there in the sky a mortar bomb will be descending upon me, and I shall be expected not just to roll up into a foetal position with my head wrapped in my hands, but to make some pretence of trying to catch it. At least I didn't know then what my cousin Jean, Phyllis's daughter, has recently told me – that my great-uncle Robert died in agony as a result of being hit in the kidneys by a cricket ball. My father was evidently keeping this bit of family news from me.

Football isn't quite as bad. The ball is at any rate large enough to be sometimes visible, and there's a bit of flatness and a faint suggestion of give when it hits you. I have some success at football, in fact – I score a goal. Unfortunately it's against my own side, and my parents have to take it in turns to sit on my bed far into the night, trying to soothe my tearful shame. Years later still I'm at a school where they play hockey. One day my father and sister secretly come and watch me, to see if somehow hockey suits me any better than football or cricket. It doesn't. It combines the worst features of both. There are twenty-one other players in studded boots, there's a cricket ball flying unpredictably about – and all twenty-one players are waving clubs around. 'You just stood there!' says my father despairingly afterwards. 'You didn't *do* anything!' echoes my sister. 'You just watched them all run past you!' says my father. I'm chastened. I just stood there and didn't do anything? I made no attempt to run away? I must really be as slow-witted as my father and sister think I am.

When he's teaching me to drive, and I'm hesitating for a moment about obeying his order to race an oncoming petrol tanker into a possible gap beyond the double-decker bus in front, he has a new phrase for me – I'm 'a mass of indecision'. A Smart Lad was still wanted, by my father and everyone else in authority over me, and I was not that Smart Lad. I suppose I took after my mother; I was a bit of a mother's boy. She never called me Willy, and I don't think she worried too much about my failures on the games field. Even she, though, thought I could do with a bit of bracing up. When I was at the football school she would give me sixpence sometimes for coming top of the class. And when I whined to her that the other boys had started bullying me, possibly for coming top, or possibly because of that ill-considered goal, she was sympathetic but brisk. 'Just get your back against the wall and keep your fists up.'

Perhaps, though, it was my father who did more to give me my character. He observed my doziness and made me see it myself. Hung it on me, like a tailor measuring up a customer and gauging his taste, then hanging a well-fitted suit on him. He probably drove me still further into doziness. Away from hard balls and hard mathematics, into the soft landscapes of language, of grammar and metaphor, of assonance and dissonance, where I felt more at home.

He had a relish for words himself, it's true, particularly rather ambitious ones with a bit of a swagger to them – 'gallimaufry', 'plethora', 'rodomontade', 'prestidigitation'. It went with his hats and brogues and lightness on his toes. I suppose I inherited the logophilia together with a bit of the bantering manner, and some of the impatience. When I attempted to help my children with their maths homework I was as impatient as he had been – worse, perhaps, since I couldn't really understand it myself – and it had much the same effect.

I look again at that snap of my two-year-old self gazing at the coloured ball, and I see something else in it as well as doziness and astigmatism. I see a touch of incipient rebelliousness. I think I do know it's a ball. I think I do know I'm supposed to bash it or boot it in some kind of way. I just won't, for some reason.

You can back yourself into being who you are, just as easily as you can walk or get pushed into it. Many years later I discovered that I enjoyed playing tennis and squash – even an occasional informal game of football. I needn't have dug my toes in quite so hard as a child. I could have done a bit more to meet my father halfway. I could have bashed or booted *something*. To our mutual advantage.

6

Fire Resistance

My parents like to take their holidays at the start of September, when the crowds have gone back to work. We go in the firm's car, almost always to the West Country. The journey starts early, at fresh young hours unknown in the normal course of life, and proceeds by way of places whose names still seem to me almost as charged with promise now as they did then: Basingstoke, Andover and Stonehenge, or, on a more southerly track, the Hog's Back, Winchester and Shaftesbury. At some point Crewkerne, Wincanton and Dorchester are likely to come into the story. It's raining, of course, but, as one of us remarks every few minutes, the sky looks a little brighter in the west. Which is where we're heading. By the time we've reached Bridport or Honiton something has gone wrong with the car. Steam is coming out of the engine. My father has found a roadside pond, and a rusty tin can to bale with.

One year we go to Newquay. By the time we have established ourselves at our hotel, just by the harbour, that promise in the sky to the west has been made good. The tidal pools among the rocks and across the endless yellow shine of the sands are glittering in the late summer sun. September is always a good month for me because it's my birthday on the eighth, and this year I'm going to be six, which is something I've been wanting to be all summer. My parents, though, are irritatingly reluctant to take me down to the beach, or to pretend not to know that we're now less than a week away from the eighth. They're spending long hours of the day sitting in the lounge of the hotel with all the other adult residents, smoking and listening intently to the wireless. The air's grey with cigarette fug and boring official voices.

I suppose they must have explained to me what those voices

were saying, but the only thing I can remember is a dream that I have some days later. The Germans have bombed all the roads leading back to London. Along their entire length, from Yeovil to Shaftesbury, from Axminster to the Hog's Back, they're nothing but lines of bomb craters. We're never going to get home.

I have another, even more vivid, dream some weeks or months later. I have studied, in George Davis's manuals, pictures of the British seaplane built by Supermarine in Southampton that established itself as the fastest aircraft in the world when it won the last Schneider Trophy race in 1931. It's a single-seater, and in my dream I'm landing in it all by myself on the calm surface of a deep blue sea, among little islands off a rocky coast. I feel as calm and profoundly happy as the sea is calm and blue. The coast, I know, is Massachusetts. I have been evacuated to America.

So this is my war, in those first few months – two dreams, and of things that never happen. My handsome cousin Maurice, meanwhile, George and Nelly's son, the schoolboy in the holiday snaps from the twenties, is a lorry driver with the British Expeditionary Force in France. In May 1940 he's force-marched from Fresnes, south of Paris, to Dunkirk, and evacuated from the beaches. My handsome cousin Philip, George and Daisy's elder son, has by this time joined the Navy, and is serving aboard a destroyer escorting convoys in the North Atlantic.

The war touches our street. Archie Dennis-Smith exchanges his tennis togs for oily overalls, and cycles off each day to work as a foreman in a factory on the Ewell bypass that makes aircraft parts. The Fieldings' simple-minded son now pedals slowly off on his pushbike each morning to work as a labourer on the local farm, growing food for the War Effort. His handsome brother-in-law, the fighter pilot, is somewhere up there above our heads on fine summer days, chalking the story of the war in a shifting scribble of condensation trails across the blueboard of the sky, incomprehensibly but we know gloriously. A plane – one of ours, *his* even – swoops low across the gardens, waggling its wings in triumph. Another, trailing black smoke, dives and vanishes behind the rooftops. One of theirs. We hope. This is 1940 – I still haven't got my specs. It's a wonder that I can make any sense of the war at all.

Two Irish navvies come down the street, knocking on all the front doors looking for work building air-raid shelters. Spending money on some passing craze like an air-raid shelter is exactly the kind of thing that my father would never dream of. In the unlikely event that his friend Kerry, or someone else at work, somehow persuaded him that we actually needed a shelter he would wait till the end of the war and get an old discarded one from someone, or improvise something out of his samples and a few bits off Bert's rusty bicycle. The war's changing everything, though. He agrees a price with the navvies and they dig the biggest hole I've seen in my life so far. It occupies one whole corner of the garden, where the blackcurrant bushes were. In the hole they erect a framework of curved steel tubes, and clad them with corrugated iron. It looks rather like one of the standard Anderson shelters recommended by the government and named after the Home Secretary that are being installed in back gardens all over London. But Andersons are for the lower social orders – ours aspires a little higher. The metalwork is stencilled with the name of the manufacturer, Boulton Paul, the firm that also makes the Defiant night-fighter. I have detailed drawings of the Defiant in the albums of pictures of RAF planes that George Davis has passed on.

The navvies cover the corrugated iron with the soil they have dug out. They install a plank floor and plank beds, and carve out a neat earthen staircase down to the door. So now we have an extra room – a country retreat, even – which is also a weapon of war built by the makers of the Boulton Paul Defiant. We're the only family in the entire street who take the navvies on – the single family out of seventeen to have an air-raid shelter of any sort. We have suddenly caught up with the Joneses and overtaken them.

One night the warning sounds. My sister and I are got up and wrapped in dressing gowns. It's still the middle of the night; this is even better than going on holiday. Nanny refuses to leave the house. She knows she's going to die very soon, one way or another, and she prefers to do it in the blazing ruins of her own room. The rest of us trek down the garden through the warm late summer night and make ourselves snug in a little world of candlelight and emergency snacks. Somewhere up there in the darkness Boulton Paul are engaging with the incoming Dorniers and Heinkels. Down here Boulton Paul are enclosing us in the damp earth smells and the excitement of being all four of us together.

The war's wonderful.

Winter comes. There are more air raids. Bombs, though, are not the only things that fall out of the sky. There's also rain, and it turns out that a hole in the ground, even one occupied by a Boulton Paul air-raid shelter, behaves in a way which neither my father nor the navvies have foreseen. It fills with water. The sharply cut earthen steps soften into a mud slide that leads down into a foul-smelling stagnant pond. The chances of dying in the shelter, either of exposure, drowning, or some waterborne disease such as cholera or bilharzia, are visibly much higher than of dying through enemy action in the house. There's no question of sheltering in it again after that once.

My father realises, though, that there's another way in which the shelter can be used to help the War Effort. We need to supplement the egg ration, as some of our neighbours are doing by raising chickens. Chickens, it occurs to him, are not the only birds that produce eggs. So do ducks. And ducks like water.

My father makes another of his rare large-scale purchases: five Khaki Campbells – four ducks and a drake. They will feel particularly welcome at a house called Duckmore, and are to have sole occupancy of what is now effectively an armoured duck-pond, where they will be safe at night, even if we won't, from the Blitz which is now beginning. During the day they're to be allowed to roam freely about on the surface, eating kitchen scraps supplemented by balancer meal, perhaps so-called because my mother will have to buy it by the sack at the seedsman's shop in Ewell

Village, and struggle home with the sacks balanced on the crossbar of the second-hand gents' bike that my father has by one means or another acquired for her. He has laid out yet more money on a handbook devoted to the raising of Khaki Campbells. They have encouragingly few requirements, he has established. They can eat almost anything. Except lupins, which will poison them instantly.

The garden's full of lupins, so my father erects a fence around the shelter to keep the ducks away from them. It's constructed out of sheets of TAC roofing, stuck endwise into the mud. Ducks, however, rather like holes in the ground, turn out to behave in ways that my father has not foreseen. They fly. They take one look at the underground swamp they have been made free of, and instantly want to be elsewhere. They flap their wings and fly over the sheets of TAC roofing into the less waterlogged parts of the garden, where the first thing they do is to eat all the lupins.

They survive, for some reason, and continue to feast on the lupins for the next four years. They eat most of the other flowers, too. The sea of mud and duck-droppings around the walled swamp in the corner laps out to occupy the entire garden. But, scattered in the mud each day around the devastated plants are the large blue-green eggs that keep us going for the rest of the war. They're one of my father's successes in life – and the least likely one yet. It goes some way to counterbalance his failure to provide England with a new opening batsman.

Now that the Blitz has got under way and the ducks have taken over the shelter we retreat at night into two windowless spaces inside the house. My parents spread a mattress for themselves in the cupboard under the stairs, next to the bare fuses, and sleep with their heads jammed up against the two violin cases and the ever more tightly compressed layers of junk in which they're embedded. My sister and I sleep in the dark corridor that leads to Nanny's room. It's not quite as enjoyable as the shelter was. I feel a certain unease as the sirens start up, one after another, rising and falling like the voices in some forgotten oratorio – and feel it still when I hear the same familiar polyphony now, in war museums and television documentaries. I don't much like the colossal racket made by the local anti-aircraft guns, and I like even less the characteristic steady throb of the German bombers. They sound so dogged, and so alien, and they pass overhead with such painful slowness. And yet, when the sirens start up again, one after another, in the long steady gloria of the All Clear, I can't help feeling a slight disappointment. The excitement's over, and nothing has happened after all.

My father's Fire Captain for the street. Every week he posts a schedule on the telegraph pole outside with the list of neighbours who have to stay up on Fire Watch. The Fire Watcher wears a helmet, to protect him not from the Germans but from ourselves – from the shrapnel that rains down from our ack-ack. He doesn't have to watch for the kind of bombs that explode, because they announce themselves perfectly clearly, and would in any case blow any nearby Fire Watcher off the face of the earth. What he's on the lookout for is incendiaries, which might otherwise lie unnoticed on roofs and sheds until the white blaze of the phosphorus had set the whole property on fire. If he ever saw one he would have to come running to our house for the famous bucket of sand and long-handled shovel, or the official stirrup-pump that as the war goes on we use to water the tomatoes and spray screaming children with on hot summer afternoons.

One night something actually happens, though it's not the Fire Watcher but George Davis in his pyjamas who comes running wildly across the road. 'Tom! Tom! I've got an incendiary on my veranda!' My father, also in his pyjamas, rushes into the garage to look for the stirrup-pump, but soon gives up the struggle to squeeze between the car and the tangle of rusty bikes. From somewhere, I think from behind the garage, in the confusion of beanpoles and raspberry canes at the back of the stagnant water butt, he manages to produce the long-handled shovel, though not I think the bucket of sand, which my sister and I have been playing with, and between them they get the white-hot phosphorus off George Davis's veranda and out into his back garden, where it leaves an impressively large blackened clearing in the jungle.

Mostly, though, the Fire Watcher's nights are quiet. When it's my father's turn, and the sky is clear, he takes a pair of binoculars and a map of the constellations with him, and from the virginal skies of the Blackout learns probably more about the universe than he ever did at school. One night he wakes me and takes me out to watch one of the big raids on the City and the docks, a dozen miles north-east of us. I recall not just the red of the northern sky, but a fairy palace of lights built high overhead, with searchlight beams supporting a multi-coloured ceiling of gently parachuting flares. His office, in the Borough, is somewhere on the edge of all this. Kerry for some reason has to do his fire-watching at the office, and up on the roof. The bombs exploding nearby rock the building so badly one night that Kerry looks over the side and sees the whole structure keeling over beneath him like the Leaning Tower of Pisa, then runs to the other side and gets there just in time to see it keeling over in that direction.

So Kerry says. Or so my father says Kerry says.

It's difficult to know, when you look at someone's life, what you should give them credit (or blame) for, and what you should put down to luck. My father didn't start with many advantages. Sharing two rooms with six other people and leaving school at fourteen isn't a privileged upbringing. Finding himself with not just one but two collapsing families to support wasn't much of a gift from the gods, either. But he made a go of his life, and not only because he was able to move out to Ewell and wear a homburg hat. I think that most of his success, and the happiness I'm fairly sure he enjoyed, have to be attributed to his own efforts, to his hard work and quick wits. But he had a bit of pure luck as well. His date of birth, for a start; just as he was too young for the First World War, so he was too old for the Second. Then again, however little else he inherited, he was somehow endowed with the confidence that enabled him to make use of his abilities. He must also have had some experience of the love that he was able to show to me and my sister, and that we in our turn felt for our own children. And then the biggest bit of luck: going to the party with poor Bert Crouchman that night in 1919. All these turn-ups for the book had lasting consequences. There's not many more of them to come, though.

Actually, my father could never have been called up for the second war, even if he had been younger or they had started taking men in their forties. He's becoming increasingly deaf, which isn't such good fortune. I don't know when it first became noticeable, but by the middle of the war he's just about as deaf as his brother and sisters. He has to get a hearing aid. It comes in a black granulated leather case, with the name of the manufacturer, Ardente, imprinted in gold, and I long to possess it. The case opens with a pop, and there on the midnight-blue velvet lining sits the polished black amplifier and earpiece on its silky cord. You put the box in your waistcoast pocket and your hands in your trouser pockets, so that your jacket's pulled back to leave the microphone facing your interlocutor. It's a discreet and magical instrument, as beautiful in its way as my mother's violin; and it's not the slightest use.

He has to start again with something much clumsier and more complex, a serious instrument prescribed by a specialist. This is a Bonochord, made by Allen & Hanbury. If I remember it rightly the microphone and the amplifier are separate, and they're attached to half a pair of headphones, which covers one ear completely. There are certainly two batteries, a low-tension one about the size of a pocket Bible, and a high-tension one more like a Bible that you might carry to church each Sunday. A web of wires runs between jacket and pockets and waistcoat, between waistcoat and back trouser pocket.

I watch him winding himself into this harness before he leaves the house in the morning, like a medieval knight arming himself for battle. The wires become tangled. He taps the microphone, or gets Vi or me to say something into it. He listens anxiously; nothing's coming through. A hidden connection somewhere is loose.

One of the batteries is flat. A switch here or a knob there is in the wrong position . . . And, then, when he gets home in the evening, I watch him unwind himself from it all again and lay the various components and leads out in good order on his dressing table. I have no desire to own this grim array, unlike the last one, even though it seems actually to work.

I never asked him what it was like, being deaf, and getting deafer. I never asked him what he felt about this very visible muddling of his dapper appearance, this invisible undermining of his quick understanding of the world around him on which all his sharpness depended. How on earth did he manage to carry on with his job? I realise now that nerving himself to go bouncing in with his big smile had always cost him more than he ever revealed; my cousin John says that at some point in the thirties my father came to stay with them to recuperate from overwork, which I suppose means stress. Now, before he goes into battle, he has to sit in the car plugging in the batteries and switching on all the switches, tapping on the microphone, checking all the connections . . . Then he has to establish friendly relations with a stranger whose personality he can't quite assess, or re-establish them with an old acquaintance whose familiar joshing and banter he can't quite catch. How does he field all the objections and prevarications, all the technical inquiries about the product, all the haggling over discounts and delivery dates, when they come to him from beyond this widening invisible ocean, this confusion of unwanted ambient noise that the hearing aid so impartially magnifies as well? Where does he find the courage to struggle on with it, day after day, week after week?

One technique he develops to help him through is to make himself more of a character. He puts on a performance, and in so far as he can he keeps the conversational initiative. He doesn't leave the person he's talking to much chance to say anything that needs to be heard. He joshes and banters, and smiles, of course, so that all the customer has to do is to be an audience, and smile back. And if the customer does say something inaudible which seems to need a response, my father uses his natural bent for exaggeration to invent a humorous distortion of it that will make his interlocutor laugh and then repeat himself. 'But, Tom, how many square feet per hour of this stuff can an unskilled fitter actually run out on site?' – 'How many *what* at night?' – 'On *site*. Square *feet*.' – 'I suppose so, but safer if they wear boots.'

There are some inaudible announcements, though, that he can't joke his way around. 'I'm driving through Herne Hill this morning,' he tells us, 'and I'm just thinking, "That's funny. Why are there all these people lying in shop doorways?" – when *woomph*! About two streets away, I should think.'

For many years I waited to inherit the family deafness in my turn. My hearing is now, in old age, getting decidedly shaky, and so is my cousin John's, but neither of us, nor any of our siblings or cousins, has suffered anything like the curse that dogged the two previous generations. The performance that my father put on to cope with it, though, set an example that came to hand later when I had other difficulties of my own – then stayed with me, and became a professional resource, rather as it did for him.

There's another reason, too, why he would never be called up. He's in what's known as a reserved occupation. As a rep? Yes, as a Technical Representative, which is what he now is, and it's reserved because of the importance of what he's selling and who he's selling it to.

The 'TAC' on all his stationery and brochures stands for Turners Asbestos Cement, and the customers to whom he's now representing the firm are the government and the armed services. The firm's logo shows a female figure in Greek robes doing rather what my father's doing as Fire Captain. She's confronting a sea of flames, armed not with a stirrup-pump or a long-handled shovel but a shield made of asbestos. This is the great selling point of the product, particularly now that the Luftwaffe's attempting with some success to repeat the effects of the Great Fire of London: unlike wood and various forms of wood substitute it's non-inflammable (and it doesn't rot). Unlike corrugated-iron roofing and cast-iron drainpipes it's also rustproof. Asbestos has no vices. Everywhere we go my father can point to great grey corrugated cliffs and hillsides of asbestos cement, most of it manufactured by Turners, the industry leader, some of it sold by himself, and a lot of it housing aircraft and munitions, locomotives and troops. There's something profoundly dreary about its lifeless greyness, even to my uncritical eye, but at least it will remain grey and not go charcoal-black or mouldy-green or rust-red. My father probably hasn't had to struggle to hear many objections or rejections from the civil servants and senior officers he deals with, now I come to think about it. The nation can't get enough of the stuff. He's part of the War Effort.

He even has a petrol ration. Archie Dennis-Smith's Triumph Dolomite retires to the garage for the rest of the war, like almost all the other cars in the district. Barlow is spared any further expenditure on petrol for his heap of rust. Our car is the only one left in the street. What do the neighbours make of this? Particularly when we somehow manage to go by car to the West Country for at least three summer holidays in the war.

The samples of asbestos that my father brings home are another of our resources against wartime shortages – a version of the carver's perks that he appropriates from the ever-smaller weekly meat ration. The samples, though, unlike the Sunday joints, grow bigger and more numerous – no longer pocket-handkerchief-sized miniatures but complete sheets of roofing and lengths of piping. They're one of the chief raw materials that we improvise things out of. The anti-duck fence is not the only asbestos in the garden. There are also many heavy rectangular boxes, about the size of orange crates and the same grim industrial grey as the hangars and warehouses. What purpose they're intended to serve in the building trade I don't know, but we use them as planters. We turn them over and punch drainage holes in the bottom by hammering a rusty screwdriver through them with the back of the rusty chopper, then grow tomatoes and lavender in them. I build an aircraft out of them. I saw the samples up with a rusty hacksaw from the coal shed, filling the air with asbestos dust. The result doesn't fly, of course. It doesn't even look much like an aircraft – it doesn't look *anything* like an aircraft – but it's large enough for me to sit in and imagine that it's an aircraft.

Our other great resource is Uncle Sid. He keeps bringing the cigarettes, on which life in wartime apparently depends even more heavily than in peacetime – Senior Service now, in packs of five hundred or a thousand from the NAAFI. He's an RAF officer – not a fighter pilot, like Fielding's son-in-law, but a controller in Bomber Command. He sits in the tower at base and solidly, reliably, reasonably talks down shattered crews limping home after a long night of fear over Germany and occupied Europe. They're sometimes off-course, lost, low on fuel. They're flying on three engines, have half the undercarriage gone or a live bomb jammed in the bomb bay, crew dead or dying. He sits through the small hours waiting like a patient parent for them to be back in radio contact. He smokes and drinks cocoa and joshes them and is the voice of normality and home in the darkness. They all call him Uncle, just as I do. His avuncularity, like my father's smartness, has been channelled into the War Effort.

In the daytime, though, he gets on his blue-and-chrome sports bicycle and cycles round the Lincolnshire farms buying eggs and an occasional rabbit, which he brings to us at the weekends with the cigarettes. He also brings his own carver's perks – small scraps that have fallen from the overflowing tables of the armed services. The RAF has more parachute silk than it can ever make parachutes out of – and there are many things apart from parachutes that waiting wives and sisters-in-law and their mothers can use it for. Late in the war the RAF also finds itself oversupplied with thick yellow felt. It has acquired it for aero engines to sit on when they're taken out of aircraft to be repaired and serviced. Uncle Sid has done a deal, involving perhaps farm-smoked Lincolnshire bacon, with a contact in the workshops, and out of his laden kit-bag, together with the cigarettes and the silk, emerge fat yellow rolls of felt. He comes to us, on a 36 or a 48, for a short break from the war – to relax in the health-giving cigarette smoke and asbestos dust of the Surrey Hills; but he spends his leave just as busily as he did when he was cutting up and gluing cardboard models of the Tower Bridge and the *Coronation Scot*. Only now he's cutting up the yellow felt and sewing it together with huge stitches of red thread to make slippers. Soon everyone in the family is shuffling about the house in thick yellow slippers with red stitching.

On Sunday evening he pushes aside the felt trims and tangles of thread that now cover the dining-room table and three-piece suite, and gets out his RAF officer's tunic and overcoat. Still wearing his own pair of yellow slippers, he fetches his brass button-stick and a tin of Duraglit. Also wearing yellow slippers I sit watching him, as four at a time he traps and buffs the gleaming buttons, each with the embossed RAF eagle and crown that I love to run my reverent index finger over. Still as good-humoured and phlegmatic as ever, he's preparing to return to the long nights in the tower alone with the unseen crews, and the days scavenging for food and scraps to keep us going. Back to the War Effort, back to his modest part in levelling the bricks and mortar of Germany.

My father, meanwhile, wearing *his* yellow slippers, writes his reports and checks the batteries of his hearing aid, ready for Monday morning. Back to the War Effort on the home front, back to his modest part in raising the asbestos roofs and pipes of Britain.

7

A Glass of Sherry

And on the war goes. By this time I have forgotten, even if my parents haven't, that there was once a time before the Duration. The Duration is the duration of the war, but it has become a freestanding abstraction in its own right, and is the condition of our life. It's the reason why the beaches on the South Coast are blocked with forests of slimy green scaffolding, why there are pig-bins on the corner and mosquito-infested static water tanks in back streets, why cakes taste of baking soda, and ice cream of . . . I don't know what: something grey and neutral . . . asbestos dust, possibly. It has become not so much a period of time as a purpose in itself. What are we fighting for? – For the Duration.

Not all the effects of the Duration are bad. The shortages that everyone now faces make the scruffy compromises of our life-style a little less egregious. Then again, in the thirties London was advancing relentlessly upon Ewell. The fields over the hill just above our house had already ceased to grow any crops except half-a-dozen species of new house, and bald concrete roadways through the overgrown wasteland where more new houses would one day be. Sooner or later the developers would be in Hillside Road itself, driving a concrete roadway between Miss Hay at No. 4 and Miss Johnson at No. 5, where a narrow entrance, choked with nettles and elder, old paint tins and piles of abandoned asphalt, leads to the little landlocked triangle of countryside behind the houses. Then the farmlands just beyond us would go the same way. On over Epsom Downs the houses would march . . .

Only now the whole unstoppable advance has been stopped. For the Duration.

For the Duration the enormous wastelands of the estate being developed by Gleesons over the top of the hill, and the tangled triangle behind Hillside Road, have become patched with allotments where the adults of the district Dig for Victory, and overgrown with rank grasses where the children build camps and huts, where they smoke and bake potatoes and bully each other. In the reprieved farmyard we maintain foul-smelling sloshy contact with agricultural life, and in the vast prairies of the meadows we wander at random – this way, that way – walk, run, lie in the long fallow and look at the sky. We cycle up to Epsom Downs and gaze out over the panorama of London and the Thames Valley under their attendance of silver barrage balloons. No one worries that we will be run over; there's no one on the roads to run us over – only my father when he gets back from work, only Dr Wilde on his rounds, only a few army dispatch riders and horse-drawn milk-floats. No one thinks we will get abused or murdered; all the abusers and murderers are in the services, abusing and murdering someone else.

Yes, for some of the other people out there the Duration is not so enjoyable. I'm chastened now when I read the histories of the war or see the film archive, and am reminded once again of the horrors that are occurring while we are so blithe and uncaring. Even at the time I'm occasionally aware of events in the wider world, and not just the Battle of Britain and the Blitz. I sense the sudden lightening of mood among the adults in the summer of 1941, when Germany invades Russia, and people begin to feel that we really might have a chance after all. On one of our mother's half-term treats for us in London we see an exhibition about Bomber Command, with a huge model of Essen burning, a thousand red and orange fires pulsing in the darkness, though with no sign of the burning bodies among them. Another treat: a family visit to a show at the Kingston Empire on 8 September 1943 – my tenth birthday – when the manager comes on stage and stops proceedings to announce Italy's surrender. Then at Christmas 1944 a shadow falls over the festivities as the Germans counter-attack in the Ardennes, and for a few weeks seem to be on the way to driving the Allied armies back to the Channel and re-occupying Europe.

What do my parents think and feel about these great events, and all the other aspects of the war that they must know so much more about than we do? For them, presumably, the war's more than the Duration. Is their confidence that we shall win in the end absolute, even before the Germans take on Russia? Do they believe unquestioningly in the things that we're fighting for?

I don't know. I can't recall ever hearing them talk about it. The questions never arise. But then I've very little idea of what they think about any of the issues of the day. From the way my father behaves and the jokes he makes I have some sense of how he sees the world, which is still to a considerable extent how it must have looked to him from the standpoint of those two rooms in Devonshire Road. He remains, for instance, a lifelong supporter of the Labour Party, undeterred by being probably the only one (apart, I think, from my mother) in East Ewell; though he's so uninterested in the actual details of politics that at a local election in later life, before party affiliations are shown on the ballot paper, he manages to vote not for the six Labour candidates he supports but for three Conservatives and three Communists.

He respects any activity that requires human skill and human effort, from performing music and observing stars to spinning a cricket ball and double-entry book-keeping; and any notable products of that activity, from cathedrals and synchromesh gears to hand-made shoes and well-written newspapers. He's inclined to be disrespectful, on the other hand, about all claims to social or moral ascendancy, and his scepticism remains unaffected by his own rise in life, or his elevation to the Fire Captaincy. Being a general, or a king, or a managing director, or a clergyman are all fundamentally comic conditions, rather like Barlow's Scottishness or Kerry's Irishness. So is being what he calls, talking about a customer or a colleague at work, a ten-to-two, or indicates by sketching the gesture of a hooked nose. I assume that he's as unware as I am at the time of the possibility that his wife, mother-in-law and son are all ten-to-twos, and all have invisibly hooked noses.

He certainly has no kind of religious beliefs, and nor, I think, does my mother. One of the things I remain most grateful to them both for is their failure to transmit to me that burden of indefinable constraint and unlocated guilt, that overarching cosmic awkwardness, which often seems to be so difficult to shake off. He has no formal ethics, either – no set code of right and wrong. He does what he does; though what he does often has a moral dimension. He shines his shoes and he expects me to shine mine; I understand, without being told, that shining your shoes and everything that goes with it are the keys to success in life. He supports his mother and his disabled sister, then maintains his parents-in-law, without any sign of impatience that I can recall. He endures his deafness, and the worse things that are to come, with courage and humour.

He isn't a great disciplinarian. I can remember only one attempt, early in our relationship, to punish me for something. Whatever it was I'd done, it irritated him so much that he suddenly lashed out at me in fury, and booted me up the backside, as if we'd both been eleven or twelve, instead of something more like thirty-six and four. The well-shone shoe didn't connect with me. Cross as he was, it was probably more a demonstration of a boot up the backside than a seriously intended one.

If there's an abstract quality that he values it's persistence. He's reluctant to allow me to go to Crusaders, some kind of Low Church Sunday school that I long to join because my best friend David has; but when he finally gives in to my pleading, and I immediately hate it, he won't let me leave until I've endured a salutary year or more of sanctimonious Sunday afternoons. He reminds me of this when later I plead to be allowed to join the school Cadet Corps. I persist in my nagging; he gives in; I'm once again immediately repulsed by it; he won't let me leave until I have endured another salutary year or more of marching round the school playground every Friday in undersized ammunition boots and oversized battledress.

But none of this, so far as I can see, springs from any general faith or particular beliefs – any set of assertions that unverifiable states of affairs are the case, or ought to be.

I suppose, with hindsight, that he loved my mother. And loved me and my sister, though he never said. Perhaps, it occurs to me now with a shock of surprise, he loved us as blindly and helplessly as years later I love my own children – was filled with the same joy at the sight of us as I am at the sight of them. Is this possible? The extraordinary discoveries one makes in life! And once again, as so often, only long after the event, only when one has stepped into the shoes one saw before on someone else's feet.

The lack of religion in the house is a further cause for Nanny's nervousness. She sometimes furtively invites my sister and me into her room and gets us down on our knees among all the dim lights and lavender smells, with our eyes closed and hands pressed together, to say our prayers. We pray for our mother and father, and address further prayers, rather confusingly, to another father which art in heaven. His name, unlike the father which art writing his reports in the dining room, is Harold, and there's no mention of any mother which art in heaven with him, or of any Nanny which art in his little back bedroom. Our own Nanny's too flustered and whispery about these surreptitious occasions to offer explanations. She seems to fear that at any moment our father (the one which art not in heaven) might burst in and drag all three of us off to be burnt at the stake. He's rather more likely, of course, given his taste for persistence, to have my sister and me down on our knees to Harold every single day of the year.

Nanny gives me a Bible. I have it still on my bookshelf, inscribed 'Xmas 1943', its spine worn away by being pressed against the lever of my bicycle bell as I cycled to Crusaders each Sunday. And maybe it's her piety that wears away my unbelief a little, too. At some point in the war, certainly, I write two poems of a religious nature. One is about the heroism of the people of Dover under bombardment by the German cross-Channel guns, the other about the invention of the electric telegraph by Samuel Morse. Each stanza of the latter ends with a repetition of the first message that Morse sent on his newly installed line from Washington to Baltimore: 'What hath God wrought!' I have also developed a feeling, which I suppose is essentially religious, that any fun or pleasure in life is unseemly, and has to be balanced out in some kind of moral double-entry system. On Christmas morning – perhaps in 1943, the same year as the Bible – after my sister and I have been awake since four o'clock, agonisingly counting the minutes until we finally hear faint signs of life from our parents' room, I insist that before we can go downstairs and open our presents we must kneel up on our beds and hold an extempore Christmas morning service of prayers and carols. I pray aloud at great length. I know a lot of carols, and we sing them all. My poor sister.

Eventually the more acute symptoms of religion pass off, and for a year or two I'm in remission. I don't know what brings this about. Sunday school, perhaps.

In spite of my father's political sympathies we pay for the doctor who comes rather frequently every winter to put a thermometer under our tongues and feel the swollen glands in the corner of our jaws. The only alternatives would be to become panel patients, as working men (not women or children) lucky enough to have national insurance are called, and wait to be seen at the doctor's surgery in Epsom on a Thursday morning, or to get some form of charity. Nobody in Hillside Road is a panel patient. By the time you'd waited your way through enough Thursday mornings to get to the head of the queue your glands would have subsided, your broken bones knitted up, your mortal remains been laid to rest.

Nor do my parents ever consider educating my sister and me in state schools. The local Council School, a large purpose-built municipal structure in Ewell Village, where the lavatory tiles covering the walls are decorated with the pupils' daubs in vulgarly bright poster paints, is visited by the middle classes only on Sunday afternoons, when Crusaders is held there. The rest of the time it, and the Council School children who emerge from it at the end of each schoolday to spread vulgar Council School infections such as ringworm and impetigo around the district, and litter the streets with dropped aitches and double negatives, are simply below our conceptual horizon. The Central School that my father went to in Holloway, with the French teacher who had with such personal attention beaten French out of his head, are aspects of the past that he has turned his back on.

So my sister goes to the kindergarten at Sutton High School for Girls, three miles away, wearing a pale mauve blazer and an anxious look on her face, with a velour hat in winter over her mass of blond sausage curls, and in summer a straw boater. But where am I to go? I've finished the top class in Nonsuch School, the delightful little local academy run by Miss Dunk and her father, and accommodated partly in a decayed Victorian mansion and partly in a raw new house on another of Gleesons' estates. I've had a good time there, and a productive one. I've learnt to read, and have written the essay that moved my father to suggest a career in journalism. I've served as official scientist in Diana Baker's gang, in its camp under the laurels in the old shrubbery. I've mastered the triangle in the school's percussion band, and sung a song that represents the call of the yellowhammer, 'A Little Bit of Bread and *No* Cheese'. I'm ready for something more demanding.

My parents decide to see whether I might get into Sutton High School for Boys, a few hundred yards along the road from the girls' high school. The blazers here are purple instead of a discreet mauve, and there are other differences, in spite of the similarity of the name. The girls' school is owned by the Girls' Public Day School Trust, a non-profit body that runs well-reputed and academically oriented schools all over the country. The boys' school is owned by the Reverend J. B. Lawton, who is also its headmaster. The girls are housed in a substantial spread of classrooms, laboratory blocks and gymnasia, tree-shaded tennis and netball courts, and a spacious hall where we go later to see my sister play Seventh Rat in *The Pied Piper of Hamelin*. The boys are in one single-storey building. Its front wall, visible to the public, is built of brick, and all its other walls of corrugated iron lined with tongue-and-groove boarding. The whole school shakes whenever a door's slammed.

There's no hall where the boys might be distracted by amateur theatricals. A wobbly partition between two of the classrooms is folded back each morning to make a space where the school assembles for prayers.

My mother takes me for the entrance exam. It's conducted orally, by the Reverend J. B. Lawton in person. He wears a clerical collar and heavy priestly boots. His grey hair's cropped as close as his little unblinking eyes are set, and his cheekbones gleam from the closeness of his shave. In the corner of his study is a rack with a selection of canes of various thicknesses. Hoping no doubt to head him off from investigating too closely my progress in arithmetic, which is still limited in spite of my father's efforts, my mother lays stress on my literary abilities, and the success I have had with titles such as 'The House I Should Like to Live in When I Am Grown Up'. The Reverend J. B. Lawton obligingly concentrates the examination upon the arts side.

'Spell "beautiful",' he says.

'B-u-e . . .' I begin, but realise at once that this draft could be improved. 'B-e-u . . . B-a-e . . .'

My restless search for perfection evidently impresses the learned and pious proprietor. I've passed. I'm in.

At Sutton High School for Boys, he explains to my mother, I can prepare to take the Common Entrance Examination, and go on to any of England's great public schools. Or, if she and my father prefer, I can stay on here, in the venerable corrugated-iron halls of Sutton High School for Boys.

For another ten or eleven years, if Eton or Winchester don't appeal.

Every now and then the war comes closer to home. Fielding's handsome son-in-law is shot down, and loses both his legs. I don't know when this happens. I just remember him later, I think at the end of the war, in trim civilian suit, handkerchief in breast pocket, off with all the other commuters each morning to catch the train at Ewell East station, swinging himself bravely down the street on two tin legs and two crutches, pipe clamped in the determined jaw, a hero still. He and his wife are living with her parents, like so many other returned war heroes with nowhere else to go – until the marriage breaks up. He departs, and the glory at No. 12 with him.

It's the Blackout that does for my beloved grandfather. He was knocked down in the unlit streets by a taxi, says Auntie Phyllis in the little memorandum she wrote for me years later, and this starts up an old injury sustained a dozen years earlier when he fell down a flight of cellar steps. He was still living in digs in Kentish Town, still 'fending for himself', and apparently was reduced at one point to hanging around the Carreras works in Mornington Crescent at the lunch hour, waiting to touch Phyllis for a discreet cash hand-out. Everyone in her office knew about it. People would tell each other, 'Oh, there's Lawson subbing her old man again.' By the time of his death things seem to have looked up a bit, and he was working as a clerk at Cable and Wireless. The post mortem, as recorded on his death certificate, says nothing about injuries caused by cellar steps or taxis. It mentions only a heart problem – and cirrhosis of the liver. I have no recollection of his drinking more than the odd pint with my father at the Spring Hotel in Ewell Village. Can both my grandfathers have been boozers?

The next victim is closer still. Christmas 1943, and things on the home front are looking notably bleak. 'The Government', records my almanac of the twentieth century for 22 December of that year, 'says there are only enough turkeys for one family in ten this Christmas.' Our family's one of the other nine. Not even Sid has been able to raise any eatable birdlife from the farmers of Lincolnshire. My father decides that one of us must be sacrificed. He goes out after breakfast and chases the drake round the garden. Through the bare winter flower beds and the desolate vegetable patch. Round the coal shed. Over the asbestos fence into the stinking quagmire around the air-raid shelter.

Within an hour or so he has caught it, and conducted it to the garage to wring its neck. He has consulted the Khaki Campbell handbook and found out how to do this, swiftly and with a minimum of suffering to either victim or executioner. The drake, however, exemplifies the national spirit of defiance invoked by Winston Churchill in his famous response to the prediction that England would have her neck wrung like a chicken: 'Some chicken . . . some neck.' Some drake, it turns out – and its neck, reports my father later, is as rubbery as a garden hose. The scene in the garage is kept from us, but it plainly gets more and more like the murder of Rasputin, until finally my father has to fetch the rusty chopper from the coal shed. Though since the rusty chopper's too blunt even to chop firewood . . .

Eventually the drake's dead and plucked, and my mother has cooked it. Even after two or three hours in the New World cooker, however, it's still, like England, defying its enemies. None of us can get so much as the prong of a fork into it.

Tuesday, 6 June 1944. A Tuesday morning like any other at Sutton High School for Boys. Latin, I think . . . Until the walls of the classroom shudder in anticipation as the door's flung open and the Reverend J. B. Lawton makes a solemn entrance. We all freeze. Any faint sounds – of breathing, perhaps, or of a page being cautiously turned in *Kennedy's Eating Primer* – cease. The good pastor has already caned his way through a queue of fifteen or twenty boys waiting after prayers, perhaps a fifth of the school, and has no doubt dispatched a few more in shifts since then. What does this unscheduled visitation portend? The solemnity of his expression suggests the worst. A really shocking new offence has come to light. A pen nib has gone missing, perhaps. The entire class is going to be caned. He's going to take off his jacket once again and roll up his sleeves. He's going to put the same effort and concentration into every stroke of the cane as he always does, rising a little on his heels, with his eyes opening suddenly wider for a moment in concentration, as he brings the weapon down with such impressive force and accuracy on to that small outstretched hand, that awkwardly vertical behind . . .

But no. The kindly shepherd of our souls is simply passing on some war news he has just heard on the wireless. The Allies have launched their long-expected invasion of Europe. We give a faint cheer, and no one's punished for it.

A week later comes further war news. This time it announces itself.

It's in the middle of the night, and presumably the air-raid warnings have sounded, because we're sleeping downstairs, our parents as usual next to the live fuse boxes, my sister and myself in the corridor outside Nanny's room. A familiar racket of ack-ack, but this time so loud that Nanny comes out of her room to join us, uttering little cries of terror. And she's right, because now there's a sound the like of which we have never heard before in any previous raid – an angry buzzing, deafeningly loud, like a giant bluebottle, that passes directly over the roof of the house as if almost touching it. The whole house shakes like Sutton High School for Boys – and then shakes even more violently as the buzzing suddenly ends in a gigantic explosion.

We're all dead! We must be! Nanny's certain of it. She keeps shouting that she knew we were going to be killed and now we have been. It's not just Nanny – we're all screaming and shouting. We're all crawling around trying to find each other, unable to see anything because the air has gone thick and white. It takes some time for our parents to establish that they still have two children, and for us to understand that we still have two parents. All five of us, it slowly emerges, even our late grandmother, are not only alive but unhurt.

The air's thick and white because this is where the plaster ceilings of the house now are, hanging in suspension, and spread fine over the floor and the Bentalls three-piece suite. Also scattered about, in a very deteriorated condition, are all the windows on the north side of the house in their Arts and Crafts lead mullions. The front door has deserted its post in terror, and is leaning shell-shocked against the wall on the opposite side of the lounge. Upstairs in the front bedroom, where my sister and I would have been sleeping if my parents had ignored the warnings, as they sometimes have in the past, a tangled mass of window-lead set with broken glass is curled up as peacefully as Goldilocks on my pillow.

It's only when day breaks and we hear the BBC news that we can begin to establish what's happened. The Germans, it seems, have started using a new form of weapon, a small pilotless jet aircraft packed with explosive, that flies until it runs out of fuel and crashes. One of the first of these, engine still running, has passed over the roof of our house. It must have missed us by a matter of feet, because it failed to clear a house in the next street, on slightly higher ground about two hundred yards away. The family who lived there are now all dead.

Nobody in Hillside Road knew them, though, so there's no damper on the excitement of all the local children at the sudden change in our circumstances. A team of men from the council comes down the street, nailing shiny linen over the empty window frames, and the lounge is filled with the soft white light you wake up to after an overnight snowfall. A white Christmas! Except that it's June, and the powdery white icing has transformed not the outdoors but the indoors.

My father puts on his official Fire Captain's steel helmet to protect himself from any bits of the house that may still be falling off, and gets up into the loft to investigate the state of the roof. Bathroom stool – knees flexed twice – foot on bedroom door handle – foot on architrave – push lid – grab edge; even the climb up there is already an excitement to watch. And then, as he lifts the trap out of the way with his helmeted head, there's not the darkness of the loft but the brightness of the open sky above it. My sister and I run out into the front garden – and sure enough, there's the Fire Captain's helmet, where no Fire Captain's helmet ought to be, emerging cautiously from the wonderful hole in the middle of the Dutch tiles. The helmet, like the homburg around my study door twenty or so years later, is followed by my father's head. He's smiling down at us, as amused as we are. This, one of my sister's sons told me recently, is the only thing that his mother could remember about our doodlebug: our father's head emerging from the hole in the roof.

It's a memorable summer. The leftovers of the white linen from the windows are a good new raw material for the camps that we build on our patch of wasteland behind the houses. The tangled lead from the mullions is even more interesting. You can melt it in an old tin lid on top of the New World gas stove and make little pools and balls of quicksilver. You can tip the molten lead into water to form fantastic shapes, or use it for a hundred other things, if only we could think what they might be.

Our house is changed even further by the acquisition of a Morrison shelter, which is not something for waterfowl to live in at the bottom of the garden, but a perfectly practicable steel table, named after the current Home Secretary, like the Anderson before it, and set up indoors. My parents must have been more alarmed than I realised by that first doodlebug. They have abandoned the trusted habits of improvisation and acquired a proper official air-raid shelter, without waiting for passing navvies or for someone to give us a discarded one when the war's over. It makes our kitchen as excitingly overcrowded as the dining room sometimes used to be on Sundays, and perhaps for my father more reminiscent of the kitchen in Devonshire Road. It has wire cage walls on three sides, and is floored with mattress, so that it makes a snug nest like a children's camp. We sleep in it at night, and during the day fling ourselves into it, if we have enough warning, whenever a doodlebug threatens.

The entertainment provided by the flying bombs continues. Never again does the angry buzzing come as close and loud as it did that first night. Even in the distance, though, it provides an agreeable touch of tension. Some fresh excitement may be just about to happen. A bigger bang. More dramatic destruction. We listen as the uneven racket gets louder – watch sometimes from the back garden as the persistent little insect with the tail of flame approaches . . . Until suddenly the noise stops. 'It's cut!' shouts everyone, and we all fling ourselves into the Morrison, or flat on the ground.

Silence. Wait . . . It's going to be a really big one!

And always we're disappointed. Six thousand people are killed by flying bombs before they're through, and after that first one they're always somewhere else.

A team of tilers works its way along the street, replacing the temporary tarpaulins on the roofs. One of them is a handsome young American called Mike, who wears gym shoes instead of boots like all the others. He has bad feet, he explains, which is why he isn't fighting his way through Normandy. All the children in the street fall in love with him. We gaze at him adoringly as he runs lightly over the tiles on his rubber soles, and stands with casual disregard for either height or doodlebugs on the very crest of a roof against the summer cumulus. We sit on the ground at his feet as he drinks coffee. On the pocket of his shirt is embroidered 'Stella, Chicago, USA, 1942'. We fall in love not only with Mike but with Stella, the beautiful girl who's waiting for him so heartbreakingly three thousand miles away. We fall in love with Chicago.

Actually I'm already in love with Chicago, even before I know that Stella lives there, perhaps because it's my mother's legendary birthplace, or because 'Chicago' is such a romantic word. Or perhaps simply because it's in the USA, which I'm also having a love affair with at the time, I think because of a Puffin book about the history of the country, which has pictures in brightly coloured poster paints of covered wagons and the Liberty Bell, and which mentions the Sioux, who have almost as romantic a name as Chicago, though I discover many years later that I've been mispronouncing it. I have the Union Jack and the Hammer and Sickle as well as the Stars and Stripes arrayed above my bed, but the Stars and Stripes is the only one of the three that I'm in love with, and at the centre of the array is a photograph of not Winston Churchill or Joseph Stalin but Franklin Delano Roosevelt. I'm in love with Franklin Delano Roosevelt. How could I not be in love with someone called Delano? Even though, as with 'Sioux', I discover years later that I've been mispronouncing it.

By this time, I think, at the age of ten and three-quarters, I'm no longer so much in love with Janet, whom I've glimpsed each afternoon coming home from Sutton High School for Girls on the same train as me, in an aura charged with romance by the scent of train oil and railway upholstery. I've never managed to speak to her, but for a whole term I've been dreaming about her shock of frizzy hair and her mauve gingham dress, to a secret background music of (for some reason) 'I Love a Lassie'. Every time I've come to the line 'She's as sweet as the heather, the bonny blooming heather' I've almost fainted from sheer erotic overload. (Later, even without any one particular girl in mind, I'm overcome by the intensity of the emotional field around a waltz called 'The Waves of the Danube' and the intermezzo from Wolf-Ferrari's *The Jewels of the Madonna*.) Now the term has ended, and I've transferred my affections to Mike and Stella and Roosevelt, but I'm still also in love with girls in general. How could I not be, when they have such romantic names? Janet . . . Wendy . . . Rosemary . . . And wear dresses. And run in such a funny way. And laugh among themselves. And are called girls. And are accompanied everywhere they go by a private soundtrack of waltzes and intermezzos . . .

I'm also, as it happens, in love with one girl in particular: Jennifer, the Dennis-Smiths' elder daughter. I certainly talk to Jennifer, unlike Janet, because we've grown up together, and I've always talked to her, and she's one of the gang who sit at Mike's feet. She's a strapping, suntanned girl with white teeth and a loud laugh. I've just unearthed a snap of her, and I see why I've fallen in love with her. It's not just her irresistibly romantic name – she's amazingly beautiful.

We spend a lot of time together that summer, even after Mike and the rest of the tilers have gone. The great meeting place for all of us is the garden of No. 6. The Locatellis (and the light fittings) have long since departed, and the Laverses are not yet back. The garden has reverted to jungle. We swing on the rusty swing (which somehow later, in the way of the world's rusty rejects, ends up in our garden). We lie about in the sunlit meadow that was once the lawn, and bicker and sneeze, and sometimes take a scythe to the grass and let it lie to make hay for the Dennis-Smith rabbits.

On other days Jennifer and I move across the road to her own garden. We sit in her summerhouse for whole afternoons at a time. It smells of coolness and dry straw, and there's a hamper full of back numbers of a comic called *Girls' Crystal*. We guzzle them one after another without stopping, a forbidden pleasure as intoxi-cating as Craven A. In the long summer evenings, made longer still by another of the innovations introduced for the Duration, Double Summer Time, we dart about in the gloaming, evading our parents' efforts to fetch us home. Jennifer laughs and spins around in her wide dirndl skirt. In the half-light she's all white teeth and sparkling eyes and darkness, and I'm even more in love with her than I am with Franklin Delano Roosevelt.

The seat of the swing vanishes. We believe that Miss Johnson next door, jealous of our idle summer amusement, has confiscated it, and we work ourselves up into a fury of indignation, to which I, as spectacles-wearer and therefore intellectual, feel obliged to give expression. I copy out Cowper's *Boadicea* in lurid red ink with various adaptations such as 'Miss Johnson' and 'she' for 'Rome', then, watched by my admiring friends, post it through Miss John-son's letter-box.

> She shall perish – write that word
> On the swing-seat she has ta'en;
> Perish, hopeless and abhorred,
> Deep in ruin as in pain.

As soon as she reads it she identifies me as the author (my specs again, I suppose) and comes round to complain to my father.

Angry as he is about the poem, whatever he can see of Jennifer and me in the gathering darkness evidently makes him a great deal uneasier, because he finds a quiet moment to give me one of his rare pieces of moral advice: I should try to play less with girls. Just as well that he doesn't know I'm also reading all those old *Girls' Crystals*, because I can tell from the tone of his voice that he's seriously worried, and with hindsight I realise what it's about: the same as all the other fathers up and down the land who are uneasy because their sons are too interested in *boys*. He thinks that I'm in danger of contracting girlishness.

Would he have been relieved, I wonder, if he'd known about the feelings I also have for Mike the tiler and the President of the United States?

My mother, so far as I can recall, says nothing about all this. Is she, too, worrying about my incipient girlishness? About the fact that she has corrupted me even before Jennifer has – all those sixpences for coming top! – and that I'm already a bit of a mother's boy?

She has enough to worry about even without my shortcomings. Not that I ever notice at the time. A mother's boy, a potential girl and housewife myself, yet I never give a moment's thought to what her life must be like, trailing from shop to shop in the Village – the grocer's, the greengrocer's, the butcher's, the baker's, the fishmonger's, and queues at all of them – racking her brains to conjure food for five, and often for more at the weekend, out of a few crumpled ration books. Not to mention food for the ducks. It's often my sister and I who wait on them; the sour smell from that battered bowl of long-boiled food waste is in my nostrils still. But it's she who has to make them the meals: mince up the peelings, simmer them by the hour, and stir in the balancer meal she has dragged back by the fifty-pound sack, uphill all the way from the Village, on the crossbar of her gents' Raleigh.

And now the doodlebug, which for her means not a premature Christmas but plaster dust and fine shards of broken glass in every corner of the house, in every carpet and fabric. There's no time for the violin now, no more stories about that ship of gold waiting in Chancery. In the snaps I have of her she's still beautiful. But in 1942 the snaps cease, I suppose because it's no longer possible to buy film for the camera. I remember her as putting on a bit of weight in those later years, as looking a little more harrassed and workaday. It's part of the solid thereness of her that I take so much for granted, and that I'm sometimes fleeing to still for comfort. When I score my one goal, for instance. Or when I'm taken with a school party to the local cinema, and I'm traumatised by a passing line of dialogue in a cowboy film – a reference to an unseen rancher who has had to put down his equally unseen herd because of foot-and-mouth. 'They killed all the cows!' I sob to her, over and over again.

Sometimes I have bad dreams, or can't sleep at all, and have to take refuge in my parents' bed. Often they don't even wake as I squeeze down between their two snoring enormousnesses. It's boring, lying there awake between the walls of their backs, in the stale smell of their night breath. But even the boringness of it is a comfort.

Am I still fleeing to my parents' bed even when I'm so busy falling in love with everyone and everything? Is my mother still coming in to give us a goodnight kiss on a Saturday night, with her breath smelling deliciously of the pint of bitter she has been drinking with my father, perhaps with Phyllis and Sid as well, at the Spring Hotel in the Village? I don't think my parents are still taking my sister and me for a Sunday morning drink at the Tattenham Corner Hotel on Epsom Downs. We have another family treat now – Saturday lunch at the British Restaurant in Leatherhead. The British Restaurants are government canteens, housed in asbestos shedding which has perhaps been supplied by my father, and their function is to keep the population cheaply and adequately nourished with vast helpings of simple food, such as bright orange mashed swedes. We don't go by car – we cycle. My mother, on her Raleigh, protectively shepherding my sister, now seven, on the fairy cycle that came from our rich relations in Enfield – six miles there and six miles back, her little legs pumping away at four times the speed of ours. The most surprising aspect of these trips is that my father, too, has been persuaded on to a bicycle. He rides it in a special non-committal way indicating that it's not his – that it's his late father-in-law's (and still with us in the garage, like the violin under the stairs) – that he's not really a cyclist at all but a motorist condescending.

An even greater treat for me, though, is the special privilege that I'm accorded on Saturday evenings as a reward for being nearly eleven. I have to wait for this until my sister's asleep, which often takes an agonisingly long time, because she suspects from the way I'm remaining absolutely silent and motionless, not suggesting any dares down to the dining-room door, or into our parents' bedroom and out of the window on to the roof of the bay window below, that for some ulterior purpose I want her unconscious. At last her restless struggles to stay awake grow still. She begins to breathe regularly ... I ease myself inch by inch out of bed...

At once she's sitting up, wide awake. 'Where are you going? What are you doing?' – 'Nowhere. Nothing ...' I get back into bed and start waiting all over again.

Where I'm going, when near dawn I can, is downstairs. What I'm doing is joining my parents for bread and cheese – the whole week's ration at one go, probably. Even more delicious than the bread and cheese is the grown-upness of it, the nonchalant three-ness of it. We're as close as the three we're listening to on the wireless as we eat, in *Happidrome* –

> We three
> In harmon*ee*,
> Working for the BBC,
> Rams*bott*om ...
> ... and Enoch ...
> ... and me.

At one of these Saturday night feasts I take an effortlessly adult swig of my lemonade – and spit it out again over the tablecloth, because it's the most disgusting fluid any human being has ever had in his mouth. *Not* my lemonade – my father's beer. 'Daydreaming again, Willy?' inquires my father resignedly.

All this – the doodlebug, the falling in love, the bread and cheese – happens, I think, in the summer of 1944. In September, on the 8th, I'm eleven, and the Germans celebrate my birthday by launching the first V2s upon London. The V2 is not a pilotless plane, like the V1; it's a rocket. It travels faster than sound, so there's nothing to hear beforehand, and no sporting chance to throw yourself on to the floor or into the Morrison. The first warning of its arrival is the explosion that announces it already has. Then you hear it coming.

In theory, it seems to me now, this ought to be less stressful than the doodlebugs, because you don't need to do anything about it. If you hear anything at all you're still alive, and it's killed someone else. But for some reason – perhaps simply because I'm three months older than I was – it terrifies me. Over and over again, as the autumn and winter draw on, I'm snatched out of sleep by that peremptory notice of execution, and as the retrospective warning comes rumbling along in its wake I realise that I could have been extinguished – could yet at any moment still be extinguished – without ever realising it.

My first intimation of mortality. The war has at last come home to me.

And then it's all over. The Duration, that dour explanation for the state of everything, that had stretched ahead to eternity as comprehensively and dully as the Law of the Conservation of Matter, has ceased to be.

An official day of rejoicing is decreed, VE Day, to mark our victory in Europe. My sister and I celebrate by starting another war of our own, against each other. She marches into Poland – deliberately snaps one of the paint brushes from my watercolour set. I honour my obligations towards my paint brush. A blitzkrieg of punching, scratching and weeping ensues, followed by a second blitzkrieg of slapping, raging and screaming from our mother. I sit chastened in the garden on my own after the battle has died down, very aware of the irony, ashamed of my part in events, pierced to the heart by the sadness of things.

In the evening there's a huge communal bonfire on the waste

ground at the back of the houses, where all the neighbours sing patriotic and sentimental songs together. An asbestos sheet – not one of my father's samples but part of someone's abandoned chicken run – explodes and almost kills the man who's stoking the fire. (I don't think TAC's publicity about the fire resistance of asbestos mentions its weakness for exploding.) What we're watching burn, though we don't yet know it, is the last of the wartime communal spirit that got this bonfire built.

In August there's another day of celebration, VJ Day; even the war in the Far East is over. Peace at last, and the good years starting. We certainly have plenty to rejoice about. Fifty-five million people have died since 1939 – and in our immediate family we have all survived, apart from my grandfather and the drake. My cousin Maurice, who came through Dunkirk, and in 1944 volunteered to go back to France as a glider pilot, is OK. So is my cousin Philip, after his time as a rating in destroyers in the North Atlantic, then rising to lieutenant-commander in the Pacific. Even Nanny has managed to hang on so far, just.

On a misty Saturday evening that autumn, my parents, my sister and I are invited to another bonfire, this time for Guy Fawkes Day. My sister and I are even more excited by this one, because it will be the first Guy Fawkes with fireworks since before the war. And it's in the paddock of our wealthy neighbour Mr Warbey, the cardboard-box manufacturer with the tennis court. We're on the up and up in every way.

So there we are, waiting to go out to the fireworks that misty Saturday evening, the 3rd of November 1945. It's about 6 p.m. My father's in the back bedroom, changing, my mother's in the dining room with Nanny. Nanny (as I discover later) is suggesting a glass of sherry, and I suppose my mother's feeling, 'Well, why not?' Everything's still rationed, it's true, England's still bleak and grey. But it's the end of another week, it's Saturday. Tommy's home, the children are upstairs playing, our wealthy neighbours have invited us out, and there are sky rockets and sparklers to look forward to. And when she thinks of everything that has happened since that party in Holloway twenty-six years earlier . . . Her father's ruin, and her farewell to music. The long wait to marry. The move to Ewell. The struggle to support parents and parents-in-law, to feed the family, to keep our battered little ark afloat . . . It's a life, though, no doubt about it. She and Tommy have made a reasonable go of it. There's something to celebrate.

Or perhaps she's just thinking about a shirt collar to be turned, a sheet to be patched.

But, yes, a small glass of sherry, certainly.

My friend David and I are in the front bedroom, trying to play a serious game. My sister's with us, annoying us.

'Tommy!'

It's Nanny calling up the stairs, and there's something terrible in her voice that I've never heard before in all her cries of alarm and despair.

'*Tommy!* Quick! It's Vi!'

We all stop what we're doing, paralysed by that note in her voice. We can hear her struggling up the stairs, gasping and sobbing, and my father running down them.

The 3rd of November 1945. About six in the evening. My father's fortune, after forty-four years, has just run out. So has Nanny's, such as it was, so has my sister's and mine.

So, absolutely and finally, has our mother's.

PART TWO

I

Childcare

'Had she *touched* the sherry, though? Had she *drunk* any of it? That's very important. Dr Wilde will want to know that.'

The weird forensic detachment of my father's question has made it stick in my mind – one of the few clear recollections I have of that evening. It's like something written down on the page, or spoken by a character in a drama – something out of someone else's story. Our own story has suddenly become incomprehensible. We have all been plunged into a world where nothing has any recognisable outlines any more, nothing any continuing substance. My father's trying to find some footing in practical reality. So, I suppose, am I, in my memory.

My grandmother had poured my mother a glass of sherry. My mother had walked across the room to take it. But, no, she hadn't touched it. She had never reached it. She had died halfway.

I can remember my father's actual question, but not my grandmother's actual reply, only her weeping wildly and saying, over and over again, 'It should have been *me*! It should have been *me*!' I know the general outline of the events in the dining room, but the particular words it was constructed from have vanished. My mother has had a heart attack and died – though how I know even that much I can't remember. How exactly did the event unfold? If Nanny was pouring sherry then she was probably by the sideboard, using not the sherry decanter, which is always empty, but a bottle taken out of the cupboard beneath it. If my mother had to cross the room to take the glass then she must have been at the other end of the room, perhaps by the fireplace. To get to the sideboard she will have had to pick her way around the settee. How far did she get? Where exactly did she fall? On the floor?

Across the arm of the settee? Was she already unconscious by the time my grandmother put the glass down and got to her? Already dead, even? How did my mother spend the last few seconds of her forty-one years in this world?

When, for that matter, does my father's interrogation of my grandmother occur? Some time in the next half-hour, I suppose, before Dr Wilde has arrived. And where? Upstairs somewhere. The dining room has become a forbidden area, a non-existent space in the geography of the house. The whole ground floor has become infected by non-existence.

Yes, I remember that my sister and I have had to stay upstairs. My friend David has somehow vanished from the picture.

What have my sister and I been doing while my father and grandmother were still downstairs in the dining room with . . . with . . . with what can't be thought about . . . and we were waiting upstairs alone? What have we said to each other? What have we been thinking and feeling? Do we really understand what's happened? Has our father come upstairs and explained to us? If so, how? How could he have even begun to explain?

David's mother has appeared round the bedroom door at some point. Has said something. Said what? What *could* she have said?

There's a time later, I think after the doctor has been, when my father, my sister and I are sitting in a row along the edge of my bed, and we're all three of us howling like animals.

'You know who'll miss her most?' cries my father. 'Me, because I've known her longest.'

I remember those precise words, and I remember feeling even in the midst of that formless swamp of uncomprehending grief that there's something absurd about them, something inappropriately childish about the claim.

There's another point, later still, when the District Nurse is there. The undertakers must already have called and removed the . . . removed the . . . removed it, because we're all now in the dining room, sitting on the three-piece suite. The District Nurse is drinking a cup of tea, very straight-backed. Conversation is difficult. It suddenly comes into my head that I should give her a brave smile. She looks taken aback, and I realise with a belated shock of embarrassment how inappropriate my impulse was.

Then what? I suppose my sister and I must eventually clean our teeth, put on our pyjamas, and go to bed. Sleep. Wake up . . .

In the morning Auntie Phyllis arrives on an early train. She has come to look after us.

On the Monday I'm back at school. I'm obliged to wait after class to explain to the Reverend J. B. Lawton why I haven't done my French homework. 'My mother died on Saturday,' I tell him. I'm aware that my voice is hushed and self-important.

His close-set eyes rest neutrally on me for a moment, assessing the plausibility of my claim. Then he nods briefly. He has accepted my excuse.

And that's the end of my mother. My sister and I aren't allowed to go to the funeral, I suppose for fear that it would upset us. What do we do instead, while our father and the rest of the family are at the graveyard in Ewell that November day, and my sister and I are staying behind at home, not being upset? Are we on our own? Am I looking after my sister?

One thing we're certainly *not* doing is talking about our mother. So far as I can recall, she's never mentioned in our house again. Not by any of us. Not by my father or grandmother. Not by me or my sister.

She has been airbrushed out of the historical record, like one of Stalin's victims. She has become an unperson. And when I'm grown up, and have to explain to people about my past, I find it difficult to be exact about even the date of her death. Was it 1945, or was it 1946? I tell some people that I was thirteen, others that I was eleven. Now, as I write this, sixty-five years later, and try to recapture the past as fully as I can, I'm able to fix the date from the death certificate. But of what actually happened on that date the scattered recollections above are the only ones I have left. I spent so many years not thinking about it too closely, or not thinking about it at all. My sister couldn't remember anything about it, even though she was already eight at the time. Her son says that she told him our mother had died while she was cycling to the shops. This is a confabulation with something that one of our neighbours said much later. She had seen our mother struggling back with the shopping on her bicycle during the war, and believed that this was part of the strain that had overtaxed her heart. In my sister's memory, evidently, not even the most general outline of the events on that November night remained.

One of the reasons that my sister and I never mentioned her is that we lacked the words. We had no name for her. We couldn't call her Vi, as all the grown-ups did when she was alive, because we never had. 'Our mother'? We'd never called her that, either, not to each other, and to start now would have been ridiculously formal. No, worse than formal – impersonal. It would have placed someone with whom each of us had a unique relationship, and for whom each of us had a unique personal name, in a general class. I did try it once, nearly sixty years later, when my sister was very ill, and I thought that she might want to talk about some of the things that we had once shared so intensely, and that we had never spoken about since. But it sounded wrong, and she didn't respond.

We *had* had a name for her when she was alive, of course. We had called her what most English children call their mothers. Somehow, though, we could no longer say the word. I'm not sure I can even now, even to myself. I'm not sure I can write it down . . .

Yes. She was Mummy. It was Mummy who had died.

There – done. For the first time in sixty-five years.

Why couldn't we say it? I don't know. But we couldn't.

Naming her wouldn't really have been a problem for our father. He could have said 'your mother' to us, in the way that divorced and separated fathers do – even, in a humorous tone of voice, fathers who are still happily married. It wouldn't have been too painful. Our grandmother might have done the same. But I don't think either of them ever did. Or perhaps they *did*. They must have done! They must sometimes have said *something* about her!

Yes – my father somehow conveyed to me at some point that she had once played the violin in the Queen's Hall Light Orchestra. I can't remember precisely what words he used. Perhaps *I'm* suppressing something.

For thirty years it never occurred to me to visit her grave. It was only in 1979, when I was making a television film about the streets I grew up in, that I went to the churchyard in Ewell to look for it. I found two headstones for other people marked with dates just before and just after the 3rd of November 1945, and between them an unmarked plot, so I suppose her bones must have been down there. It would have been characteristic of my father not to put up a stone. I'm tempted to say, not unless George Davis or our relations in Enfield had happened to have one spare. I don't think it was meanness. It was simply not his style to fix the flow of experience in possessions and portraits and speeches and gravestones. When someone was dead they were dead, and there was no palliating it. It was part of his matter-of-factness. No, it went deeper than that. He had a certain lightness of being. And I think on the whole he was right. Gone is gone – until thirty or sixty years later, when just for once you want to revisit that lost land, and then a few words in a letter or on a stone are a sudden blessing.

I've no letter from her, now I come to think about it. Not so much as a birthday card. It never seems to have occurred to anyone that I might be interested to have a photograph of her, until I started asking around the family half a century later. But then why hadn't I asked sooner? No one for that matter had ever thought that I might care to have a copy of her death certificate, and I can't remember now how I first came by it – only the painful irony of the history that it at last began to reveal.

I have it in front of me now. In Column 6, Cause of Death, as certified by the Surrey Coroner after a post mortem without inquest, it records (a) myocardial degeneration, and (b) mitral regurgitation. This is a slightly odd way of putting it, because what it presumably means is that the first was the cause of the second – that she had a long-term condition, a deterioration of the heart, as a result of which a particular event occurred – the heart attack that I had (somehow) always known about. Heart disease is often hereditary, so that, before I found the certificate, I had for years been reporting, as I was required to, my mother's premature death from it to doctors and insurance companies; and it sometimes occurred to me that the implications of this might not be purely theoretical – that just as I might inherit my father's deafness, so I might actually suffer a similar fate to my mother's, and at a similar age.

So far, though, I have survived, and without any protest from my heart, for thirty-five years longer than her, and the certificate may help to explain why, because under Cause of Death it also lists (c) scarlet fever. This is again a somewhat curious formulation, because what (I assume) it's trying to say is that this was the start of the causal chain. One of the complications of scarlet fever in childhood is rheumatic fever, and one of the possible effects of rheumatic fever is long-term damage to the heart and the heart valves.

Yes, said Phyllis, when I asked her, my mother as a child had had scarlet fever. According to my cousin Jean it had begun as measles, but her GP wasn't sure about his diagnosis, so he'd sent her to hospital. At the hospital she was put in the isolation ward with the scarlet-fever patients. From a simple case of measles, and the efforts of her doctor and parents to treat it, she had traded up, cause by cause and effect by effect, to death at the age of forty-one.

And why had the hospital put her in with the scarlet-fever patients? To be on the safe side, because there were no doctors on duty to examine her. They were all off playing cricket. The effects of cricket on my mother were in the end as catastrophic as the cricket ball in the kidneys had been for my great-uncle Robert.

But she's *not* dead!

She's not dead at all! It was some kind of mistake, some ridiculous misunderstanding! She's right here! In the room with me, just as she always was! She's laughing at my silliness, and hugging me to reassure me. I can't believe it! How can I have got things so wrong?

Never mind, though, because now that terrible time's over, and everything has been put right, everything is as it was. I'm so happy, so helplessly, childishly happy!

Now the grey morning light is filtering through the curtains of the front bedroom. I'm awake . . . and yes, it's still true! It wasn't a dream! She's alive, and nothing has changed after all! I lie basking in the sweet intensity of my joy.

And then, gradually, the certainty begins to fade . . .

Night after night I have the same dream. Night after night I make that same wonderful discovery, feel that same rush of overwhelming happiness. Morning after morning I have the same joyous awakening, then suffer the same agonising desolation as the joy ebbs away and I find myself back in the empty grey world where nothing will ever be right again.

Is my sister, in her bed a few feet away, having similar dreams and similar awakenings? Is my father, in the bedroom on the other side of the landing, alone in the double bed where his body and hers had breathed and snored side by side each night in all the irreducible substantiality that had so reassured me? Is my grandmother, in her little nest of chiffon and sepia downstairs? Or my mother's sister, cramped and aching on the mock-leather settee in the dining room? Is each of us shut away alone in that same parallel alternation of illusion and re-emergence, of joy and anguish, that can never be shared?

I can't recall ever at the time lifting my eyes above the greyness of my own waking world and trying to imagine what it was like for the others. Now, with children of my own, I can hardly believe that I never wondered what that time must have been like for my grandmother. My mother was her *child*! This is not something that ever occurred to me at the time. She has lost her *child*! Her firstborn! For a child to lose its mother is terrible. But to a child – in the waking hours, if not in dreams – the world is what it is. You're motherless? So, you're motherless. But for a mother to lose her child . . . How can she ever stop thinking that it might have been otherwise? How can she ever reconcile herself? As she said that night, over and over again, it should have been *her*, it should have been *her*.

Where was she, I wonder now for the first time, while the rest of us were sitting howling on the bed? Downstairs in her own little room, presumably, howling alone. My father had forgotten that there was someone else in the house who had known her for even longer than he had.

And my father, yes. Now I begin to imagine for the first time what it was like for him. His claim that he was the one who would miss her most, it seems to me now, even if he has forgotten her mother, is not so out of place. It's twenty-six years since he marched up to her so cheekily at that party, when he was eighteen and she was fourteen. Since then it's been Tommy and Vi. Tommy and Vi's house. Tommy and Vi's kids. Tommy and Vi's holiday snaps, back garden, Sunday tea parties. He's never known adult life without her.

Now he wires himself up in his hearing aid in the empty bedroom, and comes down to the confusion in the kitchen, where Phyllis is coping heroically, only she doesn't know where the special glass is that Jill drinks her milk out of, or what consistency Michael's porridge has to be if it's not going to make him sick, or how to keep the boiler in, or what to do about her mother sitting in her room weeping and saying it should have been her, or how she can keep her job if she's late yet again.

I suppose Tommy gives her a lift, and they sit side by side in silence until he drops her on the Northern Line at Colliers Wood or Balham. Then he drives on through the grey South London boroughs, alone with the grey samples on the back seat of the car, the grey photographs of asbestos warehouses and carriage-washing sheds. Turns left up some grey back street, left again up another. Everything greyer and shabbier than ever after five years of war . . . Switches his hearing aid on to hear the silence of all the colleagues who know what's happened, but not what to say about it, the joshing of all the customers who don't know, and who are smiling already at the cracks that old Tom Frayn always comes up with.

Then, at the end of the day, back to the shabby house, with the green gates sagging on the rotten gate-posts. Back to my sister and me. We're his biggest worry, of course. We seem quiet enough. What's going on inside us, though? Should he try to say something to us, or will it just upset us? What could he possibly say? Perhaps we'll broach the unbroachable subject ourselves. Mention her name. Ask about her – whether it hurt her when it happened, whether she's in heaven. He almost wishes we would. The silence between us all is like a pall of grey dust in the house.

Or he could pull us to him, one on either side of him, and put his arms around us, and push our heads into his chest. It would make us cry, of course. It would make *him* cry. He doesn't want to upset us again.

What's it going to do to his lovely children, though, having this terrible thing in their lives? Twelve years old and eight years old . . . How can he ever begin to make things all right for them?

He sits in his chair by the wireless, doing his reports, keeping an eye on us. I'm at the dining table with my homework spread out in front of me. My sister lies on the floor under the darts board, making a cat's cradle, unmaking it, making it again. We seem to be keeping ourselves occupied. Perhaps we've already stopped thinking about what happened in this room. Perhaps we're already beginning to get over it . . .

A huge practical problem remains, though, and is getting more urgent by the day: how is he ever going to be able to look after us? He can't give up work. He can't expect Phyllis to go on coping for ever.

It's another of the tests he's been set in life. Twelve years he had to wait to get married, while he supported his mother and his disabled sister. Then another dozen years keeping his parents-in-law afloat. At least he had someone to share all that with. But now . . .

What on earth is he going to do?

At the weekend Uncle Sid arrives. With him he brings the plans for building a working model sailing boat, together with the wood for the hull, the aluminium for the keel, the fabric and cord for the sails, the enamel to paint it and the tools to do it all with. It's a big step up from the cardboard *Coronation Scot* and the cardboard Tower Bridge, but he's chosen a simple design, with a broad, flat hull carved out of a single piece of timber, because this time it's me who is going to do the work.

But it's the same story as the rusty chopper that hammers the nails in crooked, and the toy cricket bat that didn't reach the ball. We don't have a workbench, of course, or a vice. I saw away on the top of the Morrison shelter in the kitchen, struggling to hold the wood flat with my free hand. Patiently Uncle Sid removes my thumb from underneath the teeth of the saw – then snatches the saw as it bounces out of the groove towards where the thumb has taken refuge . . . Gradually he takes the work over, and I fall once again into the role of spectator.

With therapeutic slowness and dullness the boat takes shape. Is sanded, undercoated, painted white on top and black below. Is tested in the bath. Is taken to the boating pond on the recreation ground in Epsom. Struggles slowly across it, flat and broad in the beam, among all the sleek ocean racers around it. The boat is the physical embodiment of my uncle's imaginative kindness and sacrifice of his time. When I think about those weeks after my mother died this is what I see – the flat, broad-beamed little boat struggling slowly across the sunless waters of the boating pond, then being turned around, and struggling slowly back again.

By this time, I suppose, Sid has been demobilised. He has done his bit towards slaughtering the civilian population of Germany and gone back to his old job at Carreras, making his modest contribution towards slaughtering the civilian population of Britain. He and Phyllis both. And both of them taking thought, and time out from their work, to help their brother-in-law and his children through their wretchedness. Have I ever done anything remotely as generous?

Another of my unpaid debts.

*

Childcare

The answer to our father's problem emerges, I should imagine, because no one can think of anything else: our grandmother. Nanny's going to look after us.

It seems obvious enough at the time. There she is, in the house – has been, ever since we moved into it – is still, when Phyllis and Sid, after their noble work as emergency stopgaps, have to go back to North London. Now, though, as I for the first time really think about it, I see how desperate the plan is. She's seventy-three – and not seventy-three in the way that people are now, but in the way that they were then. Even by those more modest standards she's decidedly frail. She moves with some difficulty. In the last ten years she has not, so far as I know, walked further than the back garden. She seems perpetually short of breath. She's always laying her hand to her breast, as if about to suffer the heart attack which should have killed her before. She hasn't run a household since she moved in with my parents when they first got married, fourteen years earlier, or looked after children of our age since the First World War. I suppose she has helped my mother about the house, particularly with little cries of alarm and warnings of disaster, and no doubt with private prayers. But she has always expected to spend a lot of time each day in her room, resting and writing letters to her sister Lal.

Now she has to start doing everything. Cooking and ironing. Making the beds. Washing and cleaning, with no machinery to help her apart from a second-hand Goblin vacuum cleaner which I doubt she ever has the courage to switch on. There's a gas fire in the lounge, but we never use the lounge, and a single disintegrating electric fire, because why buy another one when you can move the broken bits of the one you've got from room to room? – but she has to carry the anthracite for the kitchen boiler, then get down on her knees to rake it out and cart the ashes. She has to carry the coal for the dining-room fire and hold a newspaper over the grate to make a draught while the fire catches, then hurriedly stuff the blazing newspaper up the chimney before it sets fire to her and the rest of the house.

No doubt my father does what he can with the boilers and fires, at any rate, before he goes off to work and after he gets home. My sister and I probably sometimes get shamed into helping a bit. We don't darn our socks, though, or turn our shirt cuffs and collars, or patch our sheets. Nanny does that in the evenings, after everything else, sitting at the dining-room table, peering close with her weak eyes in the light of the single overhead bulb. Socks are made of wool, and develop holes in the toe and heel about once a week. They're never thrown away, and nor are worn-out shirts and sheets, because clothes are rationed.

Yes, she has to cope with the ration books, for food as well as clothes. Almost everything apart from vegetables and bread is still rationed, and almost everything has to be queued for. And even before she starts queuing and sorting out the ration books she has to get to the shops.

It's at this point that not only my memory but my imagination fails. The shops are in Ewell Village, a mile away. She certainly doesn't cycle there, as my mother did. Nor does she walk. What – a mile there, a mile back? There's a bus – but Nanny wouldn't get on a bus! Would she? And even the bus stop's a quarter of a mile away. Can she walk a quarter of a mile? I just can't bring an image before my mind of her even walking out of the front gate, let alone going a hundred yards to the corner, any more than I can see her flying to the Village on a broomstick. I think we still have the ducks at this point, so she's boiling up kitchen scraps and taking them down to the mudheap at the end of the garden twice a day. But the balancer meal that has to be mixed with them? The fifty-pound sacks that have to be fetched from the village? I suppose my father and I help with the shopping and the balancer meal, though I can't remember it.

But then, worse than everything else put together, she has to cope with my sister and me.

Up to now, I think, she has managed to preserve some illusions about us. She's able to see us not only as the bespectacled, awkward, squabbling little lumps who sprawl about the house each day, and have to be shouted at to tidy our toy cupboard, but, on some higher plane accessible only to the inner eye of a fond grandmother, fallen angels trailing a last few shreds of innate glory. She's devoted to us. She would make any sacrifices for us, and, now I come to think about it, is probably feeding us most of her rations. She must know, though, as she takes on her new role that bleak winter, what little devils we can be if we get half a chance.

We *have* now got half a chance – and a good deal more than half. Little devils is what we promptly become.

We're rude and disobedient. Of course. But what we fasten on most mercilessly is her fearfulness, her readiness to clutch at her heart and get short of breath and foresee calamity. She has a particular fear of heights. Not on her own behalf, because she'd never dream of going near anything that might constitute a height. It's the sight of *us* near the edge of anything more than a foot or two above ground level that makes her head spin. Heights, therefore, are what we're irresistibly drawn to.

It's difficult to find any very convincingly dangerous heights around a two-storey house. We can't get on to the roof now that the hole in it has been retiled, and we don't (of course) possess a ladder. It's impossible to climb very high in an elder or a buddleia. We do our best with what's available, though. We dare each other, when we're supposed to be in bed, not just down to the dining-room door, but out of the back bedroom window on to the narrow leads above the bay window in the dining room, or out of the front bedroom window to balance on the six-inch-wide ledge in front of it. We get up on to the roof of the coal shed, the felt over which has worn away to reveal the fragility of the boards beneath. We balance on the edge of the rotting barrel that collects rainwater, and inhale its stagnant green miasma as we haul ourselves up on to the fence behind it, and then work our way along the edge of the fence between our garage and Miss Hay's. The wood is full of splinters, and is a foot or less from the garage on either side. One slip, and we're going to end up with a leg wedged between fence and garage. Or with one leg down one side of the fence and one leg down the other, so that the edge of it is . . . But already we're off the fence and crawling up the tiles to the crest of the garage roof.

I discover that I'm now tall and brave enough – just – to follow my father's route up into the loft. Bathroom stool – a few books on top of it to make up the difference between his height and mine – knees flexed twice – one foot on bedroom door handle – other foot on architrave – push trapdoor with head – wild grab for edge . . . From up here I discover that I'm looking down not just on the landing, and the tiny target of the bathroom stool which, if I ever want to get back, I will somehow have to find blind with my exploring foot as I hang from the trap – I hadn't thought of this, or I should never have started! – but also the dizzying drop of the stairs.

With Nanny running up them, clutching her heart and scream-ing at me to come down, most satisfactorily terrified. A lot of my memories of her from this period are as seen from above, hav-ing trouble with her breathing, her thin grey hair flying in the wind, ineffectually threatening me with what she's going to tell my father when he gets home. Once, shouting hopelessly up at me as I gingerly work my way along those thin boards on the roof of the coal shed, she's reduced to calling me a limb of Satan. Or so I have it recorded in my memory. I must have got this out of a book, though. Surely.

In my most painfully sharp recollection of her, however, I'm at ground level, and so is my sister. We're not frightening her – she's frightening us.

We're standing in the lounge, where no one ever goes, except to telephone, and in our case to open our presents at Christmas. It's not Christmas, though, nor is anyone telephoning. Nanny's in her room, with my father and Dr Wilde, but the door must be open, because we can hear her. She's uttering little cries of distress. They come at intervals of a few seconds, as regular and inhuman as if they were from a machine, and whatever's happening to her must have been going on for a long time now, since my father has evi-dently had time to get the doctor. I can hear Dr Wilde's soothing

Irish voice, trying to reassure her. On and on that terrible noise goes, though, on and on.

My sister and I are standing close to each other in the lounge, and we're both crying. 'She's going to die as well, isn't she,' sobs my sister. 'We're not going to have anyone.' There's nothing I can say to comfort her. Nanny's predictions have finally come true. She *is* going to die, and we *shan't* have anyone – and it's us who have killed her. The circumstances are so painful that we've even managed to allude obliquely, if only by implication, to our mother's death.

Somehow, though, Nanny manages to postpone death once again. She recovers from whatever it was – no one explains anything to my sister or me, of course – and on she goes. Cooking, carrying the coals. Clutching her heart and screaming up at us in terror as we gaze mockingly down at her.

Perhaps it's the heart attack, or the panic attack, or whatever it was, that persuades my father we can't go on like this. Somehow he finds a housekeeper.

She's called Olive, and she's everything that Nanny's not. Still, I would guess, in her thirties; strong, calm, intelligent, self-confident and capable. Used to dealing with children – she has a daughter of about my sister's age. Unshakeably reasonable. Reads the *New Statesman*, and sends her daughter as a weekly boarder to a famous progressive school in Epsom. Unlikely to be impressed by our exploits ten or twenty feet above ground level, if only because she's the widow of an RAF squadron leader. And, in social class, way above the heads of all of us.

I see now how desperate my father is. But I also see how much more desperate Olive must be to have to move into someone else's house – and our run-down house at that. To have to accustom herself to the kind of furniture and appliances that we have – the Bentalls suite, the blunt chopper, all the things made out of asbestos samples. How has she come to this? A squadron leader's pension must surely enable her to keep her head above water. Is it her daughter's school fees? Loneliness? Altruism? Perhaps altruism comes into it. We're her charity cases. I hope so. It's too painful to think of an educated woman with a life of her own being *reduced* to this. A terrible picture of her comes to me, sharing my sister's bedroom, sleeping in the bed I used to sleep in, while I move to a camp bed in my father's room . . . But this *must* be false. The camp bed in my father's room was later, surely. She would have taken over Nanny's room downstairs when Nanny moved out. She would at least have had her own room! Wouldn't she?

I find it very difficult now to sort out the chronology and exact arrangements of those bleak years. One bizarre detail, though, has stuck in my memory – something that got us off to an unfortunate start. It's a Saturday afternoon, and Olive and her daughter Angela have just arrived. They're sitting on the three-piece suite in the dining room; their suitcases are in the lounge. Olive's drinking tea and making pleasant, measured, middle-class conversation to my father, of a sort with which I became entirely familiar later in life, but which has never been heard before in our house. My father has his hearing aid switched on and his ear cupped, but he still evidently can't hear much of what she's saying in her agreeably modulated tones. Angela, a white-faced, unsociable child (spoilt, as we come to think, by her progressive education), is sprawling on the settee reading a comic, pointedly ignoring my sister and me. My sister and I (spoilt, as I imagine Olive already thinks, by our conventional upbringing) are sitting up stiffly, speaking when spoken to, pointedly ignoring Angela. Angela has already decided that she doesn't like us. We have already decided that we don't like her. Our mutual feelings are not going to change.

Nanny, meanwhile, is moving out. Which is to say that she's fluttering blindly about the house, hand to heart, dabbing at her eyes with a lavender-scented lace handkerchief, unable through her tears to find anything she's looking for or to know where to pack it. Every tear, every sigh, every silence make clear that she is with the utmost reluctance and certainty of disaster surrendering her two little innocents to someone who has probably learnt her trade working in a concentration camp.

At last she's as ready as she's ever going to be. I suppose my father's about to drive her, together with her scarves, shepherdesses and silver-framed photographs, over to Hendon, where Phyllis and Sid, now married, are lodgers in a semi-detached house on the main road to Edgware. She must have made a final trip to the lavatory before the journey – and now the social awkwardness of this painful occasion leaps to a new level altogether. Suddenly she's rushing back into the dining room in the middle of some kind of hysterical breakdown. It's almost as bad as her earlier attack, and almost as difficult to understand what's going on.

She has seen something. Something in the lavatory. She can't bring herself to specify what it is – but she has never in all her life seen anything like it! She has warned Tommy that something of this sort would happen! She knew she should have stayed with us, even if it had killed her! What kind of world are we living in? She has never in all her life . . . has warned Tommy over and over again . . . always knew it was going to be a disaster . . .

'Calm down, Nanny,' says Olive, in her most good-humoured and well-modulated tone. (She calls her Nanny! She's that much at her ease socially!) 'Something the matter in the lavatory? I'll have a look.'

I know what Nanny has seen, because I've seen it already. I'm just as unable to talk about it as she is. I have never in all my life seen anything like it, either. I'm just as shocked, only into silence rather than hysterics.

On the forest-green wall of the lavatory, a good three feet away from the bowl itself, a small brown heart-shaped decoration has appeared. Nanny must have bent down curiously to inspect it, as I did, and discovered, as I did, that it was a dollop of excrement.

How had it got there? It seemed to me unlikely that anyone in the family was responsible. Scruffy as we are in so many ways, we're all properly inhibited about matters of evacuation. I think I realised that it was also not very likely to be the handiwork of someone as socially poised as Olive. So it must be the kind of thing you learn to do at a progressive school. I suppose Nanny must have followed a somewhat similar line of reasoning.

Even allowing for the encouragement given by progressive educators to the most extreme forms of self-expression, though, I still couldn't understand how she'd actually done it. Even now, when my shock has subsided, and with the benefit of a wider experience of the world, I still can't.

In the end Nanny's got out of the house, and Olive settles everything down, sensibly, reasonably. And that's how she runs the household over the coming months – sensibly, reasonably, never raising her voice, never pressing her hand to her heart and saying that she won't last much longer. She brings some order into our lives, without trying to impose too many of her own ideas. She gets my sister and me to behave more or less acceptably, and does it without any great confrontations. She finds some intelligent compromise between what she proposes to cook and what we're prepared to eat. She has a sense of humour, and she talks to us as if we were, like her, sensible, reasonable human beings. She raises her well-modulated voice enough when she's talking to our father for him to hear at any rate a little of what she's saying.

On Saturday evenings sometimes she walks us into Epsom to take part in the social activities at her daughter's school. It's a funny sort of place. The children cycle wildly round and round an old gravel pit in the grounds, then sprawl about in the darkness with their arms round each other, farting and shouting out and drinking cocoa and watching old Charlie Chaplin films. I love the whirring of the projector, and the magical pictures on the wall, but it doesn't seem to me much of a school. No corrugated iron. No one, so far as I can see, getting caned. None of the grey gloom of fear and misery that's necessary for proper education.

Somehow, out of nowhere, our father has conjured the perfect housekeeper – the more than perfect housekeeper – the kind of housekeeper you could not reasonably hope to find, even if you had a stately home to attract her to and could pay vastly more than I imagine my father can. She's the antithesis, it occurs to me now, not only of Nanny, but of all my father's other arrangements – the rusty chopper, the waterlogged air-raid shelter, the asbestos flower boxes.

And yet, and yet . . . the arrangement doesn't ever quite work. We never take to Angela, for a start, and Angela never takes to us. Olive manages this little difficulty very diplomatically – but then we never really take to Olive. She remains an outsider in the house. She's not quite one of us.

If I have to put my finger on her single but fatal defect it's this: she's not our mother.

I wonder now, of course, what her feelings were about us. It must have been horrible for her, living in that alien house, looking after two alien children. Doing it so well, too, and with some reasonable semblance of love – but getting no love back. For whatever reason she'd taken the job on, whether out of desperation or the goodness of her heart, she must have felt in the end that it was a defeat.

I don't know how long she stayed. Six months perhaps. I don't know why she finally went, whether it was at her wish or my father's, nor where she went on to. No explanations or farewells come to mind. She's just another of the debts that I've accumulated in life – and one that I've scarcely even thought about until now. She deserved better.

Nanny returns. Again, I can't recall any explanations, or any scenes of glad reunion. Nothing. Only, as the weeks go by, the rudeness and disobedience of my sister and me. Only Nanny's little gasps and cries, the pressing of hand to breast, the predictions of her approaching demise.

Only the same familiar, muddled wretchedness as before.

Top to Bottom

What those bleak years after my mother's death were like for my father is perhaps indicated by the state of his health. I don't know what the original symptoms were, but he was diagnosed as 'run down', that vague metaphor of an overtaxed car battery, and was prescribed a daily dose of burgundy – Australian burgundy, which at the time was probably rather like topping him up with battery acid. Perhaps as a result of this his stomach became *too* acid, and after he had choked down many pints of glutinous barium meal to outline his digestive tract for the X-ray machine a duodenal ulcer was diagnosed. He had to give up not only the burgundy, but pipe and cigarettes, any thought of bread and cheese and beer on Saturday evenings, and the cheeky carver's perks on Sunday. For months – years – he was restricted to a diet of steamed white fish and milk pudding, both of which he found as flavourless as his life had now become.

He was often confined to bed. His flu one winter turned into double pneumonia. He lay in delirium in Epsom Cottage Hospital, and then in the middle of an icy January night awoke to find himself, still in his pyjamas, on an unlit path halfway home; he had to find his way back to the hospital and present himself at the porter's lodge for re-admission. Later he slipped a disc in his back, and could scarcely get in and out of his car. For months or years he was in constant pain and undergoing constantly changing treatments. When my sister and I visited him, in the Cottage Hospital once more, we found him in traction, still struggling to smile, tied into the kind of archaic industrial machine that you see in cartoons of people in hospital. In desperation he was reduced to osteopathy, a form of faith healing, as he saw it, in which he had no more faith than in the doctrine of the Trinity. He had two sessions, at thirty shillings a go – and his slipped disc was cured, never to trouble him again; the only serious challenge he ever encountered to his general scepticism. Even he must have had the smile wiped off his face for a bit in sheer surprise.

Through all this, though, he's kept things going for my sister and me. For Christmas one year he's thrown lifelong practice to the winds and somehow bought me a chest of second-hand but genuine carpenter's tools. He's dragged us out through rain and sleet for health-giving walks. Short walks, round the unmade-up roads where the Warbeys and other millionaires live. Long walks, across the farm towards the Downs – forced marches so gruelling that they have to be done in stages, like the ascent of Everest and Scott's trek to the South Pole, with rests in numbered camps along the way. He's walked us into Epsom on Saturdays, along the same path on which he awoke from his midwinter noctambulation, to have roast beef, Yorkshire pudding and two veg in a teashop. He's taken us off for weekend Easter breaks in a gloomy B&B that Kerry had recommended on the Kent coast. He's done his best to recreate the old summer family holidays. We've sat together in the car in windswept car parks, waiting for the worst of the rain to stop, my father in his trilby hat, and the passenger's seat beside him empty. When the rain moderated a little we've walked along the narrow Devon lanes, throwing a tennis ball back and forth, my sister and I shouting to warn him when we heard a car coming.

Water seems to have been the element in which all these holidays were spent, as if nature were weeping the tears that we were no longer able to weep ourselves. Not only rain, but the rainswept sea. Spray finding its way in through our always inadequate raincoats. Streams, into which I always managed to fall, so that our walks were accompanied by the dull squelching of my two shoefuls of water. Water underfoot, water overhead. In North Wales one year, after a long day tramping through the rain, the only way we could see of getting back to the car and some hope of dryness involved crossing a single narrow girder remaining after the rest of the bridge had fallen into the raging torrent in the gorge far below. My father walked insouciantly across and back to demonstrate how easy it was – it was the kind of thing he did all the time when he was inspecting the progress of TAC's roofing contracts. I realised that as a boy I had no option but to do likewise. My sister, thank God, realised that as a girl she was allowed to weep and refuse. He didn't insist. He found a detour, only four or five miles longer.

On that same holiday he walked us almost to the top of Snowdon through the freezing hurry of soaking cloud that concealed everything around us. In Llandudno, where he had been sometimes in the twenties with Vi, he took us one evening, largely I think to get us all out of the rain for a bit, to a restaurant he remembered where there was dancing. We sat at our table, long past our bedtime, while he gazed at the couples turning and turning, lost in each other, under the endlessly cascading light from the mirror ball. Gazed and gazed, smiled and smiled. Perhaps it gave him some comfort, it occurs to me now, having us with him, looking after us on his own for a couple of weeks.

I don't want to make too much of our misfortune. Our father wasn't the first man to have lost his wife, nor were we the first children to have lost their mother. It was worse for my sister than for me, since she was three and a half years younger. And I have to recognise that for me that agonising severance had some positive effects. I had been a bit of a mother's boy, with my sixpences for coming top and my failures at manly sports. Her death hardened me a little; I didn't any longer have her to run to. I find it difficult now, looking back through the grey murk that seems to cover those years, to follow what was going on inside me. The family snapshots cease after 1942 and don't resume until the beginning of the fifties, so it's impossible to see whether there was any change in the external appearance of the disconcertingly soppy little boy that I'd become. I think, though, that I was beginning, consciously or half-consciously, to reconstruct myself.

In this I had advice and assistance from a number of people.

Uncle Sid, for a start. Undeterred by his earlier failure to teach me to catch a ball, he took me out for a walk one grey afternoon and gave me a kindly but firm talking-to in his most avuncular voice. No one, he said, liked a *home man*, which is what I was in danger of becoming. A home man, he explained, was someone who hung about the house reading books instead of getting out on the playing field. The shame of being a home man, and the fear of the universal dislike this would call down upon me, has never quite left me. I'm not sure, though, how much practical effect it ever had on me. Whereas Mrs Absolon changed my life.

Among the books I'd read as I skulked shamefully about at home had been *Scouting for Boys*. I'd been entranced by the world it had opened up of knots and lashings, of tracking wildebeests through the veldt and helping old ladies across the street, of honour to God and loyalty to the King, of camp fires and wide-brimmed hats. I had taught myself to suppress a sneeze (*only* to be done when absolutely necessary to preserve secrecy!) by biting my top lip with my lower jaw. I had resolved always to drink at least a glass of hot water before setting out into the bush if circumstances should ever force me to go without breakfast, and to avoid *larking about with girls*, even though this sounded as if it was very much what I had found so intoxicating in the summer twilight with Jennifer, because apparently it caused babies. I longed to join the Boy Scouts and live the book out, but I knew without even asking that the Scouts were exactly the kind of organised do-goodery that my father disliked – particularly after he had made an exception for the Crusaders, and I had so rapidly come round to his point of view.

Mrs Absolon was the next-door neighbour of my friend David, round the corner in Queensmead Avenue. She was a widow, and her own son was growing sisal in Tanganyika, so she had time to invite David and me to tea, and to take us trainspotting at Euston and King's Cross. She was a forthright, outspoken, no-nonsense sort of person, and her late husband had been something high up in the local Scouts. She marched round the corner to see my father. I don't know exactly what she said, but within a couple of weeks I was standing on parade in the grimy church hall in Ewell Village with a wide-brimmed hat on my head and a pole in my hands – both acquired from a shop, for money, in the normal way of the world – wearing a ramshackle collection of whatever brownish bits and pieces could be assembled by the methods more usual in our family.

It was a wild success, quite unlike the Crusaders earlier and the Cadet Corps later. During the next three years I acquired a proper Scout shirt and a sleeve covered with badges, camped and tramped and knotted and lashed, rose to the rank of Patrol Leader, and led my patrol with much embarrassing fervour to win various awards. In the shade of that broad-brimmed hat my innate weediness was much less noticeable, and my threatened exile from decent society as a home man was at any rate postponed. I even enjoyed the weekly session of British Bulldogs, an even rougher game than cricket, which involved trying to subdue struggling, farting opponents, often from the lower social orders, by the kind of brute force for which I had hitherto shown little taste or aptitude. Perhaps my fellow Boy Scouts, unlike cricket balls, were simply large enough for me to see.

The most far-reaching practical consequence for me of my mother's death, though, was that it took me out of Sutton High School for Boys.

At least, I think it did. I think my father realised that he couldn't pay two lots of school fees as well as a housekeeper. By this time he may in any case have become a little uneasy about the character of the school. Not because of the caning or the corrugated-iron walls, neither of which I would have mentioned to him. It was the age of some of my classmates that unsettled him.

I was twelve, and in a class that was preparing to take the Common Entrance Examination the following year. The prospects of some of us were dubious. '*You*, boy?' snarled Mr Plummer, a former First World War officer with the face of a bloodhound and a larynx kippered by the fags he drew upon so desperately in the playground, who taught us maths and various other subjects with world-weary efficiency. 'Pass the Common Entrance to a public school? You'll never wash the common entrance to a public house!' A number of us had already taken the exam and failed, often years before. Among my classmates were hulking great layabouts with nicotine-stained fingers and smokers' coughs, whose prospects even as cleaners of licensed premises seemed far from assured. I recall my father taking sardonic note when I told him that one of them was leaving to begin employment, not in a pub, but as a teacher in another private school a mile or two down the road.

I'm probably being unjust about the Reverend J. B. Lawton and his academy. Caning wasn't the only way he related to pupils. He'd sometimes appear beside you and put his arm round your shoulders, though whether as a sign of affection or an alternative form of punishment it was difficult to tell, since he had no expression in his close-set eyes, only a distinctive and discouraging smell about him, of harsh ecclesiastical cloth and stale tobacco. And there were plenty of able boys in the school – many of them a lot more able than me – and some of them certainly survived it well enough. I subsequently met two of them who had actually passed Common Entrance and gone on to public schools. They recalled the old place with some affection. One of them, by then a leading public relations consultant, told me that he looked back on it as a haven of peace and happiness before his public school, where he had been tarred and feathered and thrown out of an upstairs window.

For me at this point, however, my father decides that he will have to find some alternative. I will have to get, not just a place at a public school, which he could afford even less than Sutton High, but a scholarship. I borrow a set of old papers from a boy who's going to take the scholarship for Dulwich, and my father and I sit at the dining-room table and work our way through them. Neither of us can begin to answer any of the questions. More desperate measures are required. My father goes to see the Surrey Education Officer at County Hall in Kingston. It's arranged that I'm to take not the Common Entrance or a scholarship paper but some other sort of exam I've never even heard of, which I immediately suspect is really supposed to be sat by Council School children. My father has evidently had to use considerable powers of persuasion, because I'm twelve, and this exam is apparently one that you're supposed to take at eleven-plus.

In the examination room I am indeed surrounded by Council School children, and of course, since I'm a year older than I should be, I pass. I can tell that my father feels he has done well; he has carried off a considerable piece of salesmanship with the Education Officer, getting his product placed, like his roofing, in some official institution, and in spite of defects unknown in asbestos. In return he has allowed himself to be impressed by the Education Officer's advocacy of Kingston Grammar School, to which I've apparently been assigned. 'Pretty good school, you know,' he assures me, as he might about the Forty-Eight Preludes and Fugues or the Château d'Yquem, with the wink, the twitch of the head, and all the rest of it. 'Pretty good reputation in educational circles.'

My father knows nothing about Kingston Grammar School, or any other grammar school. Nor do I – only that they're all some kind of Council School, where Council School children go. Sutton High School for Boys was bad enough. In spite of all my father's winking and clicking of the tongue, I await my descent into the abyss of the state educational system with fear in my heart.

It's the town that for a start makes more impression on me than the school. I walk bleakly round the centre of Kingston in the lunch hour every day, because I can't think of anything else to do to pass the time. I'm interested in photography, so I look in the windows of the various shops selling photographic apparatus, at cameras and enlargers that I can't even dream of ever being able to afford. I look in the window of the sports and camping shop at the Boy Scout gear I can't afford either, and in another window at army surplus electronics – sturdily constructed gauges measuring quantities that no one in peacetime wants to measure any more, devices for generating signals and waves and pulses whose purpose no one can now remember. On Mondays there's a cattle market, with a section where traders lay out desolate selections of junk for sale – broken tools, rusty mangles, cracked jugs – that intrigue me partly because they look like the kind of possessions we have at home, partly because I can almost imagine being able to afford them, and partly, perhaps, because they look as dreary as I feel.

It's a town of smells, most of them bad. The urban stink of old-fashioned bus exhausts; the greasy breath from the chip shops selling the chips that boys from the grammar school are not allowed to eat in the streets; the fragrance coming from the cornets of newspaper carried by passing boys who are eating the chips all the same. The fresh scent of the timber being transferred from the barges on the Thames into the great open-sided warehouses on the bank, and the dank green smell of the river. The farmyard odours of the cattle market. In the reading room of the public library, where I go sometimes to look at the *Amateur Photographer*, the stale fug of breath from the occupationless old men who also take refuge there, which seems to have been sealed away from the outside air as carefully as the leather-bound newspapers themselves. The eastern side of the town is made depressing by the sour fumes from the Courage brewery, but in the centre the streets are ruled by the emperor of all Kingston's smells, the intimately disgusting stench of the tannery.

A lot of my time in the lunch hours of that first term is taken up with visits to jewellers. There are more jewellers in Kingston than you might think the trade could support, and I visit all of them, several times over. I'm not buying jewellery, merely trying to get my watch repaired. It's the first watch I've ever owned, and it has a luminous dial and seventeen jewels. I've been given it by Nanny for my birthday at the start of the term, perhaps partly to console me for my ejection from the Garden of Eden in Sutton. I'm so proud of it that I have to consult it, in daylight and darkness, every few minutes. Within a week, however, those luminous hands have ceased to move. The watch has died.

It turns out that Nanny has acquired it in the kind of way that most things in our family are acquired, not by handing over money in a shop, but through personal acquaintanceships, in this case involving Phyllis's landlady's sister, who lives in Switzerland. It's a smuggled watch, and somewhere along the way any kind of guarantee it might once have had has disappeared. So has the name of a supplier or manufacturer to send it back to. It doesn't even have a brand name. One after another all the jewellers in Kingston hold my watch in their hands and look down upon it, and upon me in my new grammar school cap, with varying expressions of disdain. They explain that *cheap watches* of this sort can't be repaired. I'm sure my wonderful grandfather would have had a go but cheapness in watches is not a characteristic that the jewellers of Kingston are prepared to have any truck with.

I report a tactfully edited version of these humiliating rejections to Nanny, who flutters helplessly and apologetically. My father, however, won't let it go. He's as inflexible as he was with my desire to leave the Crusaders. All the drive and determination that have made him such an effective salesman are vicariously deployed. It becomes a test of my character. I am not to take no for an answer. I am to go back and try each shop again. And again.

I fail the test. The jewellers of Kingston, far from relenting, become even more crushing at each of my reappearances. The hidden rubies have no chance to prove their durability; the phosphorescent hands never move again; the watch has become another lesson in the irreversibility of death. The humiliation is stamped upon my soul, and the watch that I was so proud of becomes an object of shame, an emblem of defeat, the focus of all my misery.

The school itself, though, doesn't make much impression on me in those first few months. It's as grindingly ugly as Sutton High School for Boys, but in a much more state-authorised kind of way. It's built of brick and is two storeys high, with a proper hall for praying in, and eating school dinners in, and putting on plays in. No one, so far as I can see or hear, is getting caned.

My classmates don't have smokers' coughs. They're all about the same age as each other, which is a year younger than me. There are ninety of us starting at the same time, and in view of my age I've been put in with the thirty thought to be the most able, the A stream. We're all industrious and well-behaved, but I've done all the work before, whereas most of the others are coming to things, particularly Latin and French, for the first time. *Hic, haec, hoc* . . . *Marcel et Denise visitent la basse-cour* . . . *Le professeur corrige le cahier de l'élève* . . . *Caesar adsum iam forte* (or, even more provocative of my classmates' respectful laughter, *aderat forte*) . . . I did all this years before! At Sutton High School for Boys I was on to ablative absolutes and gerunds: *The camp having been struck, it was meet for Caesar to give battle to the enemy.* I was at home with French irregular verbs and nouns with irregular plurals – *les hiboux sont couverts de poux.* At the end of the term I'm moved up a year – but (a note of caution) into the B stream. My classmates here, a year and a stream less inhibited, greet the swotty bespectacled upstart thrust so irregularly into their midst by turning my desk over and throwing my belongings around the room.

As that winter term in 1947 gets under way the country is brought to its knees by the most famous cold spell of the century, when temperatures in some parts of South-East England fall to minus twenty. The walk up the London Road to the school each morning is like the retreat from Moscow, the playground at break a taste of a Siberian labour camp. At home all the children in the neighbourhood are cannonading on trays and mats down the hill that had stopped the doodlebug in its tracks. I smash an old orange-box into the rough simulacrum of a toboggan, and shape the rusty springs of the vanished Morrison shelter, like swords beaten into ploughshares, to make runners; hurtle grimly down the frozen hillside with everyone else, and stumble slowly up again towing the toboggan behind me, over and over again, like Sisyphus and his stone, until it's too dark to see and too cold to endure my sodden clothes, chilblains and freezing feet any longer; then drag my tangle of split wood and buckled metal back to the cold and comfortless house. The world will never know warmth again.

In school I slowly, slowly settle into my new class and find friends. At the end of the year, though, a catastrophe occurs. Buoyed irresistibly by the great stock of datives and pluperfects that I've piled up during my years in the private sector, I come top. If you come top the rule is that you move up a stream. I protest – I want to stay with my new-found friends! My protests are brushed aside, and I have to start all over again, in a third new class.

I have to establish myself this time not as a pathetic brainbox fallen out of the A stream, but as a pathetic dumbo risen from the B stream. How am I to do it? Not by my prowess at cricket, obviously, nor at hockey, the school's winter game. Not even in the class listings, because by this time my new classmates have pretty much caught up on the vocatives and disjunctives, and because most of them are plainly cleverer than I am. In my necessity I make a surprising discovery – an unfortunate one as regards my academic success, but perhaps a first step along the road to the career that I will begin to develop twenty years later: I find I can make the class laugh and win some kind of popularity by mocking the teachers.

I take the lead, with Mumby, a new-found friend who has a similar skill, in harassing one particularly vulnerable beginner on the staff. My new vocation intersects with my old interest in photography. I bring my camera into class and surreptitiously photograph our victim as he struggles to cope with our bullying. 'The news spreads like wildfire,' I record in a wonderfully self-important diary that I'm keeping for a couple of months at this point, 'and by the end of the lesson all the form knew. In break, many boys asked me if I was Frayn, and if I had really taken a picture of [Mr H]. This, then, must be one way of acheiving [*sic*] fame.' The picture, I read in next day's entry, hasn't come out, but at the end of the term Mr H flees the school, and Mumby and I come joint bottom of the class.

The rule is that if you come bottom you move down a stream. Since I've only just arrived in the A stream, though, I'm to be given another chance. The unfairness of this outrages me. I protest – I want to stay shoulder-to-shoulder with Mumby! My protests are brushed aside. I am to mock on where I am.

As my father reads my report the corner of his mouth twitches, but not in the way that it does when he's talking about the quality of the hand-made hide upholstery in a Rolls-Royce. He's angry with me. I'm adding to the pain of whatever ailment he's suffering from at the time. He has tacitly agreed to overlook my sporting failures, and to accept that I have other abilities that go at any rate some way to make up for them. He has sold me to the local education officer, and got me installed in the best grammar school in the county. I have abused his indulgence; I have belied his claims on my behalf. I'm a piece of asbestos that has melted in the heat, or rotted in the rising damp.

I have as a matter of fact had a triumph on the playing field, or at any rate in the Cage, the rectangle of red dust behind the classrooms where most of the school plays obsessive informal hockey all the year round in every break and lunch hour. In the summer term my class, 4A, is swept by a brief craze for rounders instead. How on earth we've hit upon this girlish alternative to the manly carnage all about us I've no idea, but even I am happy to join in; I don't mind having a tennis ball tossed underarm at me, though I can no more hit it than I've ever been able to hit any other kind of ball. And then, one lunch hour, I can, and do. I swing the bat as wildly and hopelessly as ever, and for some inscrutable reason of its own, even though it's even narrower and shorter than the toy cricket bat, it connects with the ball, which flies up into the summer sky and describes such a huge parabola that it lands outside the wire netting of the Cage. I stand gazing after it, openmouthed, unable to understand what's happened. I slowly become aware that people are shouting at me. 'Run!' they're screaming. 'Frayn! *Run!*'

I run. 'The bat!' they scream. 'Drop the bat!' I run back, drop the bat, run again. First base . . . second base . . . third base . . . Home! I've gone right the way round the diamond, and the fielder's still recovering the ball! I've scored a rounder! It's the first time in my life that I've scored *anything*, at any rate for my own side. Much amused applause from my classmates, who are accustomed to choosing me second to last on games afternoons. A wild surge of joy runs through me.

Scoring a rounder means that I bat again, so my triumph will be short-lived. The pitcher pitches. I take another blind swing . . . And once again bat and ball connect. Once again the ball describes that same wonderful parabola and soars over the wire netting. Once again I stand gazing, unable to believe what seems to be happening. Once again everyone's shouting, once again I'm running . . . running back, dropping the bat, running on . . .

I've scored a second rounder. More amused clapping.

The pitcher pitches. The bat swings. The ball's high up in the summer sky. Is over the wire netting . . . This cannot be happening! A third rounder!

The ironic applause becomes serious. I'm thumped on the back. I have become a different person.

Ball . . . bat . . . thwock . . . Over the wire. A fourth rounder.

My friends – they're all my friends now! – are shouting to the hockey-players in other classes. 'Hey, come and watch old Frayn!' The games of hockey drift to a halt. The diamond's surrounded by an audience.

A fifth rounder. I can't do otherwise than hit the ball, and drive it out of the Cage. I have become a rounder-scoring machine.

A fielder's posted outside the Cage. It makes no difference. A sixth rounder.

Two fielders outside the Cage. A seventh rounder. An eighth . . .

Cheering. Applause. I'm the most famous person in the school. Everything in my life has at last fallen into place. Nine . . . Ten . . . I'm becoming too tired to run, and am generously allowed a runner to deputise for me. All I have to do is hit the ball. And hit it I do. First strike each time. Up into the sky, out of the Cage, as inevitably as the earth going round the sun, as fore-ordained as mathematics: bat + ball = rounder.

Top to Bottom

By the time the bell rings for afternoon school I've scored twenty-one rounders and am still not out. I've also learnt a painful lesson, because by this time people have become bored by the spectacle. The hockey-players have returned to their hockey. My classmates are impatient to have a go themselves. My fame has evaporated even as I continue to supply the performance that created it.

Never again do I score another rounder. Never do I score a goal at hockey or a run at cricket. At hockey and cricket I'm still the last but one person to be picked. No one in the class ever refers to this weird episode. It's as if everyone's embarrassed to have taken part in some piece of improbable collective madness like a riot or a lynching.

If only my father had seen me in action that summer lunchtime he would have forgiven me everything. If only I'd told him about it, even, as I've told it here. Rounders are not cricket, of course, and he would probably have divided my total of twenty-one by three to allow for the genetic weakness I've inherited. But even seven rounders would have made up for a great many shortcomings. Even one would have given him a moment of pride and pleasure.

As it is, though, I'm providing him with neither. Almost as irritating as my delinquency at school he must find my priggishness at home. It's a strange combination. Even as I'm seeking easy popularity in the classroom by my insubordinacy, I'm rejoicing, with many exclamation marks in the diary, in the authority which I'm imposing on my Scout patrol. My diary entries have the pomposity and condescension of an old-fashioned Letter to the Editor. A radio documentary is 'a magnificent effort, a straight story that "got over"'. On the other hand, 'I am toying with the idea of writing to the BBC' about the 'atrocious mess' made of another programme. Tchaikovsky's *Romeo and Juliet* overture 'would be bettered by keeping strictly to the themes, which are excellent. Too many frills and fancies and too many varied orchestrations come between the music and the listener, with the result of diminishing the brilliance and clarity of the real music, and tending to confuse one.' At parties, apparently, the tea is the only thing that I enjoy, after which 'the rest of the evening is a tedious round which could be spent much more profitably in the darkroom'.

Am I also saying, or shouting, this kind of thing to my father over the supper table? Even if not, he can scarcely fail to be aware that I've taken to going to church. I can't remember why – probably for the same reason that I went to Crusaders before: because my friend David does. I'm as patronising about the church in my diary as I am about Tchaikovsky and the BBC. The vicar's sermon, I record on Sunday, 1 February 1948, is 'a very poor effort – longwinded, dull, and uninteresting'. However, 'the English church service is peculiarly restful . . . and I think I would go many miles to hear the final amen.'

What my father feels about this development my diary doesn't record. Perhaps I'm doing it partly for oedipal reasons, since I'm well aware of his views on religion. My parents have never had me baptised. They've left me to make up my own mind about membership of the church when I'm old enough, as I remember my mother explaining. Old enough I now am. I make use of my freedom of choice by getting myself first baptised and then confirmed. Another moral test for my father, to which he rises as he has risen to all the others, because so far as I can recall he behaves with the most exemplary restraint, and makes no comment at all.

I don't invite him to the ceremony. At which, incidentally, I'm expecting to be struck dead. I've cheated God.

I realise with hindsight that there's something a little unusual about the vicar of Ewell, who is preparing me and another dozen or so of us for confirmation. He's an unctuous, ill-shaven man with a vast number of children, very unlike the uningratiating, bullet-smooth Reverend J. B. Lawton, and he never finishes services in the way I've grown used to, by caning selected members of the congregation. The Reverend J. B. Lawton, I think from something about the set of his eyes and the closeness of his shave, was Low Church. The vicar is High.

It never occurs to me at the time that there's anything surprising about his appearing at some services in a purple dress, at others in a green one, or about his swinging a kind of silver teapot on a chain that fills the church with agreeably holy-smelling smoke. Nor, as a member of his confirmation class, do I see anything inconsistent with normal Anglican practice when, on the last evening of the course, he tells us that each of us in turn is to go off with him to be confessed. In the Church of England the whole congregation makes a notional public confession together; it recites the General Confession of Sin, as laid down in the Book of Common Prayer, and the sin is reassuringly generalised. We, on the other hand, are to go off with this unprepossessing man one by one to some special dark corner of the church and tell him in our own words about actual specific sins that each of us has personally committed.

Not for a moment does it occur to me to question this – it's simply one of the many incomprehensible challenges with which the adult world confronts the young. I find it a particularly appalling one, though. Not even the Reverend J. B. Lawton has inflicted this particular torment on us. It's a winter's night. The church is cold, and lit only by a few bulbs over the front pew where we're all sitting cowed and silent. One by one we're picked off. I'm at the end of the pew, the last in the line, with most time to develop a full head of panic at the sheer embarrassment of the prospect. What on earth am I going to confess?

I suppose with hindsight that it's masturbation the vicar's hoping to hear about; perhaps even, with a bit of luck, something a little more precocious; at any rate a few unchaste thoughts, a few glances at *Health and Efficiency*, the naturist magazine. I'm remarkably backward in this respect, though. I've only recently discovered that the male sexual organ is not, as I'd always supposed, the navel. My classmates at Sutton High School for Boys sometimes showed me the bashful figures half-concealed behind bushes in *Health and Efficiency*, but I prudishly tried not to look too closely. One boy, particularly knowing, once challenged me 'to draw the breasts and buttocks of a woman', and I did manage two triangles facing left and below them two semi-circles facing right. I don't have unchaste thoughts, though. My thoughts about girls, overwhelming as they often are, are cloudily romantic. I didn't try masturbation until years later. I'm not sure that at the time I've even heard the word. If anybody else in our class has they're reluctant to reveal the fact; even though we will stop at nothing to torment a new teacher called Mr Bate, not one of us, difficult as this is to believe now, exploits the obvious possibilities offered by his name.

Does it occur to me that I could tell the vicar about my persecution of inexperienced teachers, or my unkindness to my grandmother? Or even my manifold moral shortcomings on the games field? I don't think it does. I'm going to be reduced to pathetic crimes like teasing my sister and failing to clean my shoes. I can't think straight for the horror of what's to come. The boy four places away from me is summoned . . . Minutes, months go by . . . He returns, cheeks red, eyes cast down, unreadable. The girl next to him, three places away from me, slides out of the pew in her turn . . .

And I slide the other way, out of the pew and out of the church, to hide my shame in the darkness of the winter night. I have failed the challenge. And God knows it, even if the vicar doesn't. When the day of the confirmation comes, and the bishop places his hand on my head, there will be a sound as of a mighty rushing wind, the veil of the temple will be rent, and a thunderbolt from heaven will fall upon me harder than even the biggest and best of the Reverend J. B. Lawton's canes.

My earthly father, though, somehow manages to remain fatherly, in spite of all my tediousness. Every now and then we listen to a concert on the radio together, even if some of the composers fail to meet my critical standards. On Sundays we often do the easier of the two crosswords in the *Observer*. ('Where the vicar and the butler keep their underclothes. 2 words: 6, 6' – 'Vestry, pantry.') When I'm away at the Boy Scouts' annual summer camp, suffering torments of homesickness in a waterlogged field in the Isle of

Wight, he drives all the way down with my sister to pay me an unannounced visit.

His car is, as ever, one of the bonds between us. In the school holidays he drives me up to town with him in the morning so that I can spend the day gazing impotently into shop windows full of Leicas and Contaxes. A little later some of the trips are to Harley Street, to an ear, nose and throat specialist who hammers a punch through the bone inside my nose to drain my sinuses and stop the catarrh that is thought to be causing me infections – almost as crude a procedure as our work with chopper and screwdriver on the asbestos boxes, though rather more disagreeable – and rather more expensive, I imagine, for my father. I'm just beginning to discover art by this time. My first experience of Van Gogh and Turner in the Tate is indissolubly connected with the sensation of blood filling the handkerchief I'm holding over my nose, and of the gathering pain in my face as the novocaine wears off. Then I go to Southwark and, handkerchief still to face, join my father and Mr Kerry for lunch in a pub called the Coal Hole.

I come out of school one hot summer's afternoon – and there in the dreary dust and noise of the London Road is the hat, and beneath the hat the smile. I'm caught off-guard. I feel a surge of helpless joy. He just happened to be in Kingston, or within half a dozen miles of it, and he has the car waiting. We're going swimming in the river at Thames Ditton. The smile's always turning up like that, unannounced, disarmingly familiar in unlikely surroundings. Sometimes for a perfectly prosaic purpose, to take me to get new shoes, say. I suppose he's lonely – lonelier than me. The sight of the joy in my face must give him some joy in return. We're growing closer even as I become more difficult.

That smile of his. It's what everyone always remembered about him. It emerged from the depths of him. When he smiled the smile became him; he became the smile.

He wasn't always smiling, of course. I can remember him angry, in pain, unhappy. Absorbed, blank. His mouth could also twitch not with humour but with impatience and irritation. In any case everyone smiles, and for many different reasons. You can smile with conscious intent – to charm and ingratiate yourself, for example – and as a salesman I'm sure my father did both. To demonstrate superiority and condescension, and there was sometimes a touch of this in his impatience with me. To conceal distress or incomprehension; and my father certainly did it sometimes for both those reasons. Particularly the latter; his smile was an adjunct to his hearing aid. Then again you can smile without conscious purpose, out of amusement, out of love, out of simple happiness; and when my father's smile came round the door, or stood waiting for me outside the school that dusty summer's day, I think there was a bit of all three in it.

Only once does his imagination fail him. I've bought an old cigarette case in the Cattle Market, filled it with the snapshots I've taken – and lost it at the bathing place in Thames Ditton. He finds me lying on my bed weeping. All his worries about the effects produced on my character by failing to catch cricket balls and running round in the twilight with girls overwhelm his judgement, and I get another lecture about manliness. I suppose it hasn't occurred to him, any more than it has consciously to me, that it might be more than an old cigarette case and a dozen grey prints that I'm weeping for.

I'm still sleeping at this point in the folding camp bed that has been set up for me next to his in the back bedroom. It must be very shortly after this that my grandmother, also repaying good for ill, insists on moving out of her little room on the ground floor and in with my sister upstairs, so that I can at last have a room of my own. When I think what it must have cost her to give up this final remaining foothold in privacy and independence I'm humbled. She has transcended herself. Another of my unpaid debts, another of the generosities that I have benefited from, and have never either repaid or matched.

Her motive, it occurs to me now, may have been not just to improve my life but actually to save it. I've set up my darkroom in the little windowless cupboard under the stairs, where the violins are kept and where my parents were sheltering on the night of the doodlebug. The covers on the fuses are still missing. There's no room to stand, so I have to squat or kneel on the floor amongst the pools of splashed developer and fixer, through which pass the frayed leads to my red lamp and enlarger, both home-made (of course) out of biscuit tins wrapped in old blackout curtains, and ancient brass electrics purchased in the Cattle Market. Several times a bolt of black lightning has leapt out of the darkness somewhere and shot up my arm, in a remarkably unpleasant manner.

Now the chiffoniers and étagères in Nanny's room are stripped of all her accumulated possessions, and my muddled books and homework and photographic apparatus take their place. Where have all the pomanders and lavender bags gone? All the scarves and shawls, all the shepherdesses and silver-framed photographs? Are the contents of 1 Gatcombe Road now crammed into one half of my sister's small dressing table? My poor grandmother. My poor sister. My lucky father, though, to have a room to himself again. And even luckier me, to have not just a room but one large enough to stand up in, with some hope of separating live wires from the pools of chemicals already accumulating on the floor. One hot summer night, in an ecstasy of freedom and unfocused erotic yearning, I climb out of my window and run round the garden in the darkness stark naked.

A year or two later it's my father's turn to make a generous gesture. When I leave school, he says, he thinks he might be able to get me into Turners Asbestos to train as a rep. Fatherly love and pride have evidently quite overwhelmed his usual sober assessment of my potentialities. But by this time I have privately decided to become a romantic poet, and with wounding loftiness I brush the suggestion aside.

On one of our trips in the car, though, he may have planted a seed which really did take root in my imagination, just like his offhand suggestion when I was seven or eight of becoming a journalist. I think I'm probably fourteen by this time. He's taking my sister and me for our annual summer holiday, and this year we're going to Norfolk. On the way we stop for an hour or two in Cambridge. My father impresses on us his respect for the place. 'Not a bad university, you know, Cambridge.' Wink, twitch of the head, click of the tongue. Of what we see as we walk reverently round the colleges I can remember only a single detail: a honey-brown stone doorway off the busy street opening on to a glimpse of sunlit emerald lawn.

I don't know which college it is. Caius, perhaps, or Christ's. That glimpse of a quiet and secluded front court, though, remains with me; and slowly over the next few years, in the recesses of my heart, as the intensity of what I have lost gradually fades, comes to stand for everything that I might one day find.

3
Skylark

It's the autumn of 1948, and three years have gone by since my mother's death. The grey light has softened a little. There's a gleam of watery sunshine in the air.

Two things have begun to change my life. For a start I have found a friend at school, with whom over the next three or four years I shall begin to discover the passionate intensities of music and literature, of intellectual companionship and romantic rebellion. Together we shall set out on the journey everyone takes, in one way or another, away from home and childhood. I shall get ever less like my father, and ever more remote from him.

I remember the precise moment it began, back in the summer term. I leaned forward in class to whisper a sardonic remark about the teacher to the boy sitting in front of me, whom I scarcely knew. He had thick black hair, an olive complexion and heroically sharp features with a touch of the demonic about them, and as he half-turned his head to hear I could see that he was smiling. And that was that. Was it the hair that did it? The dark eyes, the sculpted jaw? The smile? It was all of this and none of it. I loved him for the same reason that Montaigne loved his friend Etienne de la Boétie: '*Parce que c'était lui, parce que c'était moi.*'

His name rhymes with mine: Lane. He plays chess, so I take it up, too – become obsessed with it, to the point where people in the street seem to be checking, covering, forking and pinning each other. He has listened to a lot of Beethoven, I have listened to a little Tchaikovsky; I surrender Tchaikovsky, after a short but feeble struggle, and immerse myself in Beethoven. Beethoven's harmony and counterpoint meet my critical standards. In that first year of our friendship I hear all the Beethoven symphonies on the radio – the Eighth so many times that I can conduct my own solo but fully orchestrated performance of it inside my head more or less from beginning to end. Everyone at school knows by then that we come as a kind of corporate rhyming entity with more or less interchangeable components, simply Frayn and Lane, or Lane and Frayn. We're also both Michael, but no one at school uses first names. Not even us, now I come to think about it. 'Dear Frayn,' begin all the other Michael's many letters to me. 'Your sincere friend', they finish, or 'your most devoted critic'. Signed: 'M Lane'. Or 'Michael Lane'. Or, often, simply 'Lane'.

The second step in my transformation is brought about by a teacher. Mr Brady is a small, quietly pugnacious Irishman who wears tinted spectacles and no gown – I suspect because he has no degree, and probably no formal qualifications of any sort. He teaches us English; or at any rate he teaches us during the periods marked 'English' on the timetable. His lessons have no formal content. He maintains a soft flow of improvised yarning about whatever comes into his head, a lot of it from an Irish perspective and intended to provoke us into argument, and he recalls us to order, when the outrage or mockery he has aroused becomes too noisy, by tapping unhurriedly on the desk with the hockey stick that he always carries. Brady: 'Throughout history the English army has always been the scum of the earth.' Bristow, from the back of the class: 'But the scum always comes out on top, sir!' Laughter and cheering. Patient gavelling with the hockey stick. Slight satisfied smile on Brady's face.

I'm already in his debt because he kept me afloat, just, in the darkest days of the previous year, when I was coming bottom of the class or close to it in every other subject, by marking my essays thirty out of thirty (his own private scale – everyone else uses letters, A to D, or occasionally α to δ, modified by + or -) and reading them aloud to the class. He did much the same for Mumby, but Mumby has slipped out of the lifebelt even so, and sunk away into the B stream. Now, in the autumn of 1948, he starts to read us poetry. It's rather more gripping than the essays. 'I will arise and go now,' he begins quietly, in his soft, unhurried voice with the Irish lilt – and the whole class falls silent to listen. By the time he reaches the end we all hear the lake water lapping with low sounds by the shore, we all stand with Yeats on the roadway, or on the pavement grey, and hear it in the deep heart's core.

For some reason the poem that transforms the world for me is Shelley's 'Ode to a Skylark'. The splintered desks and the dusty floors of the classroom dissolve around me as Mr Brady softly reads, and all at once I'm beneath the high blue vault of heaven as the sun sets, with that amazing bird above me pouring down its cascading abundance of language:

> Higher still and higher
>   From the earth thou springest
> Like a cloud of fire:
>   The blue deep thou wingest,
> And singing still dost soar, and soaring ever singest.

The second stanza, and already I know that the world is incomparably vaster and more beautiful than I have ever dreamed. Every phrase sends me reeling – the golden lightning of the sunken sun, the unbodied joy whose race has just begun . . .

> As, when night is bare,
>   From one lonely cloud
> The moon rains out her beams, and Heaven
>   is overflowed . . .

Every simile opens a fresh jewel box. 'Like a Poet hidden/ In the light of thought . . .' 'Like a glow-worm golden/ In a dell of dew . . .' 'Like a rose embowered/ In its own green leaves . . .' And:

> Like a high-born maiden
>   In a palace-tower,
> Soothing her love-laden
>   Soul in secret hour
> With music sweet as love, which overflows her bower . . .

What can this possibly mean to me? What do *I* know of high-born maidens, or palace-towers, or love-laden souls? And yet I *do*! Now I *do*!

Twenty stanzas. Twenty revelations running. I've fallen in love again, as with Stella in Chicago and Franklin Delano Roosevelt – only more suddenly and more violently.

Already Mr Brady's on to the twenty-first and final one:

> Teach me half the gladness
>   That thy brain must know,
> Such harmonious madness
>   From my lips would flow
> The world should listen then – as I am listening now.

Yes! It should – it shall! Now we are to write an ode of our own, says Mr Brady. I fall upon my exercise book like one possessed. And out the harmonious madness pours, page after page of it. Another singing bird, species undetermined, up a tree this time. Another sunset in the background. No imagination, no invention. No time to break it up into lines, either, much less bother about rhyme. It's a prose ode . . . Thirty out of thirty, once again. And read aloud to the class in that soft Irish voice, it sounds wonderful. To me, at any rate. My course in life is set. I'm going to be a poet hidden in the light of thought. I shall even break up the lines, though it will be another year or more before I discover the existence of metre.

Frayn's private epiphany swiftly becomes FraynandLane's. He has got me into Beethoven; I get him into Shelley. We're *both* going to be poets. We both *are* poets already. By the following summer we have moved on from short odes to works that attempt the scale of *The Triumph of Life* or *Prometheus Unbound*. We elide our literary and musical passions by giving the poems opus numbers and dividing them into movements, then sit in the fork of an ancient oak tree next to the fairway on Surbiton Golf Course, just off the Kingston bypass, reading them aloud to each other. In terms of sheer volume Lane turns out to have a talent which I find difficult to match, though I try. In terms of pomposity and sententiousness, though, I have the edge, but then I have had some previous practice in my brief attempt at a diary. My Opus 10, *The Creation*, an improved version of Genesis in eight movements, is 'dedicated to M Lane, who showed me the way to Beethoven', and is 460 lines long. God's glory, I write, somewhere around line 400, shines through his work 'as doth the hidden sun rain down its light/ Through a diaphonous [*sic*] veil of ethereal cloud,/ Making the icèd haze a shining cloak,/ A translucent mantle of the sun.'

Diaphanous veils of ethereal cloud float around many of these poems. My Opus 14, *The Death of a Poet*, 'dedicated to M Lane, friend and fellow-poet', begins with a disclaimer:

If this work bears any resemblance in some places to the latest creation (the Pastoral) of my fellow-poet, Lane, it is not due to any complicity or to mere reproduction of each other's works, but because Shelley is our mutual inspiration. My poetry is honoured to have been created from the same spring as that of Lane, to whose latest work I bow in unfeigned admiration.

The work that follows, only too plainly inspired by *Adonais*, Shelley's elegy on the death of Keats, is relatively terse, a mere 216 lines, but its general diaphanousness makes it difficult to know whether it's Frayn or Lane who's dead, or what it is he's died of. Unless it's Keats again. Or Shelley. Or, most likely, I suppose, some emblematic figure combining the identities of all four of us. 'Dead, dead, I say, dead . . .' Leaving aside the question of which of us has got so thoroughly dead – who is the pompous idiot *saying* all this? No one *I* know, surely?

No, you've got start somewhere in life, and those veils of ethereal cloud parted eventually to reveal (for me, at any rate) the beginnings of a profession that has turned out to be a lot more secure than the asbestos industry. 'The chiaroscuro that was he/ Blended into one harmonious whole . . .' And so it did, in its way, so it did. 'For I must win to the hills and sky,/ And strive with the journey yet ahead . . .' Enough, though, enough. Let him strive away in peace, whoever he is.

I only once again ever dedicated anything I had written to

anyone. This was many years later, with my very first published book, a collection of humorous columns. The dedication was to Mr Brady, who had done so much to rescue me and determine my path in life. It was just as sincere as the dedication to my fellow poet, but not quite so sententious. I discovered where Mr Brady was living in his retirement, and took him a copy. He and his wife received me and my wife amiably and gave us tea, but he didn't seem very interested in my offering, and he plainly couldn't remember either me or his kindness to me.

I don't, of course, show my writings to my father, and I very much doubt if he ever sneaks a look. If he does he might just possibly perceive, through all the literary smog, that he has made a contribution of his own to the work. It's not just that he has got me into the grammar school and so introduced me to Mr Brady and my fellow poets M. Lane and P. B. Shelley. A number of the poems and essays, he might realise, are based on bits of the countryside that he has taken me to in the car – for weekend walks in the home counties, on Leith Hill and the Ivinghoe Beacon, or during family holidays.

Our trip to North Wales is particularly fruitful – quite a lot of that veiled majesty that I'm struggling to capture derives from one particular day driving down the Llanberis Pass, with a complex piled cloud mass hiding the mountains, out of which occasional glimpses of inconceivably lofty peaks emerge and vanish again. In the next few years I'm going to go back to Wales many times, sometimes with my fellow poet, and I'm going to become rather more closely acquainted with those high places, through the soles of my usually soaking feet and the skin of my often freezing hands. The mountains are going to become individual personalities as sharply defined and tangible as Blatcher and Janes and the other boys in my class, with names as familiar: Y Wyddfa and its outliers in the Snowdon massif, Crib Goch and Lliwedd, and on the other side of the pass the Glydrs, Fach and Fawr, and their outlier Tryfan. I'm going to see them in falling rain and falling snow, in sunlit snow and sunlit rain, and I'm going to get exhausted and lost and benighted on them. I'm going to stay in every Youth Hostel in North Wales, and from the Birmingham University climbers who spend the summer in and around Idwal Cottage, in defiance of the three-nights rule, I'm going to learn 'Ivan Skavinsky' and various other hearty standards – '*Avanti, popolo!*' (the song of the Italian Communist Party), 'I'm the man, the very fat man' ('What waters the workers' beer'), 'Queenie, the queen of the striptease show' ('And she stops . . . but only just in time') and 'Caviar's the roe of the virgin sturgeon' ('The virgin sturgeon needs no urgin'). I'm going to continue to have intensely romantic feelings about those weathered folds of ancient rock. But never again will they seem quite so lofty or so majestic. Never again will I quite recapture that cloudy intimation of grandeur that I experienced looking out of the window of my father's car.

I suppose, now I think about it, that those glimpses of mysterious mountain tops emerging through the storm clouds are perhaps an objective correlative of what's happening in my own life. Whatever effect my mother's death may or may not have had upon my character and educational prospects, it has one unambiguously positive consequence. At an age when life for many young people is becoming more difficult, things for me can only get better. From the age of fifteen or so, as the clouds at last begin to lift, more and more sunlit peaks emerge around me.

By this time I have extracted myself from the hated Cadet Corps and outgrown even my delight in the loyalties and strivings of the Boy Scouts. Another reversal, too, is occurring over the course of one single busy year, 1949. In January, aged fifteen, I'm getting myself confirmed, and surviving divine retribution for dodging the confession of my sins. That spring I cycle off to Communion every Sunday and feel God slipping down my throat, as glowingly warm as the mouthful of wine that symbolises one of his avatars (or incorporates it, possibly, in the Popish eyes of the vicar). The winey warmth spreads through not only my body but my poetry. Up the oak tree on Surbiton Golf Course that summer I'm telling God in *The Creation*, Opus 10, in case He doesn't know:

'Thou madest all, Thou art all,/ Thy parts stretch all throughout/ The homogeneous mass of Space and Time.' Two opus numbers later, the deceased Poet is 'bending his way' to the throne of God, where, 'In one blinding flash,/ He knows all.' Drenched though I am in Shelley's poetics, I seem to be impervious to his atheism.

Or am I? Already in Opus 10 a questioning note has appeared. 'All things were made by Thee, O God,' I remind Him. 'But who created sin?' I'm not the first or the last person to have asked Him this, of course. I've just Googled the question, and discovered that there are 37 million entries for it. In Opus 12 I have moved on to a rather more original assertion – though to me now a considerably more opaque one – that God is 'absolute Democracy'.

Whatever this means, I can see with hindsight that I'm beginning to depart quite sharply from the theology of the Catechism that I learned and recited so recently. That autumn, soon after my sixteenth birthday, I have an experience oddly like the blinding flash that brought enlightenment to the Poet in my Opus 12 a few months earlier. The lightning strikes as I'm running up the stone staircase to my classroom. I'm three-quarters of the way between the ground floor and the half-landing when it comes into my head with absolute clarity that *I don't believe a word of it.*

Of what? Of everything that I have since January been telling the vicar, the bishop, God and M. Lane that I did believe. It's as if a weight had been lifted off my shoulders, or the top of Snowdon had appeared sunlit through the encircling clouds. Confirmed in January – apostasised in September. A busy year. But that moment of illumination on the stairs settles the question once and for all, and I have never, in the sixty years that have elapsed since then, had the slightest inclination to go back into the darkness. I suppose the truth is that my parents never implanted faith in me, in spite of all my grandmother's efforts, at an age when it tends to mark one for life. I'm grateful to them, as for many other things; and in particular to my father, who waited so patiently for me to make up my own mind.

*

Not that I keep my father informed about the current state of my beliefs. He must be a little relieved, though, to realise that I have at last started to make a serious effort with my school work. I'm not sure why. Partly, I think, because next summer I shall have to take School Certificate, the precursor of first O-Levels and then GCSE. I'm not very clear about the career structure for poets, but you probably need to stay on into the sixth form, even perhaps to go through the gateway into that sunlit court I have so briefly glimpsed – if only to be expelled again, like Shelley, for your heroic refusal to accept what they tell you there.

I'm softening chiefly, I think, because in that crucial year we are for the most part well taught. No Mr Brady now, sadly, for English – only a dry disciplinarian who grinds suitable opinions into us on Chaucer and Shakespeare. I've begun to get interested in more than just English, though – and to regret the many holes torn in my knowledge of most subjects (some of them unfilled even today) by my earlier efforts to torment the staff and amuse the class. I remain indifferent to science and history – rather curiously, because in years to come I'm going to be gripped by both. Some of the less practical abstractions of mathematics I've at last begun to enjoy, and my imagination's stirred by the fjords and oxbows of geography, by its moraines and eccentrics, by the wheat of the Great Plains and the apricots of Mildura. I can't help laughing at *Topaze*, the Marcel Pagnol play we're reading aloud in French. I get increasingly absorbed in my struggles to disentangle the syntax of Virgil, and in the lost mythological world that so slowly emerges from it.

I'd like to be able to report that my character has been improved by conversion, but it hasn't. My fellow-poet and I remain intellectual snobs, loftily condescending to the philistinism we see around us at home and in school. We've been privately humbled, it's true, when M. Lane produces from somewhere an old textbook on prosody. As we turn the pages we discover that there's an aspect of poetry of which we have remained completely unaware, even though we've been reading and writing so much of it for the past year: metre. How we've managed to keep our eyes and ears so closed I can't think. Now we've been told about it we scoff at it, of course, as at everything else. We've long since rejected rhyme. What self-respecting free spirit would allow himself to be constrained by something so patently artificial and outmoded as anapaests and amphibrachs? Well – Shelley, we discover, for a start, now we know what we're looking for. We're deeply shaken. Like Monsieur Jourdain we've been writing prose without knowing it – but then he wasn't trying to write poetry. Production at the great Frayn & Lane verse works falls off sharply. It's difficult to go on ignoring those seductive rhythmic possibilities once you know about them – and a lot more difficult still to write verse that incorporates them. The days of the 500-line epics are over.

Our sense of being among the elect – or even perhaps of entirely constituting it – is sustained by our continuing passion for music. Here our no less profound technical ignorance doesn't much trouble us, because we've no aspirations to compose or play. We start on the libretto for an opera, it's true, though this may be earlier, when we're still in epic mode. We have a composer to hand, a boy in the class called Shutter who can actually play the piano, and who will later go on to read music at Oxford. We have a title, *Caligula*. We also have a piano – a jangly upright which has improbably appeared in the Frayn dining room to replace the grand that my father paid to have taken away ten years earlier. (Why, how, do we suddenly have a piano again? I assume so that my sister can have piano lessons, though whether it's been thrown out by a neighbour or found on a dump I've no idea.) Shutter and LaneFrayn sit down together after school at the keyboard, like George and Ira Gershwin, and Shutter improvises colossal out-of-tune chords and runs for the words that FraynLane are scribbling down and passing to him a page at a time; but since all we know about Caligula is that he was a tyrant and made his horse consul the supply of plot soon dries up, and the whole enterprise with it.

What we do with music a lot of the time is talk about it. What do we say exactly? I don't think we say anything at all *exactly*. We talk in the same kind of way as we do about the universe, the mountains of Wales, the destiny of the romantic poet and so on. In music, as in everything else, we celebrate the transcendent, the immanent, the diaphanous, the ethereal. Often we simply mention titles and opus numbers, key- and time-signatures, mood and dynamic indications – and add nothing of our own but celebratory exclamation marks. It's rather like the prisoners who have told each other their jokes so many times that all they need to do to get a laugh is to announce a reference number. 'The second section of the allegretto in Opus 95!' '*Yes!* Or that bit in the last movement of the Seventh!' 'You mean the bit like the bit in the allegro ma non tanto in Opus 132 . . .?'

Mostly, though, we do actually *listen* to music. On the wireless above all, and later on the random collection of scratched old 78s that we buy in the second-hand department at Foyles – odd choruses from *The Messiah*, odd movements from Schubert quartets and Bach partitas. Whenever we can afford it we go to concerts at the Albert Hall. These offer excellent value, because the acoustics are so eccentric before they modify the roof many years later that you hear everything twice and three times. The difficulty is to find the price of the tickets, even for a Prom, even for the standing-room high up under the echoing cavern of the roof. Until we make a wonderful discovery. There's a boy in our class called Ridge whose stepfather is an honorary steward at the hall. He gets two free tickets for the Grand Tier at every concert – and neither he nor anyone in his family has any interest in music. So Ridge passes the tickets on to LaneFrayn.

Thereafter all we have to find is the fare for the Greenline bus from Kingston after school (hard enough – if only there'd been another boy in class with a relative in London Transport!). Then we sit on the steps of the Albert Memorial and occupy the time until the concert by construing our Virgil together. The pages of our exhausted school editions have been worked loose by the slow fingerings of earlier generations, so that we have to keep jumping up to recapture them as they flutter away in the wind. Then – glory! Seats – *seats!* – in a box just over the orchestra, stage right.

Close enough to see Fürtwangler, on his first London tour after the war, mouthing at the choir – shouting aloud at them, I think – in the last movement of the Ninth.

At the end of the evening we reel home on the Greenline, uttering little cries of 'That bit in the scherzo, though!' – 'Yes, and that bit in the last bit of the first movement!' – as drunk and incoherent as homegoing football supporters. Not that we've drunk so much as a cup of tea – we couldn't have afforded it. What have we *eaten*, for that matter? Nothing, for the same reason, not since the unchewable meat and the dollops of lumpy mashed potato for school lunch nine hours earlier. All we've consumed is thirty lines of the *Aeneid*. And the music, the music.

We've also discovered politics – in the first place, I think, like so much else, through Shelley. In the form magazine we've founded I've written an article supporting the Labour Party at the 1950 General Election, and Lane, characteristically, has outflanked me and made the case for the Communists. I'm so impressed by his arguments that I no less characteristically follow his lead and shift my allegiance leftwards. The 'absolute Democracy' that I managed the year before to identify as an attribute of God we both now see as incarnated in the Soviet Union.

I don't think it occurs to either of us to join a Party organisation, or to become activists of any kind. We're not joiners or activists. We're content simply to be right when everyone else is wrong, to know the truth that everyone else is too blind or prejudiced to grasp. We two are members of the brotherhood of man, an exclusive club from which all the other people we happen to have come across so far are plainly excluded. We're the local representatives of the broad masses, and we smile pityingly at all those who are unequal to our equality. I hawk my communism and atheism around the school, trying to provoke the class enemy, interrupting meetings of the Christian Union until even the sweet-tempered and patient boy who runs it is obliged to ask me to stay away – a triumph for me, of course.

At home Nanny, hand nervously fluttering in front of her mouth to keep the terrible word from the ears of others, asks me to reassure her that I'm not *really* an atheist, and when with unsparing honesty I decline to, refuses to believe that I mean it. Even my father's patience is tested. He takes me and my sister to a performance of *The Mikado* in which the title role is being sung by one of his colleagues from the office. I sit all evening with contemptuously folded arms – and go on sitting at the end when everyone else stands up for the National Anthem. I have embarrassed him in public, my father tells me afterwards with rare bluntness. Also my feet smell. I need to take a bath and change my socks more often. God, the pettiness of the bourgeoisie!

Rather as the religious sometimes concentrate their devotions not so much on God as on one of His saints, so we focus ours less on the Soviet Union itself as on (for some reason) Czechoslovakia, where democracy has been notoriously crushed a couple of years earlier in a Soviet-supported putsch. Or so the poor dupes of the capitalist press believe. We know otherwise. We decide to combine two of our romantic enthusiasms by going climbing in the Tatras. We study maps and brochures; even the mountains look happy under socialism. We go to the Czech consulate to get visas, and we seem to be the only customers. A world-weary official with a gold tooth gives us the application forms. 'You take these home and fill them up,' he explains, 'then you bring them back here, and I throw them into the waste-paper basket.' We're shocked. A cynical relic of the old order, evidently. A few weeks later there's a report in the paper that a Second Secretary at the consulate has committed suicide, I think by jumping out of an upstairs window, as Masaryk is alleged to have done in Prague. Whether it was the man with the gold tooth I don't know. It doesn't shake our faith for a moment.

We never fill in the forms, though. I think it has belatedly occurred to us that the train to Central Europe might be even more expensive than the Greenline to Kensington. Though we were probably intending to hitch-hike, which is what we do the following year when we go to Paris and the Haute Savoie. On £7 each (I still have my old passport, in which all purchases of foreign currency have to be marked in these post-war years of perpetual economic crisis), so that we live mostly on *ficelles* spread with the English strawberry jam that we've brought in our rucksacks, together with a pack of increasingly rancid English butter.

Our form master in School Certificate year is Mr Brown, our Latin teacher, and his passion, apart from the Latin classics, is photography. He celebrates the end of the exams by taking a class photograph. His Rolleiflex has a timer, so that he's able to take his place in the midst of us – a slightly built figure, now nearing retiring age. One look at him as he sits there in his own photograph and you can see what he is: a gentleman and a scholar. He has always treated us, while he introduced us to Virgil and Caesar, as if we, too, are gentlemen and scholars – but has always also kept in hand a terrifying reserve of unpredictable fury, expressed in violent cannonades of desk lid on desk, at the occasional sudden suspicion that we're not.

I study the rows of grey-on-grey faces in the photograph as they gaze obligingly into his lens. We look a decent enough lot. Verging on the gentlemanly, most of us, a few of us even quite scholarly. Some a bit goofy, some already handsome – particularly Lane, who looks like a Mississippi gambler being played by Gregory Peck. The only visibly unsatisfactory member of the party is me. I'm sitting at Bunter's right hand, for some reason, nine feet tall and nine inches wide, with my arms defiantly folded in the way they must have been at *The Mikado*, and I have a most unpleasant sneer on my face. Have I put the expression on specially, in honour of the occasion? Or – good God! – do I look like that all the time? Is this what my demonically handsome fellow-poet has to endure as we talk about sonata form? Is this what my father sees across the supper table every evening?

Yes, my poor father. I'm now two years older than he was when he left school to start work, and assumed the responsibility of supporting his destitute mother and disabled sister. I look back at the old photograph of him, the Smart Lad with the slicked-down hair and the handkerchief in his breast pocket, the easy charm and the self-confident smile, as handsome in his very different way as M. Lane. The contrast with me is ludicrous. No sane employer would take me on as an office boy. And could I ever begin to support anyone else? I look scarcely capable of supporting my own wilting person.

While I'm clearing my desk on the last day of term my left ear's suddenly most painfully seized and twisted, as if by the claw of a giant predatory bird. I find my head turned and tilted to look up into a grinning skull-like face wandering uncertainly about above me on top of a long, cadaverous, tottering body. It's Dr Nichols, the only master in the school with a PhD, and one of the most extraordinary human beings I shall ever meet.

He's holding my ear so painfully because he can't fully control his hand movements. He can't fully control any of his bodily movements. He wobbles rather than walks – he wobbles even when he's standing still. He can write, on paper or on the blackboard, only in a series of wild approximate jabs, and speak only in much the same way. The legend in the school is that he was injured in the First World War, just as Mr Forge, the geography master, clicks at each step because he has a tin leg, and Mr Sanders, the senior English master, speaks in a high, thin wheeze because he was gassed. With hindsight, though, I'm fairly certain that Dr Nichols was born with his condition – that he suffers from cerebral palsy; he's what was then called (without pejorative implications) spastic.

He's known to the school as Gobbo, presumably because his efforts to speak involve the violent projection of a good deal of saliva. He's proposing himself as my form master for the coming year; I'm being tapped for the Language Sixth. What he's trying to tell me, in his spasmodic and unco-ordinated staccato of spit and random grunts, is that for the next two years he's proposing to teach me to speak French and German.

He has read my mind. I do want to go on with French. And I do want to learn German, the language of Beethoven and Schubert, of the German romantic poets. Another twist to my life is being applied through the lobe of my ear by those bony fingers.

And the necessity to smarten myself up and earn a living is being postponed for another couple of years.

I sometimes wonder what would have become of me if my mother hadn't died. If my father hadn't had to extract me from the Reverend J. B. Lawton's corrugated-iron academy and get me into Kingston Grammar School. If Mr Brady, therefore, had never read me the 'Ode to a Skylark'. If Michael Lane had never half-turned his head to hear my whispered witticism. Does my father, looking disconsolately across the supper table at the increasingly alien creature that he seems to have begotten, ever realise quite how much of a role he has continued to play in making me what I am?

I suppose, if my mother had lived, I should have gone on trying to earn her sixpences for coming top of the class. I should have been less obnoxious. And perhaps I should still somehow have discovered Shelley and Beethoven. Still have climbed mountains and seen the landscape opening broader and broader around me. Still in the end have found my way through that doorway to the sunlit lawn beyond.

Or perhaps it would all have turned out quite differently. According to multiple universe theory, there's a profusion of other universes in some of which this different and more presentable version of myself joins the local tennis club and the Young Conservatives, as my sister did later in this universe, where he accepts his father's offer to join Turners Asbestos and train as a rep . . .

Then I think of those two faces in the photographs, my father's and mine . . . Even without the sneer, even if I'd borrowed his pair of monogrammed and ferociously bristled hairbrushes and pounded away with them as he does until my hair was as cowed as his, I couldn't have done it. He had something, young Tommy – a dash, a cheek, a cockiness – that no version of his son could ever have imitated. Those other universes collapse before my eyes.

So does this one. If my mother hadn't died I shouldn't have gone to university, I know. I shouldn't have followed the career that I did follow. Shouldn't have made the friends I made. Shouldn't have met my first wife or my second. My children wouldn't exist, or my grandchildren either . . . Even to think about this possibility is to feel the world around me dissolving into black nothingness, to be seized by existential terror.

As it was, my infantile politics wore off, for better or for worse, and so did the rest of the cloudy romanticism. Some things from that intense and ridiculous time have remained, though. The passion for music and literature, certainly – and they have informed my whole life. As I think they have Lane's. My expression, though, has softened a bit. What I sometimes feel on my face now, from inside, is not that old rictus of superiority, but one of my father's smiles.

4

Chez Nous

By this time the grey cloud has begun to lift a little for my father, too. He's become aware of the shabbiness of our surroundings. All houses with children growing up in them show signs of the battering they've had, and ours has also been neglected for the past decade because of first the war and then the despondency that followed it. The time has come, my father decides, to redecorate.

He does not, of course, get a professional decorator to do the job. Even if he could afford to, such a straightforward manner of going about things is simply not his style – and the rare exception he made for the navvies who built the air-raid shelter isn't encouraging. So far as I can recall, the phrase 'do it yourself' hasn't yet been introduced into the language, but this is what he's now proposing – to do it himself, with the assistance of my sister and me.

From somewhere, perhaps off a barrow in the New Cut, like the gross of blunt razor blades, he acquires a supply of paint and three rollers. This is curious, because it's still only 1949 and I don't think emulsion paint has been invented yet. How can we be using rollers instead of brushes? All I remember for certain is the colour, which is pink. Strawberry pink. He also buys a tin of gold paint, and a rectangular plastic sponge, into which he cuts a pattern with a razor blade (probably one of the New Cut gross, which are perhaps just about sharp enough to inflict some damage on a plastic sponge). We're not merely going to paint the walls, and paint them strawberry pink – we're going to stipple them in gold. We're really going to brighten our lives up.

Where my father has learned about this technique – or this choice of colours – I don't know. There are no DIY manuals to consult, only, as a general guide, an Edwardian music-hall song that my father sometimes sings, 'When Father Papered the Parlour'. Gradually, very gradually, the house begins to turn strawberry pink. Not just the walls – in fact not so much the walls, because there the pinkness of the pink is muted by the colours and patterns of the old wallpaper underneath – but the floors, the edges of the ceiling, the doors, the furniture, the bath, the basin, my father, my sister and myself. Then we add the gold stippling . . .

All this, I think, is happening in the year before the full flowering of my political and religious rebellion, otherwise I might not have condescended to join in – and anyway, if he'd seen the look on my face my father might not have condescended to ask me. The differences between my father and sister on the one hand, and myself on the other, are already quite marked, but are considerably less noticeable when we're all three coloured pink with a gold stipple. It's a bonding experience.

I don't know whether my father's original intention was to turn the entire house gold-stippled pink, but in the event, after we've done the back bedroom and the lounge we never use, he evidently feels that our life is now brightened up enough and calls it a day. In the lounge, in place of *A Bit of Old London* and *St Gall, Switzerland*, my father hangs a few of the photographs I've been taking. Some of them are noticeably out of focus, some not just black and white, or grey and grey, but beginning to go brown because I haven't washed the prints long enough to get rid of the fixer. It's generous and imaginative of my father to encourage me in this way – and if I remember rightly he even pays me for them, I think thirty shillings each. Whether they enhance the general decorative effect I'm not sure. The brown and the pink don't go very well together for a start.

It's not only the house that has become more colourful – so has my father's social life. For the last few years it has been very restricted. He has been wrapped up in his deafness and his various illnesses. Barlow has moved, and been replaced by a self-employed long-distance lorry driver who seems to offer little opportunity for comic exaggeration. I don't know what's happened to George

Davis. Perhaps in peacetime public interest in the intestines of warships and bombers has waned. Now, though, my father begins to adventure a little further afield. While I've been writing *Caligula* and sitting up the oak tree with Lane, he has taken up bridge. His hosts are the Laverses, at No. 6, now returned from wherever they'd hidden themselves during the war. They're a good-hearted couple, and they must have worked hard to tempt my father out of the shell into which he'd retired. They're also remarkably dull, and they make a good foil to my father, now suddenly restored to all his old jokes and high spirits, his hotchamachachas and his turn-ups for the book; and a good foil, too, to the fourth regular bridge partner they've found, Mrs Smith, a widow who lives just round the corner in Queensmead Avenue.

Mrs Smith is a tiny bouncing bean of a woman who loves to laugh and gossip and be teased. She's no more a card-player than I am a cricketer. She's as short-sighted as me, but she won't wear spectacles because she doesn't believe in them, or in anything else associated with doctors and specialists. Who needs spectacles, when you can just screw up your eyes? However tightly she screws up hers, though, she often simply misreads the cards, or drops them. I don't think my father knows much about bridge, either, but he can certainly keep a firm hold on his cards, and count the spots on them, and mock anyone who can't. Mrs Smith is spirited enough to return his fire, though, with similar joshing aggression – and extravert enough not to mind shouting, so my father can often hear what she says.

If you stand outside the dining room, when they're playing at our house, as they occasionally do, you can hear a kind of moo-ing ground-bass from Mr and Mrs Lavers and often, over it, a humorously challenging rally between my father and Mrs Smith.

'Hotchamachacha!'

'*Now* what, Mr Cleversocks?'

'It's our trick, madam! Why are you trumping it?'

'I'm not trumping it! Oh, is that a spade? I thought it was a club . . . Anyway, spades are all I've got.'

'You've got a club.'

'You don't know what cards I've got!'

'I know you've got the four of clubs . . .'

'You think you know everything, don't you? But let me tell you, old boy – there are a lot of things you *don't* know!'

'. . . because I can see it lying on the floor there.'

'Oh, that's where it's got to . . . So now of course you think you really are the great punjandrum.'

'Cleversocks.' 'Punjandrum.' 'Chickens coming home to roast.' 'I take that with a big dose of salts . . .' Mrs Smith – Elsie, as we soon come to call her – has only a rather approximate acquaintance with ordinary words and phrases, as if she has originally heard them all through screwed-up ears. She's a good dancer, though – light on her feet, responsive to the rhythm, and bubbling with energy and excitement – and soon my father's rediscovering his own dancing days. She also has a cocker spaniel – no great recommendation to me, since I'm frightened of dogs, but a considerable one to my sister, whose ambition in life is to work as a kennel maid at Hackbridge Boarding Kennels. She has a jolly sister and brother-in-law, and a jolly niece from rural Nova Scotia who is staying with her over the summer. Soon we're all going on picnics and expeditions together, and by the end of the summer I'm composing *Lines Written for a Homeward-bound Canadian* (Opus 17).

One evening my father tells my sister and me that he wants to have a little talk with us. Odd – he's never proposed having a little talk before. He summons Nanny as well, and leads us all into the lounge. Odder still. Particularly now the walls are strawberry pink, stippled with gold and hung with fuzzy views of Surrey valleys and Welsh mountains. 'Sit down,' he says. My sister sits on one of the Bentalls armchairs that no one ever sits on, I sit on the other. My father sits on the Bentalls sofa. Nanny, who evidently knows what's coming, stands nervously behind him.

'Supposing I were to tell you,' says my father carefully, 'that I was thinking of getting married again?'

I can't remember now how we respond to this, or whether we

respond at all. I can't even remember whether it's a surprise to us, or whether we'd seen it coming. I think he tells us that Mrs Smith – Elsie – having no children of her own, is particularly pleased at the prospect of acquiring two. We shall apparently be moving into her house in Queensmead Avenue. All that strawberry paint has been applied in vain. My father's recommendation of the new house and its various advantages is the only part of his announcement that I can remember for sure.

'You'll have a much broader perspective on life there,' he says. 'There's a television set, for a start.'

This certainly makes Elsie seem quite a catch. In 1949 neither we nor anyone else we know has a television set. I think he reminds my sister about the dog. Then, for me: 'There's a bookcase in the hall, full of books. And there's a radiogram.'

It's the radiogram that clinches it for me. I have never dreamed that we might one day have a machine for playing records on. It's access to this that's going to set me and Lane on our trips to the second-hand trays in Foyles.

Though I suppose I might have guessed that if we ever were to acquire one my father would find some curiously oblique way of doing it.

They marry in Epsom Register Office that October. My father's age is given on the marriage certificate as forty-nine, though he's in fact a year younger – but then he was always a bit vague about ages and birthdays – and Elsie's as fifty-three. Their witnesses are the Laverses, who have engineered the whole event. Phyllis was evidently present, because she told her daughter Jean that she'd never seen Tommy looking more miserable. This I discovered only when Jean read the draft of this book, as I did my father's appalling aside to Phyllis: 'This is the worst day of my life.' My sister and I are not invited to the wedding, nor to the reception afterwards, if there is one, any more than we were to our mother's funeral. Once again, I suppose, the intention is for us not to be upset.

Are we upset? Am *I* upset? Or am I pleased, if only about the radiogram? Or just indifferent? I don't know. I can't remember.

This is the funny thing about the whole episode, which after all marks a considerable epoch in my life. I'm sixteen – quite old enough to remember things. It's the beginning of my School Certificate year, when I'm renouncing religion and discovering metre, listening to music and construing Virgil. Of all *that* I can remember quite a lot. But even of the physical details of the move round the corner, from 3 Hillside Road to 6 Queensmead Avenue, I can recall nothing. We're leaving the house where I've spent all my conscious life, where we were all almost killed by the flying bomb, where my sister was born and our mother died – and I can't even remember how we move our belongings. In the car? In a van? Or do we borrow a wheelbarrow? We shouldn't need a very big vehicle, I'm sure of that. Apart from our clothes and toothbrushes, my photographic stuff and my sister's knick-knacks, we've abandoned everything. Walked out on our lives.

Nanny's packed off once again to Phyllis and Sid's, where she's to spend whatever few years or months remain to her. The house itself was only ever rented, of course. But what happens to the dining table and the sideboard, the feasting cardinals and the Bentalls suite? I suppose they're taken by one of those firms that do house clearances, who sell the best of it off in places like the second-hand stalls in Kingston Cattle Market and throw the rest on the town dump.

All I know is that it vanishes behind us – mock-leather furniture, aluminium saucepans, brass candlesticks. Everything except (as I discover sixty years later) *A Bit of Old London* and *St Gall, Switzerland.*

Chez Nous, as 6 Queensmead Avenue is called, is very different from Duckmore. Elsie's late husband, Frank Smith, had been in partnership with his brothers as proprietors of a small chain of grocery stores in various inner suburbs of South London, and was founding father with them of Ye Olde Oak tinned ham. He has left Elsie well provided for, and we get to know the wonders of the house long before we discover very much more about Elsie herself.

It's large and solidly built. The woodwork's gleaming white, the wallpapers are in various respectable shades of brown, not stippled strawberry. The furniture and fittings are of good quality, and have obviously been obtained by handing over money – probably quite large amounts of it – to shops and tradesmen, not thrown out by the neighbours or won in cigarette promotions. The tables and chairs are highly polished, by a cleaner who has been in service with Elsie for years, Mrs Tunner (or Tanner, as she's probably known to herself and everyone else except Elsie). The armchairs are real hide. The leather-inlaid desk once belonged to Sidney Horler, a deceased but still slightly famous local thriller-writer. The toilet roll in the lavatory plays 'The Bluebells of Scotland' when you take the paper. If you want to get into the loft there's a stepladder to hand.

We three newcomers tiptoe respectfully through the deep pile of the carpets and squeeze cautiously between the close-packed islands of scratchable cabinetwork. One slight oddity about all this, I realise, is that our move into this world of solid bourgeois comfort coincides with my growing belief that happiness can be achieved only by living in blocks of high-rise workers' flats. Do I make any connection between my new convictions and my new surroundings? None that has remained in my mind. I seem to be living in two overlapping but largely unconnected worlds. I must surely have attempted to preserve my integrity with a little private sneer or two, but this time I've no photographic record of it.

In the hallway (a proper hallway, not a lounge doubling up, though it's almost as big as one) stands the promised bookcase, glass-fronted, and full of randomly arranged popular fiction – Sidney Horler, of course, Mazo de la Roche, Rafael Sabatini – all of it I think unread; but also for some reason *War and Peace* and Boswell's *London Journal*, both certainly unread until I get my hands on them. In the front room is the television set, the size and shape of a cocktail cabinet, bashfully concealing its polished walnut face and its small blue eye behind one of the hide armchairs, like a child sent to stand in the corner; if you want to watch anything the armchair has to be pushed back against the dining table, and then you have to look at the little picture sideways over your right shoulder. Net drapes at the windows, keeping the world out by day, and by night heavy dark plush curtains, from ceiling to floor, that absorb all the light and the sound in the house. In a basket in the breakfast room (a breakfast room!) is the black cocker spaniel, Rex. At the back of the house is the lounge – a proper lounge for lounging in, furnished with flowered chintz and china figures, together with a boudoir grand piano that nobody can play – and the radiogram, as specified, twice as big as the television set, with built-in cupboards for the records. In the cupboards, I discover to my pleasure, are two classical records – the background music from a wartime film, and the first half of the first movement of Tchaikovsky's first piano concerto.

Upstairs is a large bedroom for me – and in the back garden, at the side of the wide emerald lawn, a damp but palatial concrete-built air-raid shelter which I am to have as my darkroom. The garden is tended by another long-serving retainer, Port. Beyond the lawn is a rose pergola; beyond the pergola a kitchen garden; beyond the kitchen garden, on the triangle of waste ground at the back of the houses, an allotment where yet more vegetables are growing – most of them given away each week to Port and Mrs Tunner.

In the garage, waiting for Elsie's weekly trip to the shops, is a stately Rover, with gleaming coachwork and chromium, glowing leather upholstery and walnut fitments.

My father has come a long way from Devonshire Road, Holloway. We've all three of us come a long way even from Hillside Road, round the corner, and we're all considerably awed by the grandeur of our new surroundings. I don't think, though, that the radiogram, the abundance of vegetables or even the television set have been the attraction for my father. I think he likes Elsie, in spite of his terrible misgivings when he found himself actually marrying her. Likes teasing her, and being teased himself in return. Likes the dancing and the laughter, the sense of life returning. It takes him back to his Fred Astaire days.

Most of all, I think, he's trying to do the best for my sister and me. After the four difficult years first with Nanny, then the house-keeper, then Nanny again, he's trying to find an arrangement that will really work. A widower with two children who need mother-ing; a widow looking for children to mother. Could he ever have dreamed of a better solution?

So, our new mother.

If I think of Elsie the first picture that comes into my mind is this: a tiny woman with a vast open snakeskin handbag. She's holding the bag in front of her face and screwing up her eyes to see what she's doing, which is taking handfuls of five- and ten-pound notes out of the bag uncounted, and stuffing them into someone's hand. Mrs Tunner's. Port's. Mine. She's merrily brushing aside the recipient's polite reluctance and thanks. 'No – go on! Take it! Don't start being all hooty-tooty!'

That £7 in my passport for my first trip to France was prob-ably doled out to me from the handbag. It seems an uncharacter-istically modest sum, but her combination of impulsiveness and myopia means that her generosity is always a bit random; she may have thought she was giving me a handful not of pound notes but of tenners. Much more typical are her Christmas presents. The Toscanini *Pastoral Symphony*, for example (specified by me, of course) – and not just half a movement but all five, spread across six discs – together with the C sharp minor quartet, Opus 131, by the Busch, on another six, to be played on the great radiogram, over and over again, with the special fibre needles I've acquired, which have to be resharpened after each side (or half a side, in the case of the storm movement in the *Pastoral*). In other years it's luxuriously thick cable-knit sweaters and a goose-down sleep-ing bag for my travels, and a little later cigarettes – gold-tipped Black Russian Sobranie, and Senior Service in packs of 400. She also buys, and maintains, a subscription to the *New Statesman* for me, to further my aims of undermining the capitalist system that's providing her (and me) with the money.

My father soon finds a name for her. Just as I'm still affectionately Willy, at any rate when he's not too irritated with me, she becomes first Little Tich, like the diminutive music-hall comedian (himself, I discover from Wikipedia, called after the undersized claimaint in the Tichborne case), then simply Tich. She has to have a cushion under her when she drives her Rover, and can still barely see over the steering wheel. Not that she can see all that much, even leaning anxiously forward on top of the cushion with her eyes screwed up, and she drives very slowly, zig-zagging cautiously between the kerb and the cat's eyes in the middle of the road. My father, who is occasionally allowed to drive the Rover himself for family outings, always refers to it as the Old Box of Bells. 'I'll Old-Box-of-Bells *you!*' snorts Tich scornfully. 'The Old Box of Bells will outlast that jollapy of yours, never you fear! I've never seen such a wreck! The chromion's flaking off the rodiator already!'

She's particularly good at humorous snorting because she has a permanently stuffed-up nose. She suffers from polyps, but refuses to have them treated, or to see a doctor for any other reason. 'Doctors? Don't talk to me about doctors! They don't know anything! They give you this wonderful dognosis, then they kill you! It was the doctors that killed my dear Frank. He'd still be alive today if it hadn't been for doctors and dognosises.'

Her background's not entirely unlike my father's. Her own father was a newsagent in Noel Street in Soho, then still a poor immigrant quarter. Crowded into the houses on either side of the shop, according to the 1901 census, were waiters, cooks, tailors and charwomen, many of them hailing from France, Germany, Austria, Hungary and Russia. As a child Elsie used to earn pennies as a shabbasgoy, lighting fires and ovens on the Sabbath for her Jewish neighbours. Her family, the Rickies, had the house in Noel Street to themselves, but by the time of the 1911 census they had moved to Whitfield Street, on the other side of Oxford Street, where Elsie, her parents and her three younger sisters were now reduced to two rooms. Her father was no longer listed as being in business on his own account but as a 'worker', a dentist's mechanic, so maybe the newsagent's had failed, just as my grandfather's china shop in Plymouth did. On the Epsom wedding certificate his profession has been restrospectively upgraded from dentist's mechanic to dentist. Something a bit oedipal here, if this was Elsie's mistake – she'd no more consult a dentist than a doctor.

Like my father she left school at fourteen, but she'd started at the old French elementary school in Noel Street, so, unlike my father, who at his central school in Holloway had any traces of French knocked out of him, she actually speaks the language, or at any rate as much of it as young children use – and speaks it better and more fluently than I will achieve through two years in the sixth form with Gobbo. Most of the records in the cupboards of the radiogram, apart from the *Warsaw Concerto* and the fragment of Tchaikovsky, are French cabaret songs, some romantic, some slyly suggestive, some *faux-naifs*, sung by two of the great night-club *chansonniers* of the thirties, Jean Sablon and Charles Trenet. I have to struggle to catch the colloquial usage. Elsie sings happily along, entirely at home with them, suddenly a Paris sparrow like Piaf.

When she left school she went into the tailoring, as she always calls it, apprenticed to one of the grand bespoke firms in Savile Row, possibly Kilgour, French and Stanley, though a legendary figure called Stanbury (who may of course be Stanley) comes into the story somewhere. She seems to have enjoyed it, and I should think she was a lively, eager, pretty girl whom everyone in the workshop must have doted upon. Her sister Doris is still in the business. Instead of a wealthy grocer Doris has married a tailor, Phil Bargstedt, who has gone through the North African and Italian campaigns with the Eighth Army as a lorry driver. Phil and Dot (or Doc, in Elsie's version of her name, as if she were a member of the despised profession) live as council tenants in a single requisitioned room in Hampstead, and they work together, for John Morgan in Savile Row, he making the jackets, she the trousers. They're both as plain as potatoes, endlessly cheerful and unfailingly good-hearted. I visit them sometimes in their workshop, high up under the eaves of the West End. Phil, a huge ruined hulk of a man like a retired heavyweight boxer, sits among the other tailors as tailors have always sat, cross-legged on a great table – an English Buddha, coughing and choking in the smoke of the cigarette he keeps burning like a joss stick in the ashtray beside him. Every few stitches he stops, takes another drag on the cigarette, and cracks another soft-hearted bantering joke. Doris sits straight-backed on a chair in front him, coughing and laughing. They're sewing by hand, of course, and working so fine that the stitching can scarcely be seen even by someone whose eyes aren't watering from the smoke.

Later in life Elsie developed most of the prejudices known to mankind, but she had always lived and worked among immigrants, and no one seems to have explained to her that she could easily have extended her range to include xenophobia. When Frank Smith carried her off out of the tailoring and into the groceries they travelled all over Europe, to Holland and Denmark to buy the ham that he tinned under the Olde Oak label, to Paris because it was Paris, to Switzerland and Germany for the winter sports. Just as Frank is her lost love, so the Continent in the twenties and thirties is her land of lost content. She loves telling me about it. We've been cut off from it by the war, but, even before Michael Lane and I set out to trudge the French roadsides with our jars of English butter and strawberry jam, Abroad has been mythologised for me by Elsie's shining-eyed tales of Pullmans and wagons-lits, of the sparkling white snows of yesteryear in Garmisch-Partenkirchen, of coffee and croissants on the terrace of the Café de la Paix – all of it as remote to me as ever, of course, even when I get there, with only seven pounds in my pocket.

Actually there are unpredictable exceptions to even the most entrenched of her prejudices. She is rigidly puritanical about any reference to sexual deviancy – or to any other kind of sexual behaviour – yet she adores the extravagant dresses of Danny La Rue, the female impersonator, and laughs over and over again as she listens to a recording she has of Max Miller, the Cheeky Chappie, whose smutty innuendos shock my own highbrow sensibilities. Another prejudice she has missed out on completely is anti-Semitism, even though it's still pretty generally taken for granted in the suburbs. She seems unaware of the possibility. She was brought up among Jews and worked with them in the tailoring. They're as much a part of her life as Mrs Tunner, or an old friend she sometimes takes me to visit, Girlie. (Girlie! Were there really people then called Girlie? Or was that yet another mishearing, another mispronunciation?) At the end of her life Elsie settled in a part of Hove where most of her neighbours were Jews, was invited to all their weddings and bar mitzvahs, and sat shivah with them when they were bereaved. At her own funeral they all came and wept for her in their turn, which not too many of her Gentile acquaintances did.

She and I soon get on quite well together. I'm a little seduced, I have to confess, by the French cabaret songs, the half movement of Tchaikovsky and all the other attractions of our new home. I'm won over by Elsie herself, in spite of my intellectual snobbery – intrigued by her memories of pre-war Europe and her malapropisms, disarmed by her vivacity. I develop a slightly distanced, ironic, bantering manner with her – imitated, I suppose, from my father – which provokes her to the same kind of performance as his does.

So there we are – the perfect iconic family again: mother, father, one boy, one girl – now even a dog. Not to mention the television and the radiogram. How long can it last?

Not long, it turns out. The first problem is my sister.

I realise that I haven't said much about Jill in the course of this story so far. The trouble is I don't know quite what to say. She still puzzles me. She's so much cleverer than me, but somehow, when she's a child, it doesn't take effect in the world, either at school or in any other way. She doesn't *do* anything much. She doesn't really seem to be interested in anything, except perhaps dogs. When she marries and has children in the years to come this is all going to change – often in rather disconcerting ways. She's a late starter, though.

I try belatedly as I write this to see life from her perspective, and I do begin to understand how much harder things were for her than they were for me. Her elder son, Julian, told me when he read my first draft something that I found deeply surprising and painful: that she had always been top of the class at school until our mother died. This at last makes sense of a lot of things. But how is it that I'd never known it, or had somehow forgotten it? I suppose, with hindsight, that I'd cast a shadow over her life even while our mother was alive. In later years she came to believe that I had always been our father's favourite. I really don't think this is right. I suppose I may have been our *mother's* favourite, and perhaps, since Jill was scarcely able to remember her, she somehow transferred her sense of injustice to our father as a more accessible object. But, as *I* recall it, she and our father had a natural bond – they were both so quick, and so impatient of my slowness. And yet, slow as I was, I was always passing exams, and jumping through most of the other hoops that were held up in front of me. I see how exasperating this must have been.

I made a second surprising discovery about my sister through writing this book: that she was almost someone else altogether. My cousin Jean asked me, after she'd read the draft, if I knew that during the three and a half years between my own birth and my sister's our mother had conceived *another* child. I had not known. I've had to wait seventy-four years to hear about this little complication in the apparently straightforward creation of our iconic family, and I don't know even now whether I should have had a brother or another sister.

This potential sibling of mine apparently died in my mother's womb at the age of six months. Jean says that my mother had to spend Christmas in hospital. This would have been just possibly in 1934, but more probably in 1935, when I was two. The first memory that I can date is of my third birthday, nine months later, and even with hindsight I can't locate so much as the faintest trace of a Christmas with no mother in the house, let alone an explanation for her absence. How extraordinary, though, that no one ever told my sister or me! I suppose our mother died before she thought we were old enough to understand, and our grandmother would have

trapped any revelation so intimate behind that nervously concealing hand of hers. But didn't it ever cross my father's mind that we
might like to know? Jean was told about it by her mother, and it's
odd that Phyllis never thought to mention it in the memoir of my
mother that she wrote for me. So strange, what families preserve
of the past, and what they fail to. Jean herself didn't know, until
she read this book, that her father had served so glamorously during the war in Bomber Command. But for me not to know until
now of the existence of someone who would have been a sibling
of mine! And for my sister never to know that someone else had
almost forestalled her very existence!

When we were younger, I and the sister who has now so suddenly almost vanished before my eyes played together and squab-
bled and dared each other quite a lot. But over the years a disparity
develops. I'm always tediously *doing* things – trying to make things,
taking photographs, showing off, writing poems, being religious.
For a lot of my enterprises I require her to be involved, as assistant, disciple or audience. I can't recall ever doing the same for her.
Well, I'm three and a half years older – but the real difference is
that she doesn't ever undertake any activity that I could possibly
be involved in. She never makes me pray instead of opening my
Christmas presents. She never forces me, as I do her, to spend
hours watching inept puppet shows and incompetent conjuring.
I don't have to play bit parts in plays she has written for the local
children to perform. She doesn't make me run about the garden for
hours calling 'What am I doing now?', as I do her when I'm lying
in the darkened bedroom on a sunlit summer's day after having a
tooth out, and I discover the camera obscura – a blurred image of
outside events cast on the ceiling by light passing through a small
hole in the wartime blackout.

I recall one of my impositions on her, when I was about twelve,
with particular shame. My friend David and I have decided to
make our fortunes by manufacturing conjuring sets. We produce a
sample, which Jill is to take to school and show to her friends, so
that she can then secure orders from them, as my father does with

his asbestos gutters and downpipes. A week or two go by. Each evening I question her about her sales figures. Nothing. No orders at all. And then I discover the sample set, still in her satchel, now crushed flat. She has been carrying it back and forth every day, too embarrassed to show it to anyone.

The death of our mother brings us closer again for a while. We huddle together in our misery, and then by unspoken agreement collaborate in making the lives of her replacements impossible. By the time our father remarries, though, I'm sixteen, which is getting a bit old for this kind of entertainment, and in any case I've moved further and further away into the new worlds I'm discovering of music and poetry. Jill's part of the world I'm leaving behind. She's still only twelve, and has little life outside the family. For her, when we move into Elsie's house, everything changes. Even our father, the person to whom she's closest in the world, has become someone else in these new surroundings. She's alone. Her stepmother's recollections of Paris and snatches of French are of no interest to her. She and Elsie don't find a way of being together. And yet, since Jill's so much younger than me, she can't escape as I do. They *have* to be together. Jill is dependent on her. Elsie has to tell her what to do, and scold her when she doesn't do it.

Jill becomes more and more difficult. She has always had a temper, which I suppose suggests the frustration she has suffered. She has often exercised it on me, reasonably enough, but also on our parents. At the age of seven or eight, for example, she developed a regular morning ritual of screaming tantrums about the sleeves of her school blouse, which all seemed to her either too long or too short. (I had tantrums, too. Mine were entirely reasonable – I was screaming at the nails that bent and the wood that split as I struggled to make things.) Now her rages start again, and this time they're directed against Elsie.

What are they about? The usual things, I imagine: demands to keep her room tidy and do her homework, reproaches for leaving laundry on the floor for Elsie to pick up. I seem to remember particular difficulties about food. Jill won't eat the meals that Elsie has cooked. I sit in my large new room, memorising German strong verbs and simultaneously listening to yet another performance of the Eighth Symphony on the buzzy Bakelite radio that Elsie has dug out of store for me, and over the music, through the stout timber of the well-made door, I'm aware of raised voices and the slamming of other strongly constructed doors. I don't go out to investigate. We poets are above such petty domestic disturbances.

And then one evening, when I'm sitting in my room with Michael Lane discussing Schopenhauer or the forthcoming extinction of the bourgeosie, the door's flung open and the family's troubles come bursting in.

It's Elsie, weeping wildly. She throws herself down on her knees in front of me and buries her face in my lap. I'm frozen with shock and embarrassment, all my gallant bantering suddenly knocked out of my hand like a paper fan by a whirlwind. I've never seen anyone behave in such a way – not, at least, since the night my mother died – and I've never, even then, heard the secrets of family life broadcast in such a way to someone outside the family.

'He's going to leave!' she sobs, when she can manage to speak. 'He says he should never have come here and it's all my fault because I don't know how to get on with Jill! You and me will have to stay here, and he's going to go off with Jill and find somewhere else to live!'

I feebly pat her shoulder, completely out of my depth. My fellow poet, always more spontaneous and less inhibited than me, puts his arm round her and comforts her, then – even more like the man of the world he is – goes downstairs and pours her a stiff whisky.

5
Black Dog

My father and sister don't leave, of course. We're all shocked by the crisis, but we somehow patch things up and carry on. For some weeks my father's joshing is subdued. So, for a while, is my sister's bad behaviour. I creep about the house like a candidate for beatification, clearing the table almost before it's laid, taking the dog for walks. We all avoid each other's eye. And we get back, more or less, to where we were before.

Soon, though, another problem emerges. Not Jill this time – Elsie.

The *joie de vivre* that bubbles out of her as effortlessly as spring water, we begin to discover, can, like spring water, run unpredictably low, slow to a trickle or dry up altogether. The open handbag can snap shut. The myopic sunshine can die out of her smile. The weather can quickly cloud over and become very grey indeed.

She continues to go through the motions of family life when the depression strikes, cleaning, cooking, salting the water softener, issuing orders to Mrs Tunner and Port, doling out uncounted handfuls of banknotes, but she makes it clear that she's continuing with the whole dreary charade simply from a sense of duty. Her stories of France and life in the tailoring cease. If she has to speak her voice is mournful. If you speak to her she looks away and up, at some uninhabited spot in the air, and if she responds at all it's only with cryptic sarcasms. 'Oh, really . . .?' Derisive snort. 'Oh, you *are*, are you? I'm *sure* you do . . .' Another derisive snort. But the snorts are no longer humorously intended, and nor is the derision. These are serious snorts, seriously derisive.

She slaps the supper down in front of us on the table in the breakfast room, and it's simply a piece of organic matter which has been drudgingly boiled until soft enough to eat and then whacked on to a plate. Several times a week it's a complete Ye Olde Oak ham, still retaining the shape of the tin – a brick with rounded shoulders, narrow at the top and wide at the bottom, which I suppose is intended to suggest the outline of an inverted pig's leg. Graceless of me, I realise, to question even retrospectively the food that she has prepared for us. And pressed pig is actually a rather suitable dish for the three ungrateful pigs pressed into eating it – swine cast before swine. I grow to hate that shape, though – to hate all ham, even untinned, genuinely conoidal ham. We eat with our eyes on our plates, Elsie with her mouth open, unable to breathe through her nose.

She has good reason to be dejected, it seems to me now that I look back on it. Out of the kindness of her heart she has let three strangers into her comfortable and well-run house, three refugees who had nowhere to live but a dump painted strawberry pink. She has tried to make a life for them. They have not responded. And I think her disappointment goes deeper still. She has always longed for children; they were the one thing lacking in her perfect marriage to the perfect Frank. She had once conceived, as she tells me sometimes when she's in a mood to talk, and carried the baby to term, but after a prolonged and agonising labour it was stillborn, and she could never have another. Suddenly, years after all hope had been extinguished, she was offered another chance – two ready-made, reasonably presentable children, waiting only to be loved and mothered. I don't suppose she ever had any great hopes of me – I was too old already, and too alien. My sister, though, could still be dressed and petted, guided and shaped. And it hasn't worked out. My sister has rejected her love. She has clung to her father, and her father has taken her part. The strangers within our stepmother's gates remain strangers, intruders from another tribe. She has made her great sacrifice in vain.

Doris and Phil are not surprised to hear about her depressions; she's always been subject to them. They laugh when I go to see them in their one room in Hampstead, where they're sewing all

weekend to make ends meet. 'Oh Gawd!' gasps Doris sympathetic-
ally, snorting in her turn. 'You and Jill in the doghouse again? *And
your dad?*' 'Poor old Tommy,' says Phil. 'Doesn't know what's hit
him, does he. Be Dot and me next. Always something we've done
wrong, isn't there, Dot?' 'She's used to having things her own way,
Elsie, that's the trouble.' 'Money, Michael! Doesn't always make
you happy!' 'Poor old Else. Never mind. Chin up. She'll snap out
of it.'

And she does. She bubbles away for a bit. 'Come on, then, old
boy!' she says to my father. 'Get your hat and coat on! We're going
out! Where? Anywhere! And you can drive the Box of Bells, if
you promise not to go pronging into anything.' Even when the
effervescence begins to go a little flat I can manage to keep her
going for a while. Jolly her along, talk to her in French. Ask her
about the old days. Listen respectfully as her recollections become
increasingly mournful, particularly about her late first husband.
'Oh, Michael, he was such a wonderful man, my Frank! Anything
I wanted I could have. I'd just have to name it, and he'd get it for
me. There aren't men like that in the world any more.'

When I start learning to drive she's often pleased to let me
chauffeur her. I change the silky smooth gears on the Rover with
reverent care as we go to Streatham for her weekly descent upon
Smith Brothers to collect her groceries. She's received like a dow-
ager empress looking in on her old palace. 'And how many tins
of ham this week, Mrs Frayn? Not at all, Mrs Frayn . . . Always a
pleasure, Mrs Frayn.' Sometimes Roland Smith is there to greet
her in person – the youngest of the brothers, now running the
firm. At the sight of his plump and prosperous face Elsie comes
back to the bubble. 'Come on, now, Rowley! When are you going
to bring those lovely children of yours over to see me?' Rowley
steers her back towards the car, gallant, joshing. 'I told them to put
an extra dozen hams in the boot. I can see this handsome young
chauffeur of yours needs feeding up.'

Yes, there are certainly good times. We manage at any rate one
family holiday, and it doesn't go off too badly. Later Elsie even

introduces my father to the pleasures of foreign travel – takes him
to Switzerland and gets him briefly on to skis, then to Belgium
and Holland to stay with some of her old friends in the pig-raising
and pig-slaughtering industry. Persuades him to let her rub olive
oil into his bald patch. Lets me attempt to cook spaghetti bol-
ognese, which is then still as exotic as frogs' legs, and which I have
just discovered on my travels with Lane. She even gallantly tries
to eat the result – grey nodules of half-cooked mince floating in a
thin gravy.

And then she's down again. We're all in the doghouse, Phil and
Doris included. Even me, the peacemaker. The only creature who's
never in the doghouse is the dog. Rex is black, as black as an under-
taker's suit – the living embodiment of the black dog that Churchill, Elsie's great hero, suffers from – his name for his own recurring
depressions. Rex is never depressed himself, whatever's going on in
the house. He lies in his basket in the breakfast room, half an eye
on the general world situation, ready to be instantly as jolly as his
mistress at her jolliest at the possibility of a walk, or some suggestion of food – and he never has to eat Ye Olde Oak. He never takes
sides – he will go walkies with any of us. While my father sits with
my sister in the living room, trying to hear a variety programme on
the television, or reads *The Times* on his own, and Elsie sits, also
on her own, doing nothing, on a hard chair in the breakfast room,
Rex is prepared to sit gazing soulfully up at her by the hour, even
if she's too depressed to speak, black dog with black dog, provided
only that she scratches his stomach from time to time. But then
he does much the same for my sister – even for me and my father,
when we give him a passing scratch of the stomach ourselves.

Elsie's depressions get worse. For days she can't speak at all.
She can't even snort – it's as if the polyps have blocked her nose
completely. This is the second image of her that comes to mind, to
set beside the merry figure ladling money out of the open handbag: her sitting, too miserable even to scratch the dog, on the
leather pouffe in front of the fire in the living room, gazing into
the flames, with her knees sagging apart to reveal her long pink

directoire knickers, as if she no longer has animation enough even to maintain the normal proprieties.

Yes, poor Elsie, as Doris says. And my poor father. Well, my now rather more comfortably-off father. He's risen from Technical Representative to Sales Manager by this time, and the marriage has put money in his pocket. He's not paying rent any longer, and I suspect that he's not making any contribution to the food bills or the upkeep of the house. His appearance is changing, and not for the worse, like Elsie's. He looks more dapper than ever. The old hearing aid, with its pocketfuls of batteries and its web of connecting leads, has been replaced by something much more discreet and up to date. He takes to buying his suits and shirts in the West End – not quite in Savile Row, but in Harrods, where Vi had once served on the other side of the counter. He brushes his thinning short-back-and-sides flatter than ever, and grows his greying moustache thicker. The lines on his face are becoming more deeply etched. He looks rather distinguished – better turned out, I imagine, than most of the civil servants he's selling asbestos to.

At the weekend he takes himself off to the Members' Enclosure at the Oval to watch cricket, or to the races, where he likes to mix with the owners and trainers in the paddock. His weekend appearance is as faultless as his weekday one: pale grey suit, carefully dinted trilby, tan toecaps with a mellow glow polished into them. When I'm a little older I sometimes go racing with him (I can't face the cricket). He doesn't look out of place among the owners and trainers.

He's given up the old liberal *News Chronicle* in favour of *The Times*. He's ceased to call people Guv'nor. He's becoming – almost – a gentleman. His wits remain as quick as ever, though. There's a story about him demonstrating a sample of asbestos to someone at Heathrow to show how tough it was as fencing material. What they actually wanted, said the airport official, was not something tough at all, but something that would break on impact, to minimise damage to any aircraft that collided with it. 'Just the thing!' said my father, snapping the sample in two.

Yet he's somehow a lesser man than he was. He's living in another house he doesn't own – but now he doesn't even own the furniture. And someone else does – owns house and furniture alike, the bed he sleeps in, the table he eats off, the walls around him and the roof over his head – and contrives to remind him of the fact in every gesture. His deafness seems even more profound and more isolating in a world where all the sound is soaked up by the heavy curtains and carpets, and where there are often in any case no words being spoken for him to hear. He has always moved lightly over the earth, but among the heavy alien furnishings and the heavy silences, against which all his quickness and banter are in vain, he seems suddenly even less substantial.

Each day he escapes, as he always has done, into his own little world on four wheels. The car remains a bond between him and me, because he can still sometimes give me a lift up to town, and at the weekend he takes me out for driving lessons, which usually include a walk on Epsom Downs with the dog. The dog is Elsie's, of course. Even the car is the firm's.

Daisy, his favourite sister, died back in 1943. For the death of his brother George in 1955 he buys me a black tie. 'You'll need it often enough in the years to come,' he says. He's right, and I still use it – it's lasted longer than any other item of clothing I've ever possessed. I'm not sure exactly when poor Mabel goes. She vanishes from the electors' list in 1960, but I can't recall any opportunity to wear my black tie, and I can't now trace a death certificate. Her niece says that she went into Moorfields Eye Hospital to have her cataracts removed, and died at some point while she was lying there – stone deaf, of course, and now with her eyes bandaged as well, under orders not to move. Nellie and her family were getting ready for a day trip to Kent when the news arrived. 'Don't tell your mother,' said Frank to his daughter; 'No need to spoil her day.' Nellie takes a similarly robust view of death. When Frank dies in 1977, at the age of ninety-seven, Nellie, now ninety-four, declines to go to the funeral in favour of watching the Test match on television.

On Sunday we sometimes drive over to Hendon to see Phyllis and Sid, where Nanny's still alive, though only just. 'I shan't see another winter out, Michael.' Phyllis, Sid and Nanny don't return the visits. And none of my father's family ever comes to the house.

My sister's changing, too. She's settling down and cheering up; she's beginning to make friends with Elsie, at any rate when Elsie's in the positive phase of the cycle – becoming a little more like the daughter Elsie always wanted. Masking this new affection in mockery, just as our father does, she adopts his name for her – Tich. She also finds a new name for our father. He's no longer 'Daddy'. He's 'Pa'.

I suppose it's one of the ways in which she's making herself independent of him, her equivalent to my Beethoven and adolescent Marxism. I don't really like it. It makes him seem older, since Pa was what we used to call our grandfather. It distances him. It suggests that he's a father in a story – a humorous story. Someone else's story. Not quite the intimately familiar figure who begat us and cared for us, and with whom we have shared all the vicissitudes of life so far. All the same, I find myself calling him Pa as well – my sister's very strong-willed when she finally gets going. The dynamics of the family have altered, and my father becomes even more an outsider in the house.

The most regular visitor to Chez Nous is Michael Lane. Whenever we're not in school together, or on our way to concerts, we're back and forth to each other's houses. He lives in a small semi just off the Kingston bypass, near the old Ace of Spades roadhouse, about four miles away. We sit alternately in Lane's tiny bedroom and my large one, playing chess and reading plays together; downstairs in Elsie's chintz-and-china lounge listening to my handful of records on the mighty radiogram – then in his cramped living/dining room listening to *his* handful on a gramophone that consists of the bare machinery still frugally housed in its original cardboard box. At the end of the evening I walk him to the Spring Hotel in

Ewell Village to catch the 406 to the Toby Jug at Tolworth – he walks me to the Toby Jug to catch it in the other direction to the Spring. Sometimes, though, we've lingered so long together that the last bus has gone, or even if it hasn't we still can't bear to part, and agree to walk halfway together, talking, talking, an extra mile through the sodium-lit yellow suburbs to the Queen Adelaide in Stoneleigh, or the Bonesgate in Hook – and then sit down together on some convenient wall and go on talking some more.

Whatever do we find to talk about at such length? Impossible to reconstruct old conversations after the event, but I've had a little help from another diary that I'm keeping intermittently around this time. It's more expansive than previous attempts, which gives even more scope to my pomposity and self-importance. Waves of euphoria ('. . . anything is possible, and great things probable . . . moments of ecstatic, dreamlike happiness . . .') alternate with existential despair, precise cause unstated ('I must have sincerity. Without that, a writer, indeed anyone, is a useless shell . . . My God! how can one hope to ever know what sincerity means even, down here in this dark world of lies and deliberate blindness, where there is no air, only dust, dust, dust; the dust of decay and not realising . . .?') Some of our conversations seem to reflect the more negative moods. 'A long discussion [with Lane, of course] on subjectivity and objectivity in literature in general and our own rubbish in particular . . . a grand orgy of mutual criticism . . . I need some of his super-egoistic subjectivity, which forces everything about which he writes to become either an attribute or a gratification of his desires, while he needs some of my super-altruistic objectivity, which disconnects me from my subject as surely as death disconnects a man from life. Can a National Mind Transfusion Service be started?' On another occasion 'we tore to bits the character of nearly everyone in the sixth form, and then advanced to do the same thing with what our own were two years ago . . . agreeing that we must have been, in common with the rest of adolescents at that stage of development, living in a world of immaculate misconceptions'.

When we meet much later in middle age, after being out of contact for many years, he's a senior civil servant in Canada, and he tells me that I've caused him some professional embarrassment by announcing to the world, in a newspaper interview I've just given, that he and I had been communists, and that our friendship had had homo-erotic overtones. Did it, in fact? Well, it was certainly a love affair of some sort. I remember once waiting for him to arrive at my house. I'm standing in the living room looking out through the net curtains, as eager in my anticipation as I would be later waiting for a girl on a date . . . And here he comes, strolling in his nonchalant way, demonically handsome, in a belted raincoat of immense sophistication, like a gangster in a movie. He places a hand on the front gate, just above the plate that says 'Chez Nous' – hesitates for a moment – and then, instead of pushing it open, *vaults* it, his belted raincoat flying. My heart vaults it with him.

So love, yes. But love without the ghost of any physical expression. This may be simply because we're so ill-informed that we don't realise the possibility exists. I don't think we've heard of such a thing as homosexuality, any more than we have of metre. We don't know anything about anything! Well . . . there are some things that my fellow poet's evidently now beginning to find out about, because somewhere in the middle of our School Certificate year, I think even while he's still vaulting gates and we're spending so much time on our way either to or from the Queen Adelaide and the Bonesgate, he shows me a poem dedicated not to me but to someone called Stella. *Stella*? A *girl*? He's just met her, he tells me. They've been for a walk together. They're going to go for another walk together. I feel the sickening stab of an emotion completely new to me: jealousy. I've been displaced. Also he's found a girl and I haven't. And not just one called Maureen or Doreen, but *Stella*, like a girl . . . well, like Mike the tiler's girl in Chicago, or a girl in the dedication of a poem. Later he tells me that he invented the name, though what her real name is he doesn't reveal. Perhaps it *is* Doreen, or Maureen.

The girl herself, though, is real enough – the first indication of

Lane's growing attraction to and for the opposite sex. Or perhaps not the first; Elsie has always been rather taken by his debonair and dashing style, and whenever she gets half a chance, I think, now that she has broken the ice by bursting into tears in front of him, confides in him about how awful my father, my sister and I all are. Later he turns up in Ewell with a Rosalind, and then, in the summer holidays when we're still only halfway through the sixth form, less than eighteen months after that first walk with Stella, he establishes his ascendancy for good and all. I get a wild letter from him in Paris confessing in an agony of self-reproach that something terrible has occurred involving a woman he's met, a schoolteacher four years older than himself. He is bewildered, insane, completely uncontrollable . . . can't answer for his actions . . . has committed an offence against her . . . I take this (wrongly, I have just discovered) to mean that they have had intercourse, and am shaken to the core.

Once again I've been left far behind. My still cloudy romantic feelings fasten on girls, just as they always have; but the only practical manifestation of this, while my fellow-poet's making so much headway, is that my knees turn to water whenever I pass a girl in the street. I pass quite a lot of girls in the street, particularly in the mornings, when they like me are on their way to school. By the time I get to the bus stop my knees are often scarcely in a condition to hold me up. Then, on the bus, more trouble. The vibration induces that awkward bulge in the trousers that disconcerts all adolescent boys. Some instinct tells me, even though nothing and no one else has, that there's something shameful about this, and that when the moment comes to get off the bus it has to be concealed behind the pile of books I'm carrying. Whether I make any connection between the bulge in the trousers and the weakness in the knees I can't remember.

I realise that I must do better than this if I'm to go on talking to Lane. I must have something more than loss of muscle tone in my knees to report. I have at the very least actually to speak to a girl. In my diary for a start there are only cryptic allusions to my quest: 'And now the patient stars are looking down outside my window, asking me why I am afraid to play the aces they so unexpectedly put in my hand. What can I answer? High morality? Faint-hearted mortality, rather; it is no use deceiving myself; I can only promise myself that next time . . . ah, next time . . .'

Exactly what aces the stars have dropped into my hands from the heavenly card game they seem to be playing overhead I can no longer remember. No mystery, though, in spite of my coyness, about who it is that I'm pursuing – or rather failing to – because I don't have much choice in the matter. I only know one girl: Jennifer, with whom I was in love six or seven years earlier, with whom I shared straw cigarettes and the *Girls' Crystal* and the wartime twilight – the girl in the dirndl from whom my father worried that I might contract girlishness. (Does he ever worry about my friendship with Michael Lane? I can't remember his ever saying anything to suggest it.) I quickly start being in love with Jennifer again. Within two weeks I've actually brought myself to write her name down in the diary, and to reveal a little of my new feelings, if only to myself. 'She was, of course, as disarmingly amused and charming as ever . . . more beautiful than I have ever seen anyone look . . . intense nervous elation all evening afterwards, followed by sleeplessness nearly all night . . . Today, however, I have sunk once again into the sober depression of hopelessness . . .'

From now on there are many sighs and moonings in the diary ('. . . paralysed by suddenly hollow longing of love . . . could do nothing but walk about in the damp neighbourhood or sit and stare at my desk . . .'). I also record many attempts to contrive a meeting, which for some reason I feel must appear to be accidental. She has now left school and is working as a secretary in London. It takes me many evenings of watching the successive waves of commuters emerge from the station footpath at Ewell East to discover which train she returns on. Then, as she heads up the road towards home among all the others, I happen by some coincidence to be walking just behind her on my way back from school, even though school finished two hours earlier.

The diary's reticent about exactly how often this coincidence recurs, but quite often, I think, before at last I manage to walk a little faster, and find myself happening by an even greater coincidence to *overtake* her. I must be in danger of being pitched into the gutter by the instability in my knees at this sudden turn of speed, but somehow I remain upright long enough to just happen for some reason to glance back, and . . . 'Oh, hello! What a surprise!'

There are many painful things about being an old man, as I now am some sixty years later, but at least it means you don't have to be seventeen again.

The stars are evidently dropping playing cards out of heaven as thick and fast as Elsie at bridge, because fate repeats the same coincidence for the next few evenings, and if Jennifer's at all surprised at this strain upon the laws of probability she's too polite to mention it. Eventually our relationship progresses a little. We walk round the neighbourhood at night together. I put my arm round her. In my conversations with Michael Lane I report progress, discuss the nuances of the relationship, and humbly listen to his expert advice. Jennifer gives me an expensive foulard in gold silk. I kiss her. I question myself in the diary as to whether I'm really in love with her after all. I take her to the sixth-form social, and up to London for a night on the town. Where do we go – to a concert? A play? A night club? No – to the Ideal Home Exhibition. What *am* I doing?

And what do her parents think about all this? My mother's parents must have had mixed feelings about my father, when he first came courting in his bow tie and his slicked-down hair, but I must cut an even more unsettling figure. My father has given me money to get myself a new sports jacket and trousers. In a sober gents' outfitters in Epsom I've selected them in a discreet shade of grey, but under the artificial lighting of the shop I've misread the colour. Mr and Mrs Dennis-Smith have to watch their beautiful daughter being called for by a young man who is not only nine feet tall and nine inches wide, with a permanent sneer on his lips, but who is dressed from head to foot in pale apple-green. I must look like a dissident intellectual who's gone off to join Robin Hood and his Merry Men. Now this pale green young man is taking their daughter out to the Ideal Home Exhibition. Jennifer's mother has always had an urbane social manner, and continues to exercise it as we make conversation while her daughter gets ready (and what on earth do we make conversation about? Subjectivity and objectivity in modern French literature?), but I detect a new note of unease in her manner. She thinks that we're putting down a deposit on a house, and ordering our first three-piece suite. She thinks she's going to find herself with a pale green son-in-law.

When I think of Lane and that super-egoistic subjectivity of his that I've noted in the diary I'm abashed at the feebleness of my efforts. Or when I imagine the way my father walked into that party thirty years earlier and simply strolled up to the girl who was going to become my mother. No coincidences. No wobbly knees. No consulting with his friend about how best to proceed. Simply: 'I'm Tom – I suppose you're Vi!'

Girls and dancing, yes. I seem to be trailing rather a long way behind my father in the first department. And as for dancing . . . I sign up for a course at a local academy, and at the end of it can manage one authorised step in the waltz, provided I keep counting under my breath, one in the quickstep, and one in some South American dance which is fashionable at the time. I'm evidently better at dancing than cricket, at any rate.

My conversations with Lane and my agonisings over Jennifer are not the only things distracting me from my father's problems and the changing situation inside Chez Nous. I'm also more and more absorbed in my school work, now that I'm in the sixth form. I see from the diary that I've come up against a considerable problem for anyone studying literature, as I am, or professionally involved in it, as I shall be for most of my adult life: a growing dislike of writing essays on literary subjects ('. . . the blind, pitiful hypocrisy that is the apparently necessary way to study "Arts". One can see where literary critics are born. My God!') What I really enjoy is simply reading the books, particularly when it involves struggling with French and German, and I feel the unfamiliar words and constructions beginning to dissolve in front of my eyes, to reveal the story, the people, the places lurking inside them.

I also acquire a taste for translation which is going to last for the rest of my life. There's something deeply attractive about a task that combines the closed-endedness of the crossword puzzle, where you know that a preordained solution exists, if only you can find it, with the open-endedness of original composition, where you know that it doesn't. One particular passage we're set for translation into French, though, introduces me to a vice that it will take me seven years and some pains to extirpate – a demonstration that literature really does have the power to corrupt the young mind. We're set a passage for translation into French from Stevenson's *Travels with a Donkey*. Stevenson is four or five thousand feet up on the Mont Lozère at this point, and is spending a night in the open among the pines. At around two o'clock he wakes and rolls himself a cigarette.

The stars were clear, coloured, and jewel-like, but not frosty. A faint silvery vapour stood for the Milky Way . . . I lay lazily smoking and studying the colour of the sky, as we call the void of space, from where it showed a reddish grey behind the pines to where it showed a glossy blue-black between the stars. As if to be more like a pedlar, I wear a silver ring. This I could see faintly shining as I raised or lowered the cigarette; and at each whiff the inside of my hand was illuminated, and became for a second the highest light in the landscape.

How I cope with this quite difficult passage in French I can't recall, but it seizes my imagination in rather the same way as the 'Ode to a Skylark' did. I have fallen in love with cigarettes. I go straight out after school and buy a packet of Players, then that evening walk along the unlit tracks of the local farm under an overcast sky, with a glowing cigarette turned inwards towards my palm, trying to replicate something of the same effect with neither silver ring nor visible stars.

There's an added excitement in studying French and German

with Dr Nichols, aka Gobbo, or, as I refer to him in the diary, simply the Doctor, because of the severe difficulties that he has in communicating, and the endless drama of his struggles to overcome them. He can't even co-ordinate finger and thumb to turn over the page of one of our set texts to show us what he means. He has to lick his thumb and take a jab at it, in the hope that the paper will adhere to the saliva. The pages of our books rapidly become crumpled and loose, blotched with thumb-prints and stuck together with spit.

Before you can learn any French or German from him you have to master not only his version of English, but also the phonetic alphabet, so that he can write out for us on the blackboard the sounds he's trying to make. There's a further problem here, though. The marks he makes on the blackboard are as wildly approximate as the sounds he utters, and the unfamiliar characters of the phonetic alphabet are even less comprehensible than his attempts at the more usual one.

Insofar as possible he writes not on the board but on paper, where he can use a typewriter. This solution, though, brings yet another problem – two problems. The keys that he hits are almost as random as everything else – so he ruthlessly abbreviates and elides in order to reduce the scope for error. After two years of his teaching I become as adept as a cryptographer at reconstructing his thought and following his intentions. A friend who is also doing French for the Cambridge entrance exam shows me the list of topics for revision that Gobbo has prepared for him. It has taken most of his revision time, but he has worked out the meanings of all but one of them, which reads: *Huge pot.*

It takes me some time, too, but in the end I get there: Revise Victor Hugo as a lyric poet.

But the Doctor does it. By sheer, relentless determination and force of personality, lurching about in the ancient brown three-piece pinstripe suit that he wears day in, day out, summer and winter, he teaches us, he teaches us! Spanish, for anyone who wants it, as well as French and German. A little Russian on the side for me. He's a Christian Scientist, and I have to say that he's the most sustained and convincing demonstration of the power of mind over matter I've ever come across. Maybe the difficulties that we in our turn have to overcome to understand him are actually useful practice for linguists.

Year after year he gets the language sixth through their A-Levels. He propels them into Oxford and Cambridge. He does more – he persuades us to be interested in Racine, even if not quite in Corneille. He has us performing Schiller and reading Thomas Mann. Nor does he stop at the official syllabus. Every winter he organises an entertainment for the French Circle and another for the German Circle. In fact the Doctor and his entertainments *are* the French and German Circles, and they have the reassuring familiarity of Christmas. A boy called Loveday plays a violin solo by a French or German composer. Someone recites '*Le Corbeau et le renard*' or sings '*Die Lorelei*'. William Tell shoots Gessler. There's even an audience; the Doctor has gone round the school collecting one, largely by the lobes of their ears, or possibly, in the case of the younger boys, simply by terrifying them into acquiescence by the weirdness of his appearance. None of the audience understands a word of the performance in either language, but everyone claps and cheers, and only in part ironically.

In any case the evening always ends with a straightforward singsong – a scene set in a French café or a German beer garden, with the whole cast in Lederhosen or berets and striped vests, raising glasses of cherryade or ginger beer and singing '*Santa Lucia*' (Italian, it's true, which none of us is doing, but the Doctor has wide European horizons), accompanied by Loveday on the violin, Pratt on the piano-accordion – and the Doctor himself, lurking hugely at the back like an unsteady Eiffel Tower and playing the double bass, on which I suppose the fingering's sufficiently widely spaced for him to hit something approximating to quite a lot of the notes.

In the middle of one of these finales there's a crash like a house falling down, as the Doctor and his double bass suddenly disappear from view. They've wobbled off the back of the stage together, and fallen horizontally on to the floor three feet below. '*Santa Lucia*' wavers, and then continues. The Doctor and bass reappear on stage in time for the last chorus, the Doctor's wrinkled walnut face split by the lopsided grin with which he usually (not always) manages to greet disasters of this sort. One day in class his sudden compulsive twitches are too much for the chair he's sitting on, and with a crunch of breaking timber he vanishes behind the desk as abruptly as from the stage. Mocking cheers from the class. When his head slowly rises above the horizon, like some strange moon, he's clearly in both pain and shock. 'Remember your religion, sir!' calls Grandjean. The moon cracks into its heroic grin.

He often finds time in class for jokes. They're usually the same two, so we get to understand them quite well. The first is very short, about the Frenchman whose new trousers are *Toulouse et Toulon*. The second one's more extended. It concerns a resting actor who's hired to play the part of a major-domo at some grand occasion. All he has to do is to dress up in eighteenth-century costume, walk slowly and solemnly on to the stage, turn to face the audience, thump on the floor three times with a silver-topped staff and cry in a resoundingly authoritative voice: 'Silence!' The actor rehearses the performance many times until it's perfect. The great occasion arrives. On to the stage he slowly and solemnly marches. Turns to face the audience. Thumps three times with his silver-topped staff. Then suddenly loses his nerve. ''Ush!' he squeaks. This second joke has a serious educational message about how easy it is for even the best-prepared candidate to panic in an exam. The first, I think, has no particular pedagogic function. Both give the Doctor great delight, however often he tells them.

As well as favourite jokes he has favourite pupils, and usually about the same number of them. For a time I'm one. 'His receptivity makes it a real pleasure to teach him,' he writes in his first report on me. (Entirely legibly, I see, now that I've found it in an ancient file, so I suppose he must have got someone to write it for him.) My star begins to fade, though, as time goes on, and then sets as abruptly as the Doctor himself on the breaking chair when

I try to liven up the unwelcome prospect of writing yet another literary essay, and on a subject I find particulary dreary – 'clle & t dePictm o ancient rum' ('Corneille and the depiction of ancient Rome'), by doing it not in English prose but in French verse. In alexandrines, to be precise, the way Corneille himself depicted ancient Rome, which are not an easy form, though I don't suppose they're very good alexandrines. Most schoolteachers, in my experience, can switch with disconcerting suddenness from sunshine to thunder, and the Doctor does so now. He sends me, alexandrines in hand, to the headmaster, who finds it difficult to keep a straight face, even before he reads the verses, and mildly recommends me to stick in future to English prose. Lucky for me, perhaps, that I'm not up before the Reverend J. B. Lawton. Uncalled-for alexandrines would probably have merited the cat-o'-nine-tails.

Lane and I are both back before the headmaster for cutting French to watch the Labour Party losing the 1951 election, and my diary later records 'a series of rows with the Doctor', but in between whiles we must have made our peace. There are only four of us doing German, and it's going to be difficult to produce *Wilhelm Tell*, which has a cast of fifty, if even one of us is alienated. He invites me with the rest of the language sixth for his annual treat, chocolate éclairs in the Oak Lounge at Bentalls, then accords me an even greater favour – tea at his home, the gloomy Victorian house in Surbiton where he's looked after by his two adoring sisters, and where he takes me on a guided tour of the collection he has assembled over the years: irregular lumps of stone, indistinguishable one from another without his expert commentary, that he has broken off the leading cathedrals of Europe.

In our last term or two in the sixth form Lane and I have become grandly casual about school. We discuss subjectivity and the shortcomings of our friends not only late at night, on the bleak concrete highways of Stoneleigh and Hook – we also stroll into the centre of Kingston when we have a free period (without our caps, even!) and continue the conversation over coffee and cigarettes.

It's not quite the Flore or the Deux Magots – it's the local branch of a chain of cheap cafeterias called the ABC (the Aerated Bread Company; baffling – isn't most bread aerated?). At weekends we go up to town, when we can raise the fare, and patronise one of the new coffee bars which are beginning to open. It's in Northumberland Avenue, with no aerated bread but a chromium espresso machine as big as a cinema organ blasting steam into the cappuccinos, and a visibly bohemian clientele, where one evening there's a whip-round for one of the girls to get an abortion. And, *nom de nom*, not even Sartre or Camus could blow out a plume of smoke with as much aplomb as Lane and me.

We're coming to the end of this chapter of the story. Of school, of our great friendship. Of living with parents and step-parents, of agonising over girls under the suburban sodium lights. Just our last exams to sit, and then we shall be going our separate ways. Me into the army, Lane into the RAF, to do our National Service. Then for me, if I get in, university. Life.

We make one last trip together. We hitch-hike down to South Wales and walk over the Brecon Beacons and the Black Mountains, talking, of course, singing, drinking beer in pubs and smoking – I seem to recall a pipe by this time. I have a picture that Lane took of me on our last day. I'm in my walking boots, sitting on the upland grass and reclining against my rucksack, the wind in my hair. I look relaxed and happy. There's not the trace of a sneer on my face.

6

Closer

My father winked and clicked his tongue respectfully about Cambridge as we walked round it five or six years earlier. Now the
prospect begins to take shape of my actually stepping through one
of those college gateways myself into the sunlit world beyond –
and he baulks.

How has the idea come up at all? I think because the school
simply assumes that if you have a chance of Oxford or Cambridge
you take it. This is what good grammar schools do at the time.
You stay in the sixth form for a third year and prepare for college entrance; you try for a scholarship or an exhibition. So this
is the timetable my father sees: a third year wasted in the sixth
form, another two doing National Service, then three more frit-
tered away at Cambridge. By the time I emerge to face what's now
called the real world I shall be twenty-five – eleven years older
than he was when he first got a job and started earning his living.

I share the assumptions of the school – but I also share my
father's doubts and impatience. In a spirit of compromise, I suppose, if only with myself, I decide to miss out the third year in the
sixth form and take Cambridge entrance in the second year, which
means that I shall have to be interviewed in my first. Before my
initial shine is tarnished by the alexandrines, therefore, while I'm
still a pleasure to teach, the Doctor arranges for me to go up to
Cambridge and be seen by someone he knows personally.

I don't think I'm fully aware at this point that Cambridge is
made up of separate colleges, and that behind each of those dark
gateways lies a largely autonomous institution with its own character and peculiarities. The name that the Doctor has written down
for me, Emmanuel, or more probably Emmql, has no significance

for me except as the address where I'm to meet Dr weLbn, aka Welbourne. I certainly have no idea that Emmanuel at this time is a sporting college which particularly specialises in boxing, where existential anguish is unknown, or that Welbourne is a much-loved local character who's celebrated for his amusing anti-Catholicism and anti-Semitism. All I know is that at an interview of this sort you must be carrying the *Manchester Guardian* under your arm. I've never seen the paper before, but I buy a copy at Liverpool Street, and discover under the heading 'University News', as I read it on the train, that Dr Welbourne, Senior Tutor of Emmanuel, has just been elected Master, so with improbable urbanity I begin the interview by congratulating him. The only other thing I can remember about the occasion is one of his questions (though not my answer): 'Supposing in years to come you are married and have children. Your children go on a school exchange to France. When they come back you discover that they have been converted to Roman Catholicism. What would your attitude be?'

Impressed either by my knowledge of college politics or my readiness to subject my hypothetical children to rack and thumb-screw until they recant their hypothetical apostasy, he invites me to take the college entrance exam that Christmas, and I manage (just) to scrape a place. My father remains implacable. He declines to find the maintenance allowance I should need of some £300 a year. I suppose he sees a university as simply a way of getting into a job, and as dispensable as a ladder is for getting into a loft. I can't really blame him – not, at any rate, with the benevolence of hindsight. I've already had four years more education than he had himself, and the benefits both to my employability and to my general character are far from obvious. Any further doses of education are likely to make both even worse.

My winning (just) a State Scholarship on the results of my A-Levels that summer softens him briefly – until the Ministry of Education discovers how well-off my parents are between them. My grant will be only the nominal minimum of £30; my father will have to find the balance himself. Again he refuses. Once I've finished my National Service, when I shall already be twenty-one, I shall have to look for a job. What as? I suppose I might have some faint hope of becoming a reporter on the *Epsom and Ewell Gazette*. Or perhaps my father still nurses some even fainter hope of my becoming an asbestos rep. One way or another, though, I'm going to have to start earning my living.

I see, now I think about it, that his expectations of my future are shadowed by his experiences of the past. He looks at me and sees his father and his wife's father, neither of them – even without the debilitating effects of higher education – able to keep a job, neither of them able to support himself or his family. He has spent the first thirty-odd years of his working life maintaining them and their dependants. He can see himself spending the rest of it doing the same for me.

So what happens next is mystifying. He challenges the Ministry's decision. Is this at my urging, or the school's, or has he had second thoughts himself? Still stranger are the grounds for his challenge. He informs the Ministry that my stepmother's resources are not available for my education. This is an entirely specious argument. Whether or not Elsie is prepared to open her handbag and dole out the money to me direct, she's paying most of my father's other expenses in life. I suppose he still has to find my sister's school fees, and the cost of his new suits, and the entrance fees for the paddock at Goodwood and Ascot, but I'm obviously an indirect beneficiary of Elsie's wealth.

All this is curious enough; even less comprehensible is the Ministry's response. They accept my father's argument, though even on the basis of his income alone they will not pay me more than £168 a year. At this point he graciously concedes and agrees to give me the other £115. So in a way he has got me into Cambridge, just as six years earlier he got me into the grammar school. I'm saved from the real world for another three years. Or the real world is saved from me, as my father probably sees it.

First, though, my National Service – and this, as it turns out, is not the waste of time that I've been expecting just as much as he has. My rising tide of good fortune continues. I don't spend the next two years peeling potatoes or whitewashing coal. Nor am I sent, like so many other national servicemen at the time, to risk being killed in Korea, Malaya or Kenya. Within a few weeks of being marched with my apprehensive fellow conscripts into the grim khaki universe of the Royal Artillery's huge basic-training camp at Oswestry I'm out of it again, and have been sent off to learn Russian. Another couple of months and I'm being trained as an interpreter – at Cambridge, in fact, two years before I'm due to arrive as an undergraduate.

No literary essays, much translation. Away from home, with money in my pocket and congenial comrades. In my diary for the next few months there's no trace of existential anguish. 'Life has never been so enjoyable . . . A calm river of contentment which flows on and on . . .'

That calm river doesn't flow on for ever, of course. A few months later I'm managing to be disgusted at myself for enjoying everything so much. The rest of my life, though, at Cambridge and beyond, now that my father has helped launch me upon it, is another story, and not one that I'm going to tell here.

I'm often back in Chez Nous with my father again, first on leave from the army, then on vacation from the university. The geo-politics of the house have changed. My sister – now out at work all day, in Harrods, like our mother before her, though as a children's hairdresser rather than a sales assistant – has taken over my old room. My view of things from the little box room she has vacated has become rather more detached. 'Everything at home is too charged with the past to make present living comfortable,' I tell my diary. 'My desk is full of letters from old friends, about subjects and moods which are no longer a part of me. The drawers and pigeonholes are too crammed with old writings . . . a dreadful collection.' I feel a few evidently fading pangs about Jennifer. 'I don't suppose she has ever remembered me with more than casual regret – and she has another boy. Good luck to her . . .' I'm out of the house as often as possible, in the West End with the new friends I'm making from other parts of London. When Lane and I have thirty-six- or forty-eight-hour passes that coincide, I borrow either my father's rather grand new Wolseley or the precious Box of Bells and (I'm sorry to say) tour the pubs of north Surrey with him. No one at this time has yet remarked upon the likely results of combining drinking with driving.

My relations with my father, now I have a little more distance from him, get paradoxically closer. My journal has shrunk from substantial essays in a substantial ledger to brief paragraphs in a pocket engagement diary, but I still find space to record a number of joint expeditions. We go for walks together (one of them over the Seven Sisters, perhaps as an allusion to the road around which so much of our family's life has centred: 'a delightful day'). A concert at the Festival Hall ('I enjoyed it very much, but Pa heard almost nothing'). The races, where I try to enter into the spirit of things by putting the occasional five bob on a horse being led round the paddock by a pretty stable girl. Billiards in a hall in Epsom where no daylight has been admitted since the blackout – nor air, by the smell of it – and where we're probably the only customers without criminal records. On Coronation Day, when Elsie has invited all the neighbours in to watch proceedings on the television in the living room, my father and I, having no interest in the Queen or her crown, spend a very congenial day in the breakfast room, cutting sandwiches for Elsie's guests and drinking beer together. On Midsummer's Day 1953, when I'm home on leave again, 'Pa and I talked about the stupidity of the army, the brutality of the Russians etc until half-past twelve.'

There are also some of the same old squalls. My diary records a row with him about 'intellectual snobbery' (mine, I imagine, not his), and another about 'State of my Room'. ('What right has he got? Oh blast, fed up. Went and climbed trees . . .') When I'm commissioned, though, and have to open a bank account to get my pay as an officer, he takes me down to Barclay's Bank in Ewell Village and introduces me to the manager, then shows me how to keep a monthly tally of incomings and outgoings. It's not quite double entry, but it's good enough to save me from having my cheques dishonoured and getting myself stripped of my new commission. When I set out too late (as usual) to catch the Newhaven boat train from Victoria he drives me, weaving at speed through and around all the slow-witted weekend motorists, to pick it up at East Croydon.

The car remains a bond between us. And when the time finally comes for me to start taking up his disputed £115 a year (which in practice he has generously increased to £150), and I'm scrambling to get from my last day in the army to my first day of term as an undergraduate, he drives me to Cambridge. Or rather – two birds with one stone – allows Jill, who is now learning in her turn, to drive us both.

He comes up to Cambridge a number of times over the next three years, sometimes on his own, sometimes with Jill, sometimes with his friend Kerry, once, I think, even with Elsie. I've always remembered myself as being shamefully unwelcoming, but my diary suggests that I behave somewhat better than I thought. In summer I take him punting, in winter walk him round in the misty lamplight of the Fenland dusk. Give him lunch in my favourite Indian restaurant (where the girl who has just most painfully dumped me is sitting with her new boyfriend at the next table). I even go to watch cricket with him.

My feelings about all this are not entirely unambiguous. Tea at the Blue Boar is 'surprisingly successful', but tea in my rooms is not: 'Could scarcely bear my family, particularly father.' I have the impression, though, that he gets a bit of a kick out of these visits. He may even assure me, with the usual knowing wink, that it's not a bad old university I've got myself into. A son at the Varsity (as he probably thinks of it) may seem to him to go rather well with the Harrods suits and shirts.

Then when I come down, at the end of my three years, all his old suspicions and forebodings return with a rush. 'Pass your exams?' he asks me with careful casualness, as if they had been the Elephant and Castle. I tell him I got a two-one. The esoteric university jargon puts his back up at once.

'A do-what?'

'A *two-one*.'

'What's that supposed to be?'

'Well, you can get a first, or a two-one, or a two-two, or . . .'

'Hold on.' Quick as ever to take the point. 'So you were supposed to get a first? And you didn't? You've failed? I knew it wouldn't come to anything, going to Cambridge.'

All right, I've failed. Gratifyingly. I've wasted the last three years – wasted the first twenty-four years of my life. Now I'm going to waste the rest of it. He's arming himself against disappointment once again.

'Well, you've had your fun,' he says heavily. 'Now you've got to start looking for a job.'

'I've got one,' I tell him. I hope I manage to sound offhand about it in my turn.

'*Got* one?' He looks at me carefully. He's probably remembering that I have actually sometimes found paid employment in the past, in spite of his scepticism. I've been a Christmas postman, a van driver, a warehouseman, a sawyer's mate. Perhaps, he's thinking, I did rather better at one of these occupations than he'd supposed. It's not Christmas, and I dented the van, but maybe the sawmill thought highly enough of me to take me back. 'What sort of job?' he asks warily.

'Reporter,' I tell him. 'On the *Manchester Guardian*.'

Quick as he is, it takes him a moment or two to think of a comeback to this. He may not realise that to have got this particular job is for me more or less the equivalent for him of a five-horse accumulator coming up at Sandown, but he has certainly heard of the *Manchester Guardian*. Has never read it, but has told me, with his usual vicarious connoisseurship, what a reputation it's got.

'Are they paying you?' he says finally. 'Or are you paying them?'

This is a retreat under cover of humour. I think. For the second time the *Guardian* has come to my rescue. And a few days later he comes back from the office and says in a rather different tone of voice that he has been talking to his colleague Greenwood, whose son has also just come down from Cambridge – and also with a two-one. 'Greenwood,' concedes my father reluctantly, 'says a two-one's some kind of pass.'

So I haven't entirely wasted my life after all. He may not have to spend his declining years keeping me from destitution.

When the day arrives for me to move to Manchester, he drives me once again. From Stoke-on-Trent north it rains. The wind-screen wipers beat hypnotically back and forth, and he tells me some of the stories about his childhood that I've mentioned in this book. We sing the old songs. 'Fling wide the . . . fling wide the . . . fling wide the gates.' 'Come, come, come and make eyes at me . . .'

Now I really am finally flying the nest; no more 48s or long vacations. So far as I can recall it's the last time that he has a chance to drive me anywhere.

Did he really think I was as unemployable as he seemed to – and as I certainly thought he thought?

I'm not sure. It wasn't the style then to encourage your children too openly – and in the hard world in which my father grew up disparagement was probably thought to help form their character. Many years later my second wife's sister, who was selling prop-erty to English ex-pats in the Lot-et-Garonne, told me that a couple of her clients had met my father somewhere and he'd told *them* that he was actually rather proud of me. I couldn't help being pleased by this circuitous and belated testimony, and wanting to believe it. I'm a little cautious, all the same. I really did lack many of the qualities that my father's very different experience of life had taught him were necessary, and he really was apprehensive for me.

To me, certainly, he continued to hold my career and ambitions at arm's length. In the letters he wrote to me when I was away from home he protects himself with a rather heavy facetiousness;

but then in correspondence he's off his territory, the face-to-face joshing in which he specialises, and he knows that I have ambitions to make the written form mine. He expects, he says in one letter sent while I was still at Cambridge, that an advertisement he's seen for the *Observer* (possibly the one I'd just written myself to win the paper's student copywriting competition) 'is the genial sort of flapdoodle you yourself will be inflicting on a gullible public in the not too distant future'. Even when I was actually employed by the *Guardian*, and they had turned out to be paying me rather than vice versa, it apparently didn't occur to him to start taking the paper and reading what I wrote. 'Our only reader of the MG in the office', he says, 'has not reported any fireworks from MF.'

He seems to have softened briefly when I was away with the Royal Navy, reporting the so-called Cod War off Iceland in 1958, perhaps because it was the only way to get news of me. He's as facetiously deflating as ever, though: 'Have followed the breathtaking reports from our Special Correspondent with interest . . .' – and he can't resist adding, in case I'm getting too big for my seaboots: 'You won't always be able to make the front page.' Later on, when I was writing a column for the *Observer*, he seems to have read me sometimes. 'Good piece last Sunday,' he concedes in one letter, though the corroborating details that a writer likes to hear are missing. And I remember his being hurt at another piece in which I'd mocked family occasions where everyone talks about the clever routes they've taken to get there. He thought it was about him; I thought I'd fictionalised it beyond recognition.

I look at those letters now and I see not just the mockery but the affection that it conceals. He's pre-empting my intellectual (and social) snobbery, protecting himself from his own vulnerability. There are the usual complaints of parent to offspring about neglect, most of them facetious. When I'm in America for a few months he's 'suffering no eye strain from reading the letters that stream across the Atlantic'. Sometimes, though, he's more direct: 'I was a little hurt that you departed for Cambridge without saying farewell.' There's recognisable anguish in his letters when I spend Christmases away, once working in a refugee camp, once with some of my grand new friends. And when later I confide in him about my difficulties in a relationship with a divorced woman six or seven years older than myself he replies with quite surprising tact, gentleness and insight. He thanks me for writing so frankly, and says he trusts I realise that 'if this venture isn't successful then indeed it is a particularly sad thing for [E] after her earlier tribulations. I know you will both have given this your fullest consideration, and since you both are intelligent, you should be able to make a success of it. I won't go into all the pros and cons here but it would please me if you could come down in the near future – if this is difficult, I could come up . . . We should very much like to have [E] for Xmas.'

Why couldn't we always have talked to each other like this?

Meanwhile my father soldiers on at Chez Nous, as persistent in his second marriage as he had always required me to be in my own failed enterprises. Through the good bits – the holidays with Elsie in Switzerland and Holland; through the bad bits – her week-long, month-long depressions; with my sister on his side, with her on Elsie's side. My occasional reappearances fail to change the pattern much. 'Elsie-trouble,' says one brief entry in my diary when I'm home on leave. Then again: 'Slight relaxation of no-talking rule.' A week later: 'Row with Elsie. Air cleared. Talking.' Another visit: 'Home. Incredible hell from first moment.'

In 1959, two years after I started work on the *Guardian*, I took my future wife, Gill, down to Ewell for Sunday lunch to meet my parents. As we drove off afterwards we hadn't reached the end of Queensmead Avenue before she burst out. 'That was the most awful woman I've ever met!' she cried. I thought I had prepared her, but evidently not thoroughly enough. You get used to anything in time, and I'd forgotten quite how powerful an impression Elsie might make upon someone at a first meeting. She had evidently misidentified Gill as another Michael Lane. Within minutes of being introduced, Elsie had taken her out to the breakfast room and poured forth her venom about my father. 'She was plain, dumpy, and her voice was raucous,' wrote Gill when I asked her recently about her recollections of this disastrous encounter, and she remembered that Elsie had for good measure also denounced my previous girlfriend, the older divorcee, not because she was older or divorced – though I remember Elsie making her feelings plain to me at the time on both counts – but because she'd helped herself from the fruit bowl without asking.

She alienated Gill still further by telling her about her wonderful first husband, Frank Smith of blessed memory. Much later Gill asked Doris, Elsie's sister, if the first marriage had really been as happy as all that. 'Doris just rolled her eyes . . . Very similar problems . . . Elsie had never accepted the family's hardship when they were growing up and had never done a hand's turn to help out. She was always set on becoming a wealthy woman but it was never good enough even when it materialised thanks to Ye Olde Oak ham . . .' Elsie and my father, says Gill, were 'a complete and utter mismatch'. Gill liked my father (as he did her, in a rather awestruck way), and it was Elsie's attack on him for which Gill could never forgive her.

One of the things that Elsie told Gill about him, while Gill 'gallantly tried to adjust to the idea we were not just going to have a pleasant Sunday lunch', was that she'd found the photograph of another woman in his pocket. Neither of us can remember now for sure, but I think that this was the first that we'd heard of her – the third (I'm fairly sure) and certainly final woman in my father's life.

Gill and I are planning a very quiet and private wedding – partly, I think, to avoid any further Sunday-lunch effects – but her mother insists that we must at any rate have our immediate families present. So there we all stand in the official photograph on the steps of Kensington Register Office, with me gazing in bemused delight at my astonishingly beautiful bride, and flanking us our two families, who are meeting for the first time: our siblings and their partners, our two fathers side by side in their well-tailored dark overcoats, my stepmother and Gill's mother . . . No, I've just noticed for the first time, looking again at the copy I made of the photograph many years later, that there's no sign of my new mother-in-law. She's there in the original, Gill assures me, and has evidently got cut off in the copy because she's fled to the outer edges of the group to get away from Elsie, who has produced much the same effect upon her as she did upon Gill herself. 'She kept putting her face so close to mine,' she complains to Gill afterwards. Her mother had become 'alarmed', says Gill; and she is not someone who is alarmed easily.

It's February, and as the light fades at the end of the short winter day Gill and I drive off in our tiny Renault *quatre chevaux* for our honeymoon. Nothing's fixed, nothing's planned. We seem to be heading in a generally westerly direction, down the old Great West Road, and for the next few days we wander about the Cotswolds and the Mendips, as free as birds. Our families and the variously ordered lives they have constructed for themselves are behind us. Before us is the open road, and all the endless possibilities of a life not yet lived. We sing as we drive. 'Fling Wide the Gates', of course, and 'The Old Bull and Bush', but also new songs, the songs my father never knew, including all eleven verses of *'Auprès de ma blonde'*. The hills of Somerset and Gloucestershire, the plains of Wiltshire, fly past the windows of the little Renault. How lightly we move over the earth, and how unlike the girl in the song we are as she mourns the happiness she has lost!

Meanwhile Gill's parents are back on the South Coast, no doubt still exchanging appalled comments on the new relations they have just acquired, and mine are back in Ewell. Two months after me my sister gets married and moves out, and henceforth every evening and all weekend my father and Elsie and the ageing, increasingly evil-smelling dog are left alone together. Except for each Saturday morning, when they have a visitor – my sister, bustling cheerfully back to see what she can get for Tich on her weekly shopping trip. Until one Saturday, for reasons which my sister finds compelling but can never explain so that anyone else can understand (bought Elsie her groceries in the wrong shop, Gill says), she and Elsie fall out, and don't see or speak to each other again for eleven years.

I doubt if there are any visitors at all at Chez Nous after this. My father and Elsie are totally alone. Alone with the hide arm-chair that has its back turned towards the television set, the Ye Olde Oak on the supper table, the smell of the dog in his basket beside it, Elsie's ever-longer silences, the memory of the photo-graph in the pocket, and each other.

One day at the beginning of 1962, when my father just happens to be passing through Notting Hill, and his homburg and smile have appeared round the door of the two-room flat where Gill and I are then living, I tell him that he's going to become a grand-father. The news leaves him surprisingly unmoved; perhaps he has other things on his mind. Gill's contractions begin in the small hours of Sunday, 6 May, and at first light I drive her to the old Charing Cross Hospital. The avenues of Hyde Park are deserted in the spring dawn air, and the bright new green leaves and the fresh blossom of the horse-chestnut trees are totally still, as if the whole world is holding its breath for us.

All day Gill's labour goes on, agonising and exhausting. It's evening when our daughter is put into my arms. She screws up her eyes and utters a blast of angry sound, louder and more furi-ous than I could have imagined possible. Her tiny jaw vibrates with the violence of it – and it's this that shatters me. I have one of those sudden thunderclaps of enlightenment that makes theor-etical knowledge concrete and real. I understand, as perhaps my father did when I was put it into his arms nearly twenty-nine years earlier, that this is *another human being* – not an extension of her mother or me, but an individual quite separate from either of us, whose standpoint in the world is unique and whose will is sovereign – a self, just as each of us is. A new life has begun, and a new generation.

Forty-seven years later that little scrap of human willpower is going to persuade me to write this book, and to tell her a little more about the world, for ever lost to her, which has helped to make her what she is.

As I get back to our flat late that evening, almost too tired to take my clothes off, the phone's ringing.

'Where have you been?' says my father, audibly displeased. 'I've been trying to call you all day.'

He'd wanted me to help him move his stuff, he explains, out of Chez Nous and into a furnished flat he's found at short notice. I don't suppose there was much to move – no more than he could ferry in the back of his car, probably, but I suppose he was hoping for some moral support on what must have been a very bleak day in his life. No chance to give me any advance warning; Elsie had only just told him that the moving van was arriving first thing Monday for all the contents of the house apart from him. She has sold it from under him, and is moving to Hove.

I explain to him where I've been all day. He's not entirely mollified.

7

Legatees

The flat my father has found is in Wimbledon, in a vaguely Georgian-looking post-war block with vaguely Regency-looking furnishings – the kind of place husbands move into at short notice when they've been thrown out by their wives. My father's personal possessions are too few to make much visible impact upon it; his hearing aid and a copy of *The Times* on the vaguely Festival of Britain coffee table, perhaps a mug of tea or Nescafé that he's made for himself. (Cookery – a new activity for him, because the only thing to eat or drink that I can remember his ever making before were the sandwiches we cut for Elsie's coronation guests.) His footprint on the earth is lighter than ever. The flat has two rooms, so he's back to where he was when he started out in life sixty years earlier, in Devonshire Road. Except that in these two rooms he's alone.

Or is he? Somewhere in the background of his life lurks another person, the woman Elsie has seen in the photograph. None of the rest of us has caught the slightest glimpse of her.

I'm not sure that we know even her name yet. We're simply aware, from things he says, that he has another life going on. He's not always as we see him, sitting alone in the flat, or coming alone to tea with us. He has been for walks in the country, to concerts at the Festival Hall – and not just as 'I' but as 'we'. At some point he must actually mention her name, though, because we begin to ask politely after her: 'And how is Gladys?'

Gladys, yes. Mrs Steele. But we never meet her. My father invites Gill and me to tea, or my sister and her husband Robin, or all four of us, and there's nothing to see in the flat but the carefully impersonal furniture, the hearing aid, *The Times*, the tea things. He's making tea for one, for three, for five, but apparently never for two. Often, though, you have an indefinable feeling that somebody else has just been there but left no trace. We boldly ask him if he'd like to bring her when he comes to lunch or tea with us. It's never possible for her, though; she has an elderly mother to look after, who seems to require attention at every imaginable mealtime.

Why is he so bashful about her? Why doesn't he tell us that he wants to have a little talk with us, as he did when he first took up with Elsie? Sit us down on the Regency-style soft furnishings. Say: 'Supposing I were to tell you that I'm having a relationship with someone? She doesn't have a dog or a radiogram – but on the other hand she's not manic-depressive, and we don't all have to move into her house.' I suppose he's embarrassed. He's still married, after all, and he's more conventional than he seems. Gladys, he makes clear, is divorced. What we don't know yet is that she's thirty years younger than him.

Then again, time has continued to change the politics of the family. My sister and I are both married, and it would be difficult to catch us on our own for a little private talk. He would have to address all four of us together, half of us still comparative strangers; it would be like testifying at an evangelical prayer meeting. And we've all become so respectable. Gill and I are acquiring a second daughter, my sister and Robin their first son. We're family people, with homes to guard and the values and ideals that this entails. We've committed ourselves to a way of life that perhaps seems to exclude enjoying yourself in the company of young women you're not married to. My father's a bit in awe of my sister now, in any case; she's helping Robin to set up a new business and, as my father reports to me with an astonishment and respect that none of my efforts in life has ever elicited from him, has mastered double-entry book-keeping. I think he might have taken me into his confidence if I'd been on my own. I could have returned some of the understanding that he showed me when I confided in him about that relationship of my own a few years earlier.

Now that both his children have parents-in-law he's no longer the single head of the family, merely one of three, and he's being absorbed into the increasingly complex cat's cradle of relationships that we're weaving to cocoon our children. My sister and Robin (soon with a second son) are part of a network that also involves all Robin's relatives; Gill and I (with a third daughter) of a network that also involves hers. The two networks overlap; we supply each other with the extra uncles and aunts that our children need. We spend alternate Christmases with each other, we designate each other as potential foster-parents. Each set of children needs a pair of grandfathers, so our father finds himself as half of each pair. Saturday with this one, Sunday with that. Lunch here, tea there. Presents and birthday cards going off in two different directions by every post. Gladys bundled out of the flat as Jill and Robin arrive. Gladys back – no, out again, because here come Gill and I.

A full complement of three grandmothers the family can't supply. Only the two, one on Gill's side and one on Robin's, plus, occasionally, a step-grandmother in Hove. And the ghost of a quasi-step-grandmother, in Wimbledon.

We reopen family ties that have been effectively extinct for years. The children have more great-uncles and second cousins than they have teddy bears, more places to go to tea on Sunday afternoons than there are Sunday afternoons. On my side of the family alone there are Uncle Sid, Auntie Phyllis, Cousin Jean and Nanny. Phil and Doris. Cousin Maurice and Enid and their three sons. Cousin John and Joyce and their daughter. Cousin Philip and Hazel and their two daughters . . . And often we take our children's grandfather with us.

We're recreating for the next generation the overcrowded dining room of our own childhood, the convivial scrum around the tea table, the conversations about how to get across London. We're bringing back to life as best we can the uncle with the beetling eyebrows, the glamorous young aunt with the Evening in Paris, the whistling grandfather with the plus fours and the enormous lap. We're putting the whole show back on the road.

*

For three years my father keeps up the farcical alternation of Gladys and the rest of us. Then one Saturday morning Gill and I, in Wimbledon for some other reason, call in on him unannounced. And there she is.

She certainly makes a change from Elsie. Everything about her – her style of dressing, her whole manner – suggests that the self-effacement she has been practising for the last few years comes quite naturally to her. If the living room of my father's flat had been any larger we might never have noticed her standing there, smiling awkwardly, already getting her things together to take flight. We insist that she stays, tell her how pleased we are to meet her at long last, physically restrain her. She does a lot of smiling. She's reluctant to sit down.

She looks as if she has served in the war; as Gill notes, she has a distinctly ATS hair style. I've just discovered the registration of her birth, though, and it was in 1931 – she's only two years older than me. She speaks very gently and softly. This is the most surprising thing about her – that she speaks so softly to my father – more softly to him, I think, than to anyone else. Slowly and clearly, though, and looking smilingly straight at him. He smiles back, and seems to have no difficulty in understanding her.

She's head of the typing pool at Turners Asbestos, and in time we realise that she's probably a firmer boss than her manner suggests; although she's divorced from Mr Steele she retains some of the qualities suggested by his name. She carries herself very erect and has alarmingly authoritarian views, expressed with deceptive mildness. She lives with her aged mother in a tiny terraced house in Mitcham. Many of my father's complex short cuts on his way into work pass through Mitcham – or did while he was still living in Ewell. This is how it started, apparently, when he began giving her lifts to the office and back during a train strike.

Anyway, the farce is over. We invite them both to dinner, with Jill and Robin, and from then on Gladys is incorporated into our web of interconnected relationships. This gives my father his cue for how to introduce her at social occasions – she's 'a friend of the family'. His embarrassment hasn't disappeared. They begin to go on holiday together, or to admit that they do, but my father's careful to stress to me the difficulty of getting two single rooms. He retains his flat in Wimbledon, she the little house in Mitcham. There's no sign – or no sign that I'm allowed to see – of their ever being at only one of the addresses overnight. Perhaps they never are. I wish I could put my arm round his shoulder and say, 'Dad! Please! Simplify your holiday bookings! Don't pay more than one lot of rates and gas bills!' But I can't. I do try to persuade Elsie, since I'm still on speaking terms with her, to do what I think my father himself feels unable to suggest – to divorce him. She scornfully refuses.

It's only a year after Gladys has joined the visible world that my father reaches sixty-five, and has to retire from Turners Asbestos. He has been dreading this for some time – not so much for the loss of earnings as for the loss of occupation. He can't face the prospect of sitting around all day with nothing to do, he tells me. The skills that he deployed to insinuate me into the grammar school haven't failed him, however. At an age when no one can get a proper job he gets one, travelling South London to sell the services of a firm called Wembley Roofing. The work calls on all his old abilities, all his knowledge of the South London streets, all his old contacts. He obviously does well, because he and Gladys become personal friends of the managing director and his wife. There are photographs of all four of them together in evening clothes, with impressive ranges of wine glasses on the gleaming tablecloth in front of them. This is a good period of his life – the best, I think, since that November night in 1945.

Perhaps my sister and I *have* got the whole show going again. Found a grandfather for our children, a happy father for ourselves.

Three years this Indian summer lasts, then my father goes into hospital for tests. The results are not good. He has cancer of the bladder.

*

The hospital where the tumour's cut out of him is in Wimble-don. The drive there in the days and weeks that follow the oper-ation, through the tail of the rush hour, from south-east London to south-west, gives me an intimacy with the South Circular and its various escape routes and back-doubles that almost expunges the memory of the Elephant and Castle.

He always smiles as I approach his bed, however bad he's feel-ing. Which I think really is pretty bad. 'Not too clever today,' he often has to admit – long one of his phrases – or, a new one to me: 'All my wickets are down.' Gladys is there already, with clean pyjamas and news from his old office. On the better days he and I look at the *Times* crossword together. The hospital chaplain has come to give him comfort, he reports one evening – and succeeded handsomely, because my father derives considerable satisfaction from the smartness with which he chased the poor fellow off. We don't say that much to each other, though. It's difficult for him to hear even Gladys amid the hushed murmurings of visiting time, and anyway there isn't much to say. We smile at him. He smiles at us. Worth coming just for his smile.

I fetch him when he's discharged. The car's still a bond between us; but there's another change in the politics here, because of course it's my car now, not his, and I'm the one who's doing the driving. I take him not to the flat in Wimbledon but to Gladys's house. He's still so weak, and so in need of care, that his concern for the proprieties has had to be laid aside. Gladys has set up a single bed in a downstairs room, where I sit for as much of each day as I can while she's at work. He's in worse pain than ever, and it's frightening to be on my own with him, because I don't know what to do, except give him painkillers and get the doctor round yet again. Bits of the lining of his bladder, explains the doctor, are still coming away, and passing agonisingly through his urethra. This is where it hurts so much, he says, unable to sit or lie still – in what he calls his pipe or his John Thomas. I've never heard him use either expression before. But then I've never before heard him refer to the genitals, his own, mine or anyone else's, or anything else connected with the human sexual function. Nor have I ever seen him in such pain, not even with his ulcer or his slipped disc.

There's another inhibition that he overcomes, too. The day after his discharge from hospital he writes to thank me for visiting him – and he does it simply and truly, from the heart. I will consider the letter unnecessary, he says, but he would feel slightly uncomfortable if he failed to write it. I'm so moved by what he says next that I find it difficult even to copy it here: 'There were many times in hospital when your visits seemed the mainstay of my existence.'

And here's what I find even more difficult to say: I didn't reply.

I not only didn't reply in writing – I don't think I even mentioned the letter as I sat by his bedside in Mitcham. He had opened his heart, and spoken as we should all like to speak, and to be spoken to; and I failed to respond. Why? I can't understand it. The contrast with the way in which my children have behaved with me is humiliating. Rebecca has tried to console me for my failure. 'If there was reticence between you,' she wrote when I told her about this, 'you were both simply products of your time. As all children do, you took your cue from him and from the prevailing sensibility. I imagine he would have been very disconcerted if you'd broken the powerful conventions of emotional restraint.'

True. Except that for once he *had* broken them! And I hadn't taken his hand through the breach he'd made. I have done a number of things in life, before then and since, that I'm not proud of, but I usually know why I did them, or think I do. This one, though, continues to baffle and shame me.

It's true that the relations between me and my father were shaped by the conventions of the time, and that those conventions have changed. I wish I could believe, though, that I'd been able to give him even a little of the joy that my children have given me.

And then I think . . . perhaps I did, just a bit. In spite of my failure to be a cricketer, and my intellectual snobbery, and my failure to write home. The same strange thought recurs, and it's one that it's taken me all these years to think: the realisation that he loved my sister and me, and that we brought him happiness. Perhaps that's why he would detour halfway across South London to drop in. And when he put the hat and the smile round my door and saw me sitting there, it could be that he felt something of what I feel when I catch sight of *my* children. So this may be what it was like being him, on the other side of his smile. Perhaps, in spite of all our differences in character, he was driven in his inmost heart by some of the same helpless passions as I am.

Gladys nurses him slowly back to health. She speaks to him as softly and smilingly as ever, and he smilingly understands what she says. If ever she regrets finding herself tied to an ageing invalid she gives no sign of it. He moves back to the flat in Wimbledon and returns to work. That winter he rings me in a state of some excitement about a series of articles I've written on Cuba. 'You ought to do more of this kind of thing,' he says encouragingly. He has already been enthusiastic, just before he went into hospital, about my first television play. I think he has at last begun to see that the genial flapdoodle I inflict on a gullible public might be a halfway acceptable alternative to cover drives and leg breaks, to orders for roofing and rainwater goods.

Our visits back and forth resume, our tours of the outlying relations. We all go to Billericay together, where Sid and Phyllis have been living for many years now. Sid's as cheerful as ever, long retired from the cigarette industry but still loyally doing his best to consume its products. He has heart problems, and arthritis so bad that his legs scarcely function any more, even with two sticks to lean on. He has become what he always warned me against being – a home man; but he heroically drives himself over to see us in his specially adapted car, and heroically shifts his considerable bulk upstairs to our first-floor living room. He's still as joshing as ever. At the head of the staircase he pauses to recover from the climb, and is greatly assisted by the sight of our Matisse lithograph, a girl's head established in half a dozen skimpily sketched lines. 'Well, Michael,' he laughs happily, 'whoever sold you this certainly saw you coming. Why didn't you just get one of the girls to knock something up for you?'

By this time getting even downstairs to his own living room at home each day has become become an act of heroism. Nanny can't get downstairs at all now. My glamorous aunt with the Evening in Paris has devoted her life to caring for two long-term invalids. 'It won't be long now,' says Nanny, when I visit her in her little bedroom, 'I shan't be here next time you come.' And finally, after being wrong about her life expectancy for so long, for at least since my father first met her in Gatcombe Road in 1919, she turns out to be right, though it's taken her ninety-seven years to manage it.

I go to see her in hospital for one last time a day or two before she dies. She doesn't see me; her ancient pale watery eyes can no longer see anything. I take her hand and tell her who I am. 'Oh, it's Michael!' she cries feebly, with a delight that pierces me to the heart for all my teasing of her when I was a child, all my neglect of her since. She doesn't make any predictions this time; she doesn't need to. She just weeps and says over and over again: 'I held you in my arms! I held you in my arms!' She means when I was born, her first grandchild, thirty-six years earlier, in the flat over the off-licence in Mill Hill.

My father, though, is in another good phase. There's a photograph of him taken by Gladys when they're on holiday that summer, I think in the Canaries, and hatless. Almost all his hair has gone by now, but he's suntanned and he has a particularly wide and relaxed smile on his face. He looks in some indefinable way *young*, and as happy as I've ever seen him.

Back in London the hat resumes its appearances round the door, with the smile not far behind it. Sometimes the children are at home, and he makes far more impression on them than I realise at the time. Jenny, who's born in 1967, is too young to remember him, though she sometimes brings him to mind for me because she has a lot of his cheek and quickness, not to mention his double-jointedness. But Rebecca, who was only just eight when he died, recalls him as 'an immensely benevolent man with a dazzling smile . . . I still remember the desolation when he died, that this great warmth of spirit could possibly be finite. I also vividly remember telling my teacher at school and walking home afterwards, astonished and then sick at heart that it must be true, since she hadn't – as I had somehow hoped – denied it . . . It's his smile that remains still in my mind's eye.'

Even Susanna, who was only six when he died, has a vivid recollection of sitting in his lap on one of those days when he just happened to be passing. 'He was wearing his hat and I remember asking him where he got it. And he spun a wonderful story about the Hat Tree, accompanied by many smiles and hugs. I remember the intoxicating delight of sitting on his knee, the focus of his full attention, knowing that he was teasing me, but being entranced and amused by his tall tale. He was a very funny man. And I remember that smile. It's your smile, too . . .'

Then at Christmas the final act begins.

We're all at my sister's for Boxing Day. My father has a headache. He takes some aspirin; the headache persists, and gets worse. He withdraws from the table and sits at one side of the room with his head in his hands, suddenly no longer young and no longer happy. The headache goes on all day – and all next day, then every day. He goes back into hospital for tests, and the source of the headache is diagnosed. His cancer has followed one of the established pathways from the bladder; he has a tumour on the brain.

By March he's in a pitiable state, helpless and confused, and he has only weeks left to live. Gladys by this time has moved to a larger and more agreeable house in the outer suburbs, and she installs him there, in a sunny back bedroom. Whether she guessed what was coming, and deliberately picked a house at Banstead, I don't know, but the ambulance has only a mile or two to take him each day for his treatment in the Royal Marsden, the great cancer hospital. Soon he's no longer fully in control of his bodily functions, or fully in touch with the world around him. 'I can't help thinking there are lions in the room,' he says to me apologetically one day. 'I don't suppose there really are, but would you mind just checking? I think I can hear them . . . Over by the chest of drawers, perhaps . . .'

Gladys sits with him through the long nights. While she's out at work my sister and I take turns. I'm glad to have someone sharing the job – Jill was too busy the first time round having her second child. He doesn't seem to be in pain now, but he sometimes needs cleaning up – and in any case I'm trying to slip away from time to time to meet famous actors and actresses who may be persuaded to star in my first play. I sometimes feel as if I'm an actor myself, moving back and forth between the brightly lit artificial world on one side of a door and the makeshift gloom behind it.

But he's on a hiding to nothing. Soon the task is beyond the three of us, and the Marsden take him into their wards. The smart lad who was always so quick, and so impatient of my slowness, is now no longer capable of organised thought, and, in a reversal which would once have seemed unimaginable, I have to get a power of attorney to manage his affairs for him. He's never made a will, of course, any more than he's ever taken out an insurance policy, so what little he possesses will go by default to his wife – to Elsie, who has all the money she can possibly need, and who has done nothing for my father in the last eight years except put him on the street. My sister and I are so appalled that we confect a will for him to sign at the same time as the power of attorney, leaving the money to Gladys, who could actually do with it, who has looked after him as devotedly in sickness as in health, and who has given him a little happiness again at the end of his life. By the time various bills have been paid there's a balance of some £1,500 in his account. When Gladys gets the money she insists that we give a share of it to Nellie, his one surviving sibling – and that we somehow make it seem as if he, not she, had intended her to have it.

My father, I assure the solicitor when I send him the will and the power of attorney, 'was in a quite lucid condition when these two documents were signed. I explained the import of them both very carefully, and he understood and definitely assented to them both.' I think this is reasonably true – he's certainly conscious, and the consultant who's treating him, present for the signing, believes he can understand. He can no longer write, though, and on the power of attorney he has to make his mark, just as his illiterate grandmother did when she registered his mother's birth over a century earlier. His index finger no longer bends concave to the pen, as it did to his old silver Eversharp to produce all those columns of tiny figures on his sales reports. He can barely hold it at at all, and the mark, scarcely even an X, is as faint and wandering as the random trace left by an insect. By the time we come to the will he's too exhausted even to do this, and I have to guide his hand.

I write to tell Elsie that he's dying (though I don't tell her about the will). 'Poor old boy,' she says when she phones back, shortly but not entirely unsympathetically, and when we get to the funeral she sends flowers. I later post on to her the necessary form to enable her to claim her widow's benefits, and I think she must take it up, because I have a card in the file that was sent to my father by his local Ministry of Social Security office – apparently almost as confused as he was – to tell him, a month after he died, that his claim has been transferred to their Hove office 'as it is thought that you will find this more convenient'.

Elsie survives another three years. Even at the end – very frightened, according to her sister Doris, between a first heart attack and the second that finished her – she won't let Doris call a doctor. Almost all the other relatives from my childhood who come into the earlier chapters of this story are now long gone. Most of the relatives on my father's side that I know about die before their time, like my father himself and his father, from one form of cancer or another: his sister Daisy, his brother George, his nephew Maurice. Phil wheezes on into his seventies and Doris, who loyally sewed in Phil's cigarette smoke, continues into her mid-eighties. Sid holds on somehow until he's seventy-two. Phyllis outdoes even her mother; she died only four years ago at the age of ninety-eight. Nellie, my father's eldest sister, is the longest-lived of my father's family. I can't find the date of her death, but she's still alive in her late eighties, and able to be astonished at finding that anyone in the family was rich enough to bequeath her £300.

My father doesn't leave much else behind. In all his sixty-nine years he has still never mastered the arts of acquisition and possession. He has no house of his own, of course, and long before he's actually dead his employers have with some embarrassment reclaimed the car for his successor. When the Royal Marsden can do nothing more for him he's moved to a hospice, and after his death the matron hands me the belongings he has left. Apart from a dressing gown and a cardigan they fit comfortably into a rather small cardboard box. In the accompanying inventory he's reduced to much the same sparse list as I suppose everyone is in such documents:

> 1 pr slippers
> 1 pr socks
> Toilet bag and contents
> Sweets
> Cards, battery
> 1 signet ring
> Specs
> Hearing-aid
> Watch

Years later Gladys passed the watch on to me. There must have been a few other bits and pieces left behind in her house along with his clothes, because apart from that wristwatch she also gave me a couple of pocket watches, one a steel Ingersoll which I think he was perhaps using when I was a child, and one with a battered gold case which I recall him wearing in the breast pocket of his elegant suits in the fifties. And when, five years ago, Gladys herself died (only seventy-two, also of cancer), one of her executors gave me, rather in the manner of my father's supposed bequest to his sister, two pictures that they thought she would have wished me to have. They're ink and wash, and I recognised them instantly: *A Bit of Old London* and *St Gall, Switzerland* – the last faint, improbably preserved traces of my childhood at 3 Hillside Road.

My father left few possessions but a very adequate posterity: my sister and me; my three daughters; my sister's two sons; my seven grandchildren; my sister's four. No doubt there will be more as the years go by – the last traces of my father, spreading wider and wider through the world from one generation to the next, as long as the world and the generations continue.

To me personally he left a fortune – an intangible and unrecorded legacy more precious than money or anything he might ever have written down. The humour he used to deal with his customers and circumvent his deafness; his indifference to all systems of belief; the smile on his face that I sometimes find so disconcertingly on mine. My very existence, in the first place, of course – and the beginnings of a life that turned out to be so much easier than his. I didn't have to share two rooms with six other people, or a kitchen and lavatory with four more. I didn't have to leave school at fourteen, or go out and sell things, or support feckless parents and in-laws. He loved me, saw to it that I was fed and clothed and educated, and left me reasonably free to get on with things in my own way. What more can anyone want from a father?

I didn't even have to care for him or my mother in old age. They didn't intentionally clear themselves away with such promptitude, but all the same my sister and I were spared the burdens that the longevity of parents has imposed upon so many of my contemporaries.

Anyway, he *did* leave me physical possessions, in a way. He left me that house in Hillside Road, even though he didn't own it. He left me the Bentalls suite, even though it was going to go on the tip. He left me the rusty chopper and the flooded air-raid shelter and the feasting cardinals, even though they've all long ago vanished off the face of the earth. Perhaps, after all, my mother's story of the pirate ship contained a grain of truth. There *was* gold in the family, waiting only for me to claim it, though it was amassed by a twentieth-century salesman rather than a sixteenth-century pirate. Out of it I have made a childhood, and the person I became. Some of it has found its way into the stories I've written. And now into this true account of my inheritance.

Or as true an account as I can manage, given the weakness for fiction that my father also left me.

Looking after our father in his last illness and dealing with his death bring my sister and me closer than we've been since that other death, twenty-five years earlier. In the years that follow, though, our lives begin to change. For both of us old longings and possibilities, apparently extinguished for ever in the placid waters of family life, begin to stir. We both run a little wild, and, in the devastation that follows, both our families break apart. Has our father's death snapped some last invisible link in a chain that neither of us was really aware of? My sister strongly disapproves of the new life I make. She begins speaking to Elsie again before she dies, after eleven years of silence, but refuses, out of loyalty to my first wife, to speak to my second for the next twenty-seven years.

And now, looking over her life from this new perspective, she starts to spread her disapproval back to the father whose side she had taken in the long Cold War with Elsie. 'He was a rotten father,' she says to me one day, out of the blue. I'm so surprised that I fail to ask her why she thinks this, and even now I still don't understand what the deficiencies were that she retrospectively found in him.

Whatever my sister meant by her dismissal of our father, it's true that he did play a part in leaving her and the world at large a terrible legacy. Thirty-three years after he died she begins to suffer from shortness of breath. It takes the doctors several months to diagnose the cause: mesothelioma, the incurable and deadly cancer of the lining of the lung that emerges sometimes half a century or so after exposure to asbestos, and that was first properly understood after he died, even later than the effects on the human body that my kind Uncle Sid's cigarettes were having. The only asbestos she can recall ever being exposed to was in the samples that my father used to bring home, and that I sawed up. A hand has reached out of the remote and innocent past, just as it did from the isolation hospital where our mother had caught her childhood scarlet fever.

She's sixty-six. The doctors say she has three months to live. Her illness brings us together again, just as those two earlier deaths had. I call on her at her son's house where she has taken refuge, mistake her instructions about letting myself in round the back, and oblige her to come to the front door. It takes her many minutes; when the door at last opens she has almost no breath left in her body. Later I try, at long last, after sixty years of silence on the subject, to talk to her about our mother. I ask her if she remembers her playing the violin to us. She doesn't, and in any case the term 'our mother' is still unusable between us. We don't pursue the subject. The doctors, it turns out, are wrong about her having only three months to live. She has one.

I may yet go the same way myself; no one knows how long that hand out of the past can sometimes be stayed. In the meantime I've become older than my father was when he died. Six years older – I'm on my way to becoming *his* father. If I'm making fun of him in this account of his life – his ridiculous hopes of my sporting abilities, the lightness of his tread upon the earth, his deafness, his 'guv'nor' and his 'hotchamachacha' – it's rather in the way that he made fun of me for so many things – rather in the way that everyone seems to make fun of their father when they get around to writing about him, as they so often do in later life.

Whether he in the end felt proud of me or not, I'm certainly proud of being his son. The joshing is the way I've inherited from him of expressing my pride. Yes, and my love, that I never found the occasion to mention to him. Unlike the sons of Noah, I have impiously uncovered his nakedness. I have, though, tried to emulate another mythical son; I have borne him as best I could out of the ashes of the past in the way that the pious Aeneas bore his father Anchises on his back out of the ashes of Troy, in those pages of Virgil that fluttered away in the wind so many years ago.

*

He sometimes opens his eyes for a moment, when I visit him in the hospice where the last five weeks of his life ebb away, and gives me a smile, but he can no longer speak, and for most of the time he seems to be asleep. It's as if he has faded, like the Cheshire Cat, until only the smile remains. Behind his closed eyes his wrecked brain must still be partially functioning. Is some kind of conscious inner world continuing? What are his last experiences in life? A shifting, tangled dream, perhaps, of lions and discomfort; of rainwater goods and the warmth of the car on a summer's day; of duck eggs and tramlines. Perhaps for a moment he's back in Devonshire Road, throwing the bread under the table and eating the cheese. Or walking into the party and seeing Vi again for that first time. Or perhaps there's only confusion and strangeness.

What's going on in *my* head, as I sit there at his bedside? Nothing worthy of the occasion, so far as I can recall. Thoughts about my work. Wondering how long I should stay. Occasional pangs of helpless grief. Mostly, I think, longing for him to die, for both our sakes, and for it all to be over.

It happens at four-thirty in the morning, on 9 May 1970. I'm not with him. The last of him for me was when I visited him the previous evening. He can't open his eyes any more. I take his hand, as I did Nanny's, and tell him who I am. I feel a faint pressure on my hand in return.

Then he smiles. His old familiar smile, all that's left of him, for one last time.

Slowly the smile fades.

And that's the end of the story.

Photographs